THE GLOBAL
KITCHEN

Preparing vegetables in Turkey. *Photo by: Arlinba Blair/Colorific.*

THE GLOBAL KITCHEN

Meat and Vegetarian Recipes from Africa,
Asia and Latin America for Western Kitchens
with Country Information and Food Facts

by Troth Wells

THE CROSSING PRESS, INC., FREEDOM, CA 95019

Back cover photo: Nairobi market, Kenya. Maggie Murray/Format.
Endpaper photo: Fruit market in Tunisia. Robert Harding Picture Library.

Published in the U.S.A. by The Crossing Press, Inc. in 1995.
First published in Great Britain in 1991 by New Internationalist Publications Ltd.

Printed in Hong Kong

Cover design by Amy Sibiga
Color page design by Mark Glynne-Jones/Jump To!
Inside page design by John Godfrey. Layout of inside pages by Jo Tydeman and Peter Tucker.

ISBN 0-89594-753-6

FOREWORD

With this book—containing some 250 recipes from Africa, Asia, Latin America and the Middle East—we have brought together a range of wholesome and delicious foods. Some are quite basic, others more elaborate, but the recipes have been adapted to Western kitchens.

Testing the recipes not only gave us a great opportunity for eating some delicious meals—it also led to finding out more about why people eat what they eat, and why there is hunger, so increasing our understanding of the world of food.

Some of what we discovered is written into the book—from how Africans came to be eating maize/corn, and women's role as food producers to how the passion fruit acquired its name and what befell some Ethiopian goats eating berries from a bush...

We hope you'll enjoy the book, too, whether you browse through, dip into, read at length or simply start cooking.

Troth Wells
for the New Internationalist Co-operative

Acknowledgements

A book like this, with its many parts, necessarily has many participants. In thanking them all I begin with my colleagues at the New Internationalist for their wholehearted support for this project: Vanessa Baird, Chris Brazier, Wayne Ellwood, Alan Hughes, Guy Montgomery, Gill Moore, Clive Offley, David Ransom, James Rowland, Sue Shaw, Wendy Slack, Peter Stalker, Kate Stott, Richard Swift and Dexter Tiranti.

I'd also like to thank subscribers who sent in recipes and wrote interestingly about how they were made, or where they'd first eaten them. Testing the recipes was a major (albeit pleasurable) task and I know I could not have managed without the help of many people, especially Peter Stalker, William Beinart and Karen Bull. Special thanks too to Gill Moore, Kate Stott and Guy Montgomery for work on measurements and ingredients. When it came to the text around the recipes, Chris Brazier's sensitive editing was much appreciated.

On design, thanks to Mark Glynne-Jones (ever cheerful), John Godfrey, Peter Tucker and Jo Tydeman. At the production stage, many thanks for the hours of typesetting to Wendy Slack, Brendan McGrath, Peter Tucker and Jonathan Coleclough, and also to Alex Tucker and Dafydd Llwyd Lewis for the final preparation of the pages.

It still seems miraculous to me that we can produce text on a screen that eventually comes out as page after page of bromide artwork. I would like to acknowledge the largely unseen (by me) but much valued technical support from Peter Stalker and Kate Stott.

And having produced all the pages, there was all the proof-reading; thank you to Dinyar Godrej, William Beinart, George Fisher and Wendy Young.

Special thanks, too, to Dexter Tiranti whose enthusiasm for the book never wavered despite some difficult moments and whose help on the editorial and visuals side was always forthcoming . I'd also like to thank Ann and Gabriel, my children, and their friends Katy and Rebecca, who tried lots of new foods and were refreshingly unequivocal in their pronouncements. Finally, thanks to the close friends and relatives whose support helped me with a hidden struggle, and who have contributed to the book in countless ways.

Contents

Two children: Jinja, Uganda. At school they also grow vegetables and rear chickens.
Photo: Jørgen Schytte/Still Pictures

Sharing food at a *puja* (religious ceremony) in Nepal. *Photo by: Mike McQueen/Impact Photos.*

World
OF
FOOD

A WORLD OF
FOOD

The best restaurant in Kuala Lumpur, the sprawling capital of Malaysia, was not to be found in the business sector with its broad boulevards and high-rise offices. It was down an alley in one of the poorer districts of the city, where children were eternally playing, diving in and out of doorways. The chef in question — whom I knew only as Mr Lim — both cooked and served his delicacies at a ramshackle street-stall or *warung* put together out of planks and canvas. At lunchtime I would come out in the heat of the day to sit on the bench of his stall and eat the most wonderful *gado-gado* – a traditional Malaysian and Indonesian dish in which a cornucopia of vegetables is topped with a steaming and spicy peanut sauce.

I found this combination irresistible. I have sought out *gado-gado* in Malaysian or Indonesian restaurants in the West — and make it myself — without ever quite matching Mr Lim's original, imbued as it was with the sights and sounds around me as I ate. When I painfully stammered out the Malaysian for *'This is the best restaurant in Kuala Lumpur, Mr Lim,'* he laughed heartily at the sheer craziness of the idea. But I meant it.

And it is in that spirit that the New Internationalist co-operative and I have put together this book, for my experience in Malaysia could be repeated all over Africa, Asia, Latin America and the Middle East. Centuries of skill have gone into making meals that are unique to a culture or a region. And that is why we have gathered recipes from the Third World into this book — not just to bring different and enticing gastronomic experiences into our kitchens (though that would be reason enough) but also to convey through the pleasurable everyday activity of eating some sense of the richness and diversity of the women, children and men who make up the global family.

As the world shrinks through faster and better communications, we have the chance nowadays to learn more about other people. And people across the world can also benefit from this intercontinental exchange. For example, when I made *guacamole,* (a Central American avocado dip) for a party in Penang, Malaysia, my friend Gaik Sim was intrigued. *'We have avocados here, they were introduced by the British,'* she said *'but we don't really use them that much. I've never been quite sure what to do with them.'* The creamy dip, with its spicy edge of chili flavor was well received and, who knows, maybe it will catch on in Malaysia.

In preparing the book I saw how people have accepted new foods, sometimes at first through receiving hospitality, and incorporated them into their local diet. The European cauliflower, for instance, teams up with the local avocado pear in a salad from the Dominican Republic; African cooking abounds with dishes using groundnuts (peanuts) and maize (corn) — both introductions from South America. North Indian food shows the influence of the Persian Moghuls. I learned that *'chow'* (as in 'chow mein') is an Americanism that arose from the presence of Chinese labourers building railroads in the western US early this century. The Mandarin word, *'ch'ao',* meaning to cook or fry, became to American ears the name for the meal itself.

Enriching journey

As I thought about the preparation of this book, I found myself looking back with fresh eyes at the times I have come into contact with food, especially in Third World countries. I realized that I had picked up quite a bit over the years about food production and the causes of world hunger —important lessons which I have tried to summarize at the back of this book (see *A history of food,* p. 171). But too often hunger is the only way we in the West connect food and the people of the Third World — in famine situations with the planes and trucks full of grain sacks roaring in. Faced with famine, we lose sight of people as individuals. And when I reviewed my own travels, I realized that eating food with people from other cultures, other continents, is one of the quickest (and most pleasant) routes to understanding and valuing people as individuals.

I don't think that what I saw and learned is particularly special: you will no doubt have similar tales of markets, of crazy episodes, of poverty side-by-side with plenty, and a sense of the range of people you met who made the travel such a rich experience. My first contact with food growing, though, was in England. As a child I used to visit my uncle's small farm outside Lincoln. It was here I first saw a calf being born, the steam rising off its wet fur, its mother bellowing her delight. I remember too seeing the bright red scarlet pimpernel flowers growing by the pea fields, and the seemingly endless expanse of potatoes — the main crop in that area. Many of the potatoes ended up in Lincoln's potato-crisp factory, which I think was the first in the country. This seductive 'food' with its little blue-paper twist of salt, was an instant success. As children we made do with the cheaper factory rejects — the greasy shards from the bottom of the pan which made for marvelous munching.

At some point my uncle lost his main potato field. It was transformed into a runway for Britain's nuclear aircraft, the Vulcan bomber. The little farmhouse still shakes disturbingly each time the menacing shapes rumble along the runway and lurch into take-off.

Although I didn't know it at the time, my visits to the farm were a good introduction to some of the issues which I came to realize affect food-growing all over the world — a nutritious staple, potatoes, was sold as a cash crop and transformed into junk food; then forces beyond the farmer's control took good land out of agricultural use.

'Eat up your meal — think of all the hungry people in India' was a common admonition from my mother around this time. But luckily this wasn't the limit of my contact with India and food. My mother was the daughter of a doctor in the Indian Medical Service and I listened rapt to stories of her childhood. To bring warmth to the damp coldness of an English winter, she would make curry with left-over lamb from the Sunday meal and the exciting aroma added spice to her tales — about the cobra lying coiled on the cool stone floor of the wash-house; about her father's accounts of soldiers and pig-sticking in the Khyber Pass.

The chutneys and pickles that accompanied our curry had a sour-sweet allure for my young palate. Toying with a piece of mango I'd be fascinated by the idea that it had come all the way from India — and that something as apparently 'normal' as chutney had only become part of the otherwise staid British diet when soldiers and civil servants had brought it back from Asia. I didn't realize then quite how much else the British had extracted from the sub-continent.

Tasting non-European food in its local context was a revelation to me as a teenager in Turkey. In Istanbul it was a delight to go for a mouth-watering stroll beside the bustling Galata bridge, seeing the large round trays made of red wood piled high, some with fish, others with fruits. I remember inside one restaurant, the eager proprietor beckoned us into a dark and smoke-stained kitchen. Steaming basins of food were set there — purple aubergine (egg-plant) stews and fluffy pilaffs. Lots of talk followed about which dish to try, spoons were dipped into various bowls so we could taste them. I warmed to the obvious friendliness — the sheer openness and informality of the people was as much of a revelation as the taste of the dishes. Soon I was gesticulating and stumbling in Turkish as I selected something to eat; they laughed and spooned huge amounts of food onto my plate.

A first encounter with *doner kebab* — now a popular fast food in a more cosmopolitan Britain — came on the same trip, this time in Bursa, on Turkey's Asian flank. Here a tall vertical spit turned, bearing the mound of lamb with fat sizzling down the sides. Behind it was the red-glowing

Photo: Dexter Tiranti

The Unreal Thing: soft drinks and much of our food in the West use basic ingredients which are then preserved, processed and packaged beyond recognition.

charcoal stacked high and a little precariously. The red-faced chef carved the meat at arm's length: the heat was tremendous. And after all this the kebab had to be special, like the place. Slice after slice of succulent lamb laid on pita bread, topped off with yogurt, garnished with tomatoes and washed down with *ayram*, a local yogurt drink.

In Turkey the food and the people seemed bound together in some fundamental way, perhaps because the links with food-growing or fish-catching are still closer there than in most parts of the West. My own children for instance would never see the secret clusters of Brussel sprouts growing on the plant unless I made a point of taking them to a farm. Much of what we buy in the shops has been processed and preserved and packaged beyond recognition.

In most of the Third World this is not yet the case — the food is composed of wholesome ingredients which have not usually been chemically treated, and is intimately linked both to the farming and the cultural traditions of the region. And that is another reason why a book based on Third World dishes can be valuable: in a world where we have become detached from our agricultural roots, and where both our environment and our own health are suffering as a result, the book can help us explore other culinary cultures where the ordinary, everyday food does not come from cans and packets.

Hamburger outreach

Traveling in the United States gave me an insight into that canned, processed food culture which has since spread its tentacles all over the world. Thumbing it through the Southern states in Bicentennial Year, I got a ride with plump 13-year-old Lee and his dad. As we traveled through the scenic Smoky Mountain National Park, Lee's attention soon wavered and his thoughts turned to food. Quizzing me, he unearthed an incredible fact: I had never eaten at McDonald's. *'You mean you don't know what the "Golden Rings" are?'* He could hardly contain his disbelief. And when it became clear that Baskin-Robbins ice-cream was also unfamiliar to me, I saw at a glance that Lee now thought he knew why the US was number one in the world.

Once down the mountain road we ended up in Gatlingburg, named for the famous gun's inventor, where kind father and son treated me to a wet and sloppy Big Mac, French fries, Thousand Island dressing, and a double scoop of ice cream with whole strawberries in it. The food was tasty, no denying it. And very available. The delights of clam chowder, *succotash* and spiced molasses cake can be harder to track down if you're traveling on the Interstate.

The unhealthy diet helped explain why everyone who picked us up on that trip seemed overweight — too many stomachs resting on steering wheels born of too many roadside diner fry-ups. By contrast, the black people in the tumbledown huts we passed on the edge of former cotton fields looked thin: unhealthy for a very different reason.

Buying Egyptian cotton had become cheaper for the US than growing it in Mississippi. The little that remained was harvested by cotton-picking machines, so there was not a lot for the workers to do here now, and very little money. They didn't seem to have anywhere to grow food. *'Aaw, they could easily move to California and get work there,'* said a church minister who gave us a ride.

All over the world people find they have to move on and be uprooted because they cannot provide for themselves where they live. Farming land is concreted over as towns and road networks expand. Land that used to grow food for local people is used instead for commodities like cotton, and when the demand falls, people have no resources to fall back on.

That highway led me in the end to Mexico, where I remember being struck by the tortilla-making machines. A conveyor belt would feed the pressed-out corn pancakes down the line to where women piled them high, ready to be sold to cafes and *loncherias*. Maize corn is Mexico's traditional food grain but I soon noticed how much wheat bread there was, especially in the bigger cities. *Tortas* (white bread rolls) were replacing tortillas. In Guadalajara's market, the man behind the stall deftly sliced open the bread roll and slapped in a mixture of spicy green and red peppers and a trail of tomatoes. It may have mattered little to him that the sandwich was made from wheat flour rather than maize, but when wheat creeps in and begins to displace local staple cereals there can be difficulties ahead.

This wheat comes from the US prairies. The US grows more wheat than any other country in the world, too much for its own needs. So it sells some south of the border. Meanwhile much of Mexico's farmland that could have grown corn/maize has been taken away from *campesino* (peasant) production and turned into large farms growing tomatoes and other goods for export to the US. People leaving the land have flocked into Mexico City and other urban centers, and they have to be fed — with US wheat. The vicious circle goes round. And so Mexico City goes on growing, the largest and most overpopulated city in the world.

By Lake Atitlan in Guatemala — a beautiful stretch of water cradled by three volcanoes — the world farming economy seemed far away. Yet even here the sense that we live in one interdependent world was inescapable. It wasn't just that I, as a Western tourist, was meeting both indians and Guatemalan descendants of the Spanish conquistadores. Here too was a restaurant run by Chinese who had settled here after

3

originally sailing to Peru. The experience of matching my halting Spanish to their quite different rendition of the language was hilarious, and meant that I was never sure what I was going to be eating. But it didn't matter: the Chinese interpretation of Guatemalan food was delicious.

However the most striking food traders by the Lake were the indians, who came to the market with baskets of potatoes and tomatoes to sell, weighing out their wares with hand scales. Indian women purchasers unfolded the colorful shawls from their backs to use as shopping bags, revealing the astonishing *huipiles* — woven patterned blouses — that are distinct to each village.

Living in the hills of Guatemala, the indians were never completely conquered by the Spanish. Catholic churches and priests have bowed to this, turning a blind eye to chicken sacrifices on the steps of the church while the votive candles blaze inside. But today government brutality and market forces have changed their lives much more effectively than did the Spanish guns. On the road down to the coast truckloads of indians swayed and jostled as they travelled to the humid sugar-cane plantations to find work. These indians have always been skilled cultivators, growing maize and beans together in a harmony that nourishes the soil as well as the body. Yet here they were migrating to work producing an infinitely less nutritious crop that would not even be eaten in their own land.

The logic of the global marketplace means that countries are encouraged to specialize in crops for sale abroad. The money they earn in exchange is meant to provide the capital for 'development'. What happens all too often is that the price for a commodity such as sugar falls. The country earns less than expected and goes into debt. Any subsequent income is rapidly re-exported to service the debt. And food production for local people begins to falter as the cycle gathers momentum and resources are diverted to export crops.

Malaysian milestone

The pattern was familiar to me by the time I went to stay in Malaysia in the early 1980s. Export crops, in this case rubber and oil palm, took up much of the land. As a result rice, the main cereal, had been neglected and the country still has to import it.

Yet for all that Malaysia has one of the richest and most diverse cuisines in the world. The country's bountiful climate and fertile soil gives it a head start. In addition the population

Banana bunch: the 'logic' of the global marketplace means that countries like Dominica specialize in crops for sale abroad, and food production for home consumption falls as a result

Photo: Philip Wolmuth

is drawn from three cultural groups: Malays, Chinese and Indians — who have all contributed enormously to Malaysia's culinary traditions. For the first time, I was living in a Third World country instead of simply passing through. And that gave me a deeper understanding about crop-growing and food in the world which has been part of the stimulus for putting this book together.

All the same, my first experience of a Malaysian meal was not auspicious. It was with the parents of a woman we had met on the plane. A friend and I sat in the front room and talked with the father. There was hardly a sight of the women, who were all hard at work in the kitchen grinding the spices and preparing the vegetables. I felt a bit awkward, my 'white' skin making me an honorary man.

My unease increased as the women materialized bearing dishes of mutton curry, *biryani,* stewed okra and steaming rice. On seeing this, the old man turned gloatingly and confided that *'Food never tastes sweeter than when it is cooked and served by your wife'*. And grown by them as well, possibly. After all, women's labor produces half the world's food and women also carry out virtually all the household tasks like fetching water and caring for the children.

More typically, though, I'd walk along after work to Penang's Gurney Drive, now Jalan Ahmed Shah, where the foodstall hawkers would line up their carts by the kerb. This was where everyone met, walking, talking and eating as the final hour of daylight gave way to the tropical night. Young men on Honda bikes roared up and took away their purchases of *nasi goreng* (fried rice) or *roti canai* (flat bread and curry sauce) in little plastic bags swinging from the handlebars. The air had the salty tang of the nearby sea, and of the various foods being cooked up on the food stalls. Each had its speciality, and carried all the ingredients to make the dish: noodles piled high, rows of fish swinging from hooks above the chopping board, and tamarind pods for the Malay fish broth *Laksa*.

My favorite starting point was a stall run by an Indian man and woman. She always seemed serene despite the long hours she worked for meagre reward. But perhaps it was resignation rather than serenity that I saw in her face and in the steady movement of her hands as she made *thosai*, fermented rice-flour pancakes. The man heated sweetened milk and then held it aloft in a brass cup, letting the milk cascade down into another cup held low in his left hand. Again and again he did this, until I was hypnotized and the milk was cool enough to drink.

Afterwards, I'd wander on to another stall for *ikan bilis*, whitebait fried crisp with peanuts, or *saté*, tasty pieces of skewered mutton, pork or chicken cooked over a charcoal stove and dipped into peanut sauce.

Chinese stalls carried some of the most varied food — *mee goreng*, noodles with boiled egg, potato, beans sprouts and tofu or bean curd or the beguilingly named *Wan Ton mee* that turned out to be noodles with broth, slices of *char siew* (roast pork) and the *wan ton* themselves: dumplings.

Chinese cooking still astonishes me by its ability to incorporate just about anything. Tales of monkey brains and snakes aside, I thought I was a fairly adventurous eater. But being presented a broth for breakfast one morning I found my limits. Floating or rather sticking out of the liquid were the unmistakable yellow claws of chicken feet. My local companion slurped and sucked them with a competence born of enjoyment and habituation. *'Chicken!'* joked my friend as I went in search of a banana bun.

What people eat is obviously bound up with where they live and what they are accustomed to. Chinese people have traditionally lived with the fear of famine and the certainty of poverty — their willingness to eat (and relish) the last claw of an animal and all manner of vegetables flows naturally from that. However, this book does not explore the outer reaches of Chinese cuisine. Most of the 'exotic' ingredients turn out to be a pleasant surprise.

Malaysian friends always used to tease me about the blandness of European food. *'You know why the British really left Malaysia?'* said one of them, Anwar. *'It was because they could no longer stand the smell of the durian fruit.'* With a stench somewhere between over-ripe brie cheese and rotting garbage, he had a point. But if you can ignore the odor and get on with the eating, durians taste rather like custard. Both Malaysians and Thais are hooked on the fruit, and to some extent officialdom has had to respond to the fevered eating at durian time. Garbage collections are stepped up, while hotels and airlines warn would-be durian-smugglers of the strict penalties they face if caught with the stinking fruit.

Needless to say, durians have not caught on in Britain. But other products of the association with Malaysia are found in the sago, rice and tapioca milk puddings that we used to eat as children. I didn't know then that sago came from a type of palm tree, nor that tapioca resulted from processing cassava or manioc root. While the sago palm is a local plant in South-East Asia, cassava had been carried there by the Europeans from South America.

Women of the world

Cassava links Asia and Latin America with Africa too. The starchy root is not famed for its nutritional qualities, but it is popular because it can withstand drought and does not need much work in cultivation. Sadly where it has taken over as a staple, for instance in West Africa, cultivation of the more nutritious millet and sorghum is falling.

And while no-one would want to deny hard-pressed women farmers the slightly easier life that cassava-growing offers, it is unfortunate that more resources are not channelled into maintaining better-quality food plants alongside it. And it is worse than unfortunate that more of the women's work is not taken on by men.

5

Cassava has its moments, however. One hot sticky evening in Mombasa, Kenya, I tasted a delicious cassava dish at a Swahili restaurant in the narrow streets of the old Arab part of town. Sitting at a rickety table on the pavement, they brought *muhogo* cooked with coconut cream and it was very good. But of course I could afford to buy other food as well: *mushkaki*, for instance, small pieces of marinated grilled meat served with salad and also a drink of fresh passion-fruit juice.

Women's work: in Kenya as in most parts of the world it is women who bear the brunt of growing food for the family. And preparing it, and cooking, and doing the dishes . . .

Some of the Mombasa region's tropical fruit and vegetables find their way up to the market in Nairobi. Here in the Central Highlands area, *shambas* (small-holdings) grow maize and beans cheek by jowl with avocado and orange trees or tea. Women do most of the farming work in Kenya as in the rest of Africa. This dry fact was turned into living testimony as I moved around the country, showing the **New Internationalist** film *Man-Made Famine* to women farmers as part of an education project with the Young Women's Christian Association (YWCA).

'Nothing much has changed here since we made the film' said Dinah Mukwana greeting me with a rueful smile. She had told her story in the film's section on cash crops. Her husband is thought to be in Uganda; at any rate she does not hear from him. She farms the five acres with the help of her children and grows maize, millet and fruit — and sells enough sugar cane to be able to pay the school fees for her children.

Up in a poorer area near Sondhu in the western part of the country, the land was less bountiful yet people still insisted on giving us food and drink. *'The women grow maize, cow peas, millet and cassava,'* explained Juliette Okech of the YWCA who had accompanied me there. *'The people have been resettled here but because it is a conservation area they cannot take reeds for thatch or firewood for charcoal. There is a reservoir nearby but no pump or pipes for the water yet, so the community is struggling.'* Nevertheless, these people with so little for themselves gave us a spread which included the prized tail of the fat-tailed sheep — so esteemed that normally only men get to eat it. Their generosity and friendliness stays with me and I often wish I was as spontaneously welcoming and open as they were to me, eager to show me their homes and to ask about mine. They especially wanted to know what I grew on my *shamba*. They laughed when I told them that I'm no farmer like them, that I buy all my food in a shop.

My few words of Kiswahili just about stretched to complementing the women I met on the *chakula kienyeji*, local food, that I ate with relish in different places. For it was delicious — the nutty-textured millet or corn porridge, *ugali, irio* (corn and bean mush), the smoky-flavored *nyama kuchoma* (grilled meat) and *sukuma wiki*, spinach-like greens.

In every country you visit there are new foods, intriguing combinations of ingredients waiting to be tried — and researching this book has been like a round-the-world trip in itself. Cooking the recipes has introduced me to entirely new dishes such as *gbegiri* (black-eyed bean soup from Zambia), marinated beef from Mongolia, and *ceviche*, soaked fish with lemon from Peru. I now appreciate a much wider range of good wholesome foods than I ever did before. The variety is not just in the ingredients either. I have become more aware of the attention paid to different flavors, colors, textures and ways of cooking.

Above all this book has increased my respect for the people of the Third World who are behind these recipes. I admire the way they, especially women, connect with the land and turn its fruits into such a variety of wonderful meals. What is commonplace to them is novel to us — a beckoning world full of new tastes and different preparations. Very few recipes are normally written down, the method of passing on is by word of mouth, and then by taste and experience that shows resourcefulness and imagination. In this book of course the measurements are given, but don't let that stop you adapting and experimenting. I hope above all that this book gives you a sense of the people and countries behind the recipes and that you enjoy cooking and eating these meals.

NOTES TO THE RECIPES

In the West there is growing recognition that the way we eat, together with a sedentary life, is not good for our health. Generally we eat too much sugar, salt and fat and too little fiber. We need to eat more fresh fruit and vegetables, whole grains and legumes and to cut down the refined and processed foods. There are several publications on health, nutrition and wholefoods; a few are listed at the end.

Measures for salt, fat and sugar in this book are given as guide amounts only: if you want to use less or no sugar, that is up to you. If you prefer to cut out the salt altogether, then go ahead.

The reason this is important is not just because of your health but also because the idea of being flexible about what you put into a pot is a useful, some may say essential, part of cooking — to experiment, to add or take out something. Why not use a bit more lemon juice perhaps, or how about trying lentils instead of ground/ minced meat? This approach also reflects the way most people cook in the developing world where recipe books are few and far between, and the best cooking goes on at home with hand-me-down favorites. So while this book gives the measures required to make each dish, you might like to try a little experimentation.

With these general points in mind, you may find it useful to read the following notes on the recipes in this book, before you start cooking.

Sugar and Honey
Where sugar is listed as an ingredient, the measure is given as a guide amount. You may prefer to reduce this or even omit it altogether. Remember, brown sugar is just as bad for you as white. Honey can be substituted where appropriate. It contains fewer calories than sugar but that's still too many for most of us, and its tooth-rotting qualities are intact. However unlike sugar, honey contains fructose which is absorbed more slowly than the sucrose in sugar and so you do not experience the 'sugar-high' and its corresponding low.

Salt
Salt is always to taste in the recipes. Some people prefer not to use salt at all in the cooking, but to let people add their own when the meal is served.

Fat
Most recipes call simply for 'margarine' or 'oil'. Here it is best to use unsaturated varieties such as corn, safflower, sunflower or soybean. One or two recipes specify coconut oil or 'ghee' (clarified butter). These are saturated fats and normally best avoided as they contribute to the cholesterol build-up in the body.

However for special occasions you may like to use these ingredients for their character-istic flavor. Red palm oil, specified in a couple of recipes, is thick and red but unsaturated and not to be confused with palm kernel oil, thin and clear but saturated. In general, it is better to stick to the unsaturat-ed oils and fats and to drain any fried food on paper towels where possible. Remember too that there is fat in meat and cheese and in snack foods such as chips and crackers. Many processed foods are made with saturated fats such as palm kernel or coconut oil. The recipes are quite sparing in the use of oil and margarine but you may find you can cook with even less. The point to remember is to reduce *overall* fat intake.

Fiber
Fruit, vegetables, legumes (beans, peas and so on), seeds and whole grains provide different kinds of fiber. Oats, for example, provide soluble fiber which may help reduce cholesterol levels. Where possible, eat brown rice and wholemeal/wholewheat flour as well as fresh fruit, seeds, legumes and raw or lightly-cooked vegetables.

Preparation of fruit and vegetables
With concern about fiber on the one hand and anxiety about pesticide residues on the other, it is difficult to advise how to prepare the fruit and vegetables you will be using. Organically-grown produce is obviously the best, if you can obtain it. If not, wash the fruit and vegetables carefully and leave them unpeeled if you can. In the recipe ingredients it is assumed these items are washed and peeled as desired.

Bulgur and cracked wheat
If using bulgur, pour boiling water over it and leave to soak for about 40 minutes, then drain and use. For cracked wheat, boil for 20 minutes and then let it stand in the pan for a few minutes more, or cook these items according to the instructions on the packet.

Canned foods
Except for tomatoes and one or two other items, the recipes do not give canned ingredients. However if you want to use canned garbanzos/chickpeas or red kidney beans for instance that is fine but you may need to double-check the quantities and the cooking method for the dish you are making.

Cassava/manioc
Cassava/manioc should always be peeled and cooked before eating as it contains substances which can give rise to prussic acid. However this is readily destroyed by cooking. The most common way to cook cassava is

to cut it into chunks and then boil it for about 30 minutes, or according to the recipe.

Chicken
Most of the fat in chicken lies just under the skin. For this reason, most recipes in this book call for the skin to be removed.

Chilis, chili powder, curry powder, other spices and herbs
The measures given for these ingredients are guide amounts only, and refer to dried ingredients unless otherwise stated. If you are not sure how hot you like something, start by using a little and add more later if you wish. In general, food tastes better if you use fresh spices and herbs. Cayenne pepper can be substituted for chili powder.

Creamed coconut
Some recipes call for coconut milk or coconut cream, which is made from the grated and squeezed flesh of fresh coconut. In the West you can buy a small block of creamed coconut in health food stores. To use, you simply cut off a chunk and melt it in hot water before adding to the recipe (amounts to be used are in the recipes). You can also make coconut milk using shredded or desiccated coconut (See p. 126) Ordinary milk can be substituted.

Dried beans, peas, lentils etc.
The measures given for these are for the dry unsoaked, uncooked ingredients.

Fish and vegetarians
Some dishes in the vegetarian

section use prawns, shrimps or oyster sauce. Omit these ingredients if you do not eat sea-foods.

Flour
Unless specified otherwise, 'flour' in the recipes means wheat flour. You can use wholemeal/wholewheat interchangeably with refined, or use half and half, but bear in mind that wholemeal/wholewheat flour makes a more solid product. It is a good idea to sieve it as this helps aerate it. Just tip the remaining bran in afterwards. If you find wholemeal/wholewheat pastry difficult to roll out for a pie base, then put the mixture into the pie-dish and press it into place with the back of a metal spoon.

Meat
Select lean cuts and trim off any fat from the meat before you start. The cooking times given for meat are guides only — the actual time will depend on the cut of meat you are using, the size of the pieces, your cooking pan and stove.

Nuts and seeds
Amounts given for these are for shelled but raw (unroasted) items, unless stated otherwise. See individual recipes for toasting or roasting instructions.

Peppers/bell peppers
Where a recipe lists bell peppers these are the large sweet red or green varieties (see note below).

Plantains/green (savory) bananas
These are easier to peel if you

boil them first for about 30 minutes. If you have to peel them before cooking, cut the plantain in half and then make lengthwise cuts in each section and remove the peel.

Scallions/spring onions
Several of the recipes call for these. If you cannot get them use shallots or ordinary onions instead.

Shrimps, prawns and shellfish
The measures given for these items in the recipes is the volume/weight after the shells have been removed.

Stock or water
Where a recipe offers stock as an alternative to water, use stock if possible as it gives much better flavor to the dish.

Tablespoons
While teaspoon measures are the same, British tablespoon measures are larger than in North America and Australasia. UK readers should therefore use only a *scant* tablespoon amount.

Note: All measures in the book are in US cups and Metric. Where US and UK spell a word differently, the US version is generally used. Names for ingredients may differ in your country: we have tried to use the one or sometimes two most common names.

There are many publications on health, nutrition and wholefoods available in libraries and bookstores; only a small selection is included here.
Diet for a Small Planet by Frances Moore Lappé (Ballantine Books, New York, revised edition 1982)
New Internationalist issue 135, May 1984
The Politics of Food by Geoffrey Cannon (Century Hutchinson, London 1987)
The Right Way to Eat by Miriam Polunin (Dent, London, revised edition 1984)

A food stall in Bahia, Brazil. Photo by: Michael Macintyre/Hutchinson Library.

STARTERS, SNACKS, SOUPS

AFRICA

Cassava/manioc chips/crisps

Serves 2-4

Originally from South America, cassava takes its name from the Taino indian word *cacabi*, while other South American indians, the Tupi, gave us the word *tipioca* – tapioca – for cassava's starchy by-product. In the 17th century the Portuguese carried the root to West Africa where it is now a major crop, favored for its resistance to drought.

These chips/crisps are delicious served hot or cold with drinks as a snack.

I N G R E D I E N T S

1/2 pound / 225 g cassava *

oil

salt

* Cassava or its juice must always be cooked before eating (see **Notes to the Recipes p.7.**)

1. To begin, peel the cassava/manioc, using a sharp knife as the skin is quite thick. Then slice it very thinly, crosswise if possible. If the center core is too tough for this, slice the root lengthwise and cut again if necessary to produce the right size slices. Soak the pieces in cold water for 30 minutes.

2. After this, boil the cassava slices briskly for 10 minutes. Drain and dry them. Then, in a heavy pan, heat enough oil to fry the chips and cook several pieces at the same time until they are golden.

3. Now drain the chips on paper towels, allow them to cool slightly and sprinkle on the salt, if liked, before serving ■

SOUTH AFRICA

Chicken with lemon and cilantro/coriander

Serves 2-4

In this Cape kebab, the meat should be marinated for an hour before you start cooking. But after that, it is very quick to do and tastes delicious.

I N G R E D I E N T S

1/2 pound / 225 g chicken meat, skinned, boned and cut into 1 inch / 2.5 cm cubes

juice of 1 lemon

handful fresh cilantro / coriander leaves, chopped

1 clove garlic, crushed

1 tablespoon oil

dash of dry white wine +

salt and pepper

+ optional ingredient

1. In a large bowl, mix together the lemon juice, cilantro/coriander leaves, garlic, oil, wine and salt and pepper. Put in the chicken pieces and leave them to marinate for an hour.

2. After this, thread the meat onto skewers and broil/grill for about 20 minutes, turning often, until the meat is cooked and browned ■

SUDAN

Yogurt and tahina dip

Serves 4-6

'Whoever has drunk from the River shall return' says a Sudanese proverb speaking of the Nile River, whose power over life and death gives it magical properties. Sudan is the largest country in Africa but one of the poorest, and the civil war in the non-Muslim South is a continuing drain on its resources.

The recipe echoes the Arab and Muslim influences in the North of the country with ingredients found widely in Middle Eastern cooking.

INGREDIENTS

²/₃ cup / 150 ml tahina/ sesame seed paste *

²/₃ cup / 150 ml plain yogurt

2-3 cloves garlic, crushed

juice of 1-2 lemons

a little fresh parsley, chopped finely

salt and pepper

* available from health food stores

1. Using a mixing basin, blend the crushed garlic with a little salt and the tahina paste.

2. Then add the yogurt and lemon juice gradually, beating to make a smooth, thick cream.

3. Now sprinkle on the seasoning and then put the dip into a bowl. Scatter the parsley on top and serve with carrot and celery sticks, and pieces of hot pita bread ■

ZAMBIA

Okra soup

Serves 2-4

Okra, also known as *lady's fingers* and *gumbo*, are the pods of a tropical African plant. They produce a gluey substance when cooked that thickens soups and stews, as in this recipe.

INGREDIENTS

¹/₂ pound / 225 g okra, finely chopped

2 tablespoons / 25 g margarine

¹/₄ teaspoon ground cinnamon

2 cups / 470 ml chicken stock

salt and pepper

1. First, melt the margarine in a saucepan and then put in the okra, cinnamon, salt and pepper and the stock. Cover and bring to the boil. Now turn down the heat and let the soup simmer for 15-20 minutes.

2. After that let the soup cool a little and then transfer it to a blender. Mix well, adjust the seasoning and the consistency, adding more water, stock or milk if required. Return the soup to the saucepan and serve hot ■

IN ALL RECIPES
- PEPPER AND SALT ARE TO TASTE
- CHILI AND SUGAR ARE GIVEN AS GUIDE QUANTITIES ONLY. VARY TO TASTE
- MEASURES FOR BEANS AND GRAINS REFER TO DRY INGREDIENTS.

11

ZAMBIA

Gbegiri (Black-eyed bean soup)

Serves 4-6

Zambia is one of the most urbanized countries in Africa with about half of its seven million people living in the towns which have grown up around the Copperbelt. Food grown includes maize/corn, millet, cassava/manioc, yams, beans, peanuts and fruits.

Gbegiri, though called a soup, can also be served as a stew with corn/maize porridge or rice. It is very good re-heated the next day.

I N G R E D I E N T S

2 cups / 350 g black-eyed beans, soaked and cooked

1 tablespoon oil

1 onion, chopped finely

1 tablespoon tomato paste

1 can tomatoes, chopped

2 cups / 470 ml stock

salt and pepper

1. To begin, heat the oil in a pan and soften the onion in it.

2. While that is cooking, partially mash the black-eyed beans using a fork or potato masher.

3. Now add the tomato paste, tomatoes, stock, beans and seasoning to the onion, stirring well. Let the soup simmer for 30 minutes before serving ■

CHINA

Chicken and prawn soup

Serves 6-8

After rice and steamed bread, noodles are the most common accompaniment to meals in China. They can be made from wheat or rice flour, as well as other ingredients such as pea starch.

The noodles used here – *sei fun* or 'cellophane' noodles – are shiny, thin and transparent and usually made from ground mung beans. If you cannot find them in an oriental store, substitute thin rice noodles.

I N G R E D I E N T S

$1^{1}/_2$ pounds / 675 g chicken portions, skinned

1 large onion, finely chopped

4 cups / 950 ml water

2 pounds / 900 g prawns, shelled and cooked

$^{1}/_2$ pound / 225 g mushrooms, sliced

1 cup / 150 g cellophane noodles or rice-flour noodles

1 teaspoon dark soy sauce

2 tablespoons oil

4 scallions / spring onions, finely chopped

2 cloves garlic, crushed

$^{1}/_2$ teaspoon ground cilantro / coriander

salt

1. First, put the chicken pieces into a large saucepan together with the salt and onion. Pour in the water, cover and bring to the boil. Then turn down the heat and simmer until the meat is tender, about 20 minutes.

2. Now take out the chicken and allow it to cool before you remove the bones. Then cut the meat into long thin slivers.

3. Put the chicken pieces back into the stock and add the prawns and mushrooms. Bring to the boil and simmer for 5 minutes. Then add the noodles and soy sauce, cooking gently for another 5 minutes or so.

4. While that is happening, heat the oil in a pan and cook the scallions/spring onions and garlic with the ground cilantro/coriander for 3-4 minutes, and add these to the soup just before serving ■

Chinese date and watercress soup

Serves 4

One of China's remarkable achievements is that it feeds a fifth of the world's population on just seven per cent of the world's cultivable land. However production of basic grains including rice and wheat has fallen in recent years as people choose to grow crops like sugar which can be sold for cash.

This soup from the Szechuan region, uses Chinese red 'dates' which are not dates at all but a wrinkled fruit which has a taste similar to apples and prunes. They are imported dried to the West, and can be bought from oriental food stores. But if you cannot find them, the soup tastes good without them.

INGREDIENTS

4 cups / 375 g fresh watercress	¹/₂ inch / 1 cm fresh ginger, peeled and chopped
4 Chinese red dates	2-4 teaspoons rice wine or dry white wine
2 teaspoons soy sauce	1 teaspoon sugar
4 cups / 950 ml stock (chicken or ham bone)	salt

1. First remove any discolored and wilted leaves from the watercress and break off the thickest part of the stems. You can add these to the soup if you wish.

2. Now bring the stock to the boil and add the dates and ginger. Simmer for about 15 minutes and when the dates are soft, put in the watercress, wine, sugar, soy sauce, salt and the watercress stems if using.

3. Allow this to simmer for 5 minutes or so until the watercress is tender and then serve ■

Ham and cabbage soup

Serves 4-6

'Chow mein' may be a firm favorite in the West but it does not really exist in Chinese cuisine. One story contends that 'chow' is an Americanism, arising from the presence of thousands of Chinese laborers working on the railroads early this century. When preparing food they would use the Mandarin word *Ch'ao*, meaning to cook or to fry and this was picked up by Western ears as 'chow' to mean food or stew. White cabbage can be used instead of Chinese cabbage.

INGREDIENTS

¹/₂ pound / 225 g piece of ham, or unsmoked gammon rasher	¹/₂ pound / 225 g Chinese or white cabbage
4 cups / 950 ml water	salt

1. If you are using gammon, cut it into ¹/₂ inch/1 cm cubes. For the ham, remove the rind and bone it before cubing.

2. Now put the meat (and bone if using ham) into a large pan and add the water and salt. Bring to the boil and then reduce heat and simmer for 20 minutes.

3. While this is cooking, separate and wash the leaves of the cabbage. Lay the leaf stalks together and slice the leaves thinly, crosswise.

4. Add these to the ham and stock, bring to the boil and simmer for 10 minutes. Season before serving ■

STAPLE FOODS: POTATOES

In Russia potatoes were first known as *'the devil's apples'*. In that country, as in other parts of Europe, any food which grew underground like this tuber were suspect, being associated with dirt and the devil.

All over Europe the friendly tuber took time to catch on after its introduction in the sixteenth century. Cultivated in Peru for over 7,000 years, potatoes were deemed to be *'of good flavor, a gift very acceptable to indians and a dainty dish even for Spaniards'* by the invading Iberians. But at first Europeans favored the plant more for its full leaves and pretty flowers — a perfect buttonhole — than as a source of food.

It was a different story in Ireland, where the potato may have been washed up with the wrecked galleons of the Spanish Armada. There, the tuber was quickly seized upon: it is easy to cultivate, requiring less land and labor than grains. And, for Irish peasants, potatoes would be safe underground, away from the boots of Queen Elizabeth I's rampaging unpaid soldiers and the warring Irish chiefs.

For the English landlords who wanted wheat to be grown, these advantages made potatoes the perfect provision for their Irish tenants. They would need less land to grow food on. This would release more for the wheat. And since potatoes required less looking after, the workers could spend more time cultivating the landlord's fields.

By the seventeenth century the 'Irish' potato was established as a prime food source for the Irish and increasingly for poorer people in other parts of Europe. It was a good source of protein, giving more nutrition from less land with less farming time than any cereal. But there was a catch. The potato was highly susceptible to disease. Potato blight ravaged the crops and in the ten years following the 1846 famine a quarter of Ireland's eight million people starved to death and a further 25 per cent left to seek work elsewhere. But during the famine, grain was still exported from Ireland to England; local hungry people could not afford to buy it.

To begin with, the rich held aloof from potatoes because they were seen as poor people's food. This changed over the centuries, possibly helped by the French horticulturalist Antoine-Auguste Parmentier who persuaded King Louis XVI — and therefore the populace — of the tuber's value. Parmentier's name is still associated with a potato soup, *potage Parmentier*.

Potatoes are used for humans and for animal feed, as starch and gums, as glucose in the pharmaceutical industry and also as alcohol (*potchine* in Ireland and *schnapps* in Eastern Europe). They readily lend themselves to the local cuisine wherever they happen to grow which is just about everywhere, and increasingly in developing countries such as India and Kenya. The food industry loves them too because they are cheap and can be turned into 'value-added' processed foods, which are more expensive — like chips or crisps.

Main producers (in descending order) Soviet Union, China, Poland, United States, India, East Germany, West Germany, France, Netherlands, UK.

World production (1985) 300 million tons.

INDIA

Curried potato fries/chips

Serves 2-4

With over 800 million people, India is the world's second most populous country after China. About two-thirds of the people farm, growing a wide range of food from millet and rice to chickpeas, lentils and, increasingly, potatoes which are becoming an important staple.

I N G R E D I E N T S

4 medium potatoes	1-2 cloves garlic, crushed
1/2 teaspoon turmeric	oil
1 tablespoon sesame seeds, toasted *	salt

* To toast the seeds, put a heavy pan over a medium heat and when warmed scatter the seeds in without oil. As they cook they will jump and turn golden.

1. To begin, cut the potatoes into French fry/chip shapes and then soak them in water for 30 minutes. Drain them and leave to dry out a little.

2. After this, heat enough oil to shallow fry. Add the potatoes and the salt. Cook for 15 minutes, stirring round.

3. Next add the turmeric and mix it well to spread the color evenly.

4. When the potatoes are nearly done, put in the crushed garlic and toasted sesame seeds. Mix well and then serve with dhal (see p.39) or as a snack ■

KOREA

Naeng myon (buckwheat noodle soup)

Serves 4

Buckwheat or 'groats' was eaten first in Central Asia but it remained untasted in Europe until the Middle Ages. Dutch settlers carried the cereal to North America where the seeds took root and thrived in the Hudson River Valley. It is very nutritious and is found in health stores as whole white buckwheat or as *kasha*, which is roasted hulled buckwheat kernels.

I N G R E D I E N T S

1 1/2 cups / 225 g thin buckwheat noodles *	1 pear
1 teaspoon sesame oil	4-6 red radishes or 1 small mooli / white radish, sliced
6 inches / 15 cms length of cucumber, unpeeled	2-4 teaspoons mustard powder or bottled mustard, diluted with enough water to make a thin sauce. +
2 cups / 470 ml stock, seasoned	+ optional ingredient
2 hard-boiled eggs	

* These are available as soba noodles from oriental groceries. If you cannot find them, use thin rice noodles.

1. Begin by cooking the noodles quickly in boiling water, or according to the instructions on the packet. When cooked, drain and rinse in a colander under cold water.

2. Place the noodles in a bowl and pour in about 1/2 cup/120 ml of the stock and the sesame oil. Toss the noodles in the mixture then cover the bowl and set aside. Put the stock into a saucepan and heat gently.

3. Taking the cucumber, trim off the ends and cut it into 2 inch/5 cm chunks. Now cut each chunk lengthwise into 8 slices. Follow this by peeling the eggs and slicing them thinly. Then divide the noodles among 4 bowls.

4. When this is done, peel and core the pear and cut it lengthwise into thin slivers. Now pour the hot stock over the noodles in each bowl, arrange the pear, cucumber, radish and egg on top. Serve right away, with the mustard sauce if liked ■

PAKISTAN

Samosas

Serves 2-4

Pakistan, with over 100 million people, grows enough wheat to meet its own needs except in times of bad drought or pest attack. Other main foods grown are rice, corn/maize, barley, millet, sorghum, peanuts, pulses, vegetables and fruit.

Samosas are increasingly popular outside the Indian and Pakistani communities who introduced them to other places such as the UK and parts of Africa. They are delicious with a squeeze of lime or lemon juice, a little green salad and a cold beer.

I N G R E D I E N T S

MEAT FILLING

1/2 pound / 225 g ground/ minced lamb

1 medium onion, chopped finely

2 cloves garlic, crushed

1 tablespoon oil

1 medium potato, parboiled and diced

1/2 teaspoon chili powder

1/2 teaspoon garam masala

small handful fresh cilantro / coriander leaves, chopped

salt and pepper

PASTRY

1 cup / 125 g plain flour

1/4 cup / 60 ml water

2 teaspoons oil

}

VEGETABLE FILLING

1 small onion, chopped finely

2 cloves garlic, crushed

1 tablespoon oil

1/2 cup / 85 g peas

1 medium potato, parboiled and diced

1 carrot, diced finely

1/2 teaspoon garam masala

1/2 teaspoon chili powder

small handful fresh cilantro / coriander leaves, chopped

salt and pepper

or use 1/2 pound / 225 g frozen plain pastry, thawed

1. First of all, make the dough by mixing the flour with the water and oil. Leave it to stand for 30 minutes.

2. For the meat filling, brown the meat and cook the onion and garlic in the oil and then add the spices and cook for 2 minutes. After this, put in the other ingredients and allow them to cook gently until soft. Leave to cool.

3. For the vegetable filling, soften the onion and garlic first in the oil. Add the spices and after cooking them for a couple of minutes put in the other vegetables for 5-10 minutes until soft. Then leave them to cool.

4. Now divide the pastry into 2 pieces and roll each portion out on a floured board into a thin rectangular shape, roughly 12 x 6 inches/30 x 15 cms. The pastry should be quite thin.

5. Cut the pastry into strips measuring 2 x 6 inches/5 x 15 cms. Put a small amount of the filling in the center of each strip and fold up into the shape of a triangle. Seal the edges with a little water.

6. Cook the samosas in a little oil over a medium heat until they are golden brown in color, or alternatively place them on a oiled broiling/grill pan and dot each with a little margarine or oil. Broil/grill under a medium heat, turning a few times so they do not catch ■

(Opposite) No mod cons – housework for this Bangladeshi woman is hard with no electricity or piped water.
Photo: Shahidul Alam/Drik Pictures

IN ALL RECIPES
● PEPPER AND SALT ARE TO TASTE
● CHILI AND SUGAR ARE GIVEN AS GUIDE QUANTITIES ONLY. VARY TO TASTE
● MEASURES FOR BEANS AND GRAINS REFER TO DRY INGREDIENTS.

PHILIPPINES

Habas con chorizos (Sausage and salad)
Serves 4

More than 7,000 islands make up the Philippines, a country that is rich in minerals and a leading gold producer. Islam had taken root in the South of the country by 1450 but the Spanish conquest in 1565 impeded its spread. Spanish rule was replaced in 1868 by US control for the next 50 years.

Chorizo is a Spanish spicy sausage made from pork and flavored with garlic, chilis, cumin, cloves, paprika and vinegar. It is prepared by air-drying and you can find it in supermarkets or delicatessen stores.

I N G R E D I E N T S

1½ cups / 250 g garbanzos / chickpeas, soaked and cooked

½ pound / 225 g chorizo or salami-type sausage, sliced

2 red bell peppers, sliced finely

1 green bell pepper, sliced finely

3 tomatoes, sliced

1 onion, chopped finely

2 cloves garlic, sliced finely

2 tablespoons vinegar

2 tablespoons olive oil

salt and pepper

1. Using a salad bowl, first put in the cooled garbanzos/chickpeas and then add the sausage, bell peppers, tomatoes, onion and garlic.

2. Whisk the vinegar and olive oil together in a bowl and season with salt and pepper. Pour this dressing over the salad, mix the salad well and serve ■

Hinalog na manok
(Chicken soup with ginger)
Serves 6

This soup uses a Filipino fruit, the *calamans*, which is a small, juicy citrus but since it is rarely found outside the Philippines, lime or lemon juice can be used instead. Incidentally, the chicken pieces need to marinate for 30 minutes.

I N G R E D I E N T S

¾ pound / 340 g chicken meat, skinned and removed from the bone *

2-3 tablespoons oil

2 onions, chopped finely

3 cloves garlic, crushed

½ inch / 1 cm fresh ginger root, peeled and cut very finely

4 tomatoes, sliced

2 tablespoons soy sauce

2-3 tablespoons calamansi, lime or lemon juice

6 cups / 1.4 liters chicken stock

1-2 chilis, sliced finely or ½ teaspoon chili powder

salt and pepper

* boil up the bones to make the stock

1. Begin by cutting the chicken into cubes about ½ inch/1 cm in size. Put the chicken pieces into a bowl and sprinkle on the salt and pepper. Leave them to stand for 30 minutes.

2. When this is done, heat up the oil in a large pan and cook the onions, garlic and ginger for 3 minutes. Then add the chicken and tomatoes and stir-fry for 10 minutes over a medium heat.

3. Now pour in the soy sauce, lime or lemon juice and stock and bring to boiling point. Let the soup bubble briskly for 2 minutes, then add the chili. Cover the pan now and reduce the heat. Simmer for 10-20 minutes until the chicken is tender ■

Sotanghon soup (Chicken noodle soup)

Serves 4

Most of the 56 million people of the Philippines live in the rural areas, as plantation workers or as subsistence farmers, growing rice, maize/corn, sweet potatoes, cassava/manioc, plantains, pineapples, mangoes and cocoa. Extremes of wealth and poverty still wrack the country in the wake of the Marcos years.

INGREDIENTS

³/₄ pound / 340 g chicken meat, skinned and removed from the bone *

2-3 tablespoons oil

1 medium onion, chopped

2 cloves garlic, crushed

1 leek, sliced into thin circles

2 carrots, sliced

* keep the bones to make the stock

1 stalk celery, sliced

4 cups / 950 ml chicken stock

¹/₂ teaspoon paprika

1 cup / 150 g sotanghon noodles +

1 tablespoon chives, chopped

salt and pepper

+ ideally use sotanghon or 'cellophane' noodles, but thin rice noodles will do.

1. Start by cutting the chicken meat into very small pieces. Then heat the oil in a large pan and soften the onion and garlic in it for a few minutes. After this add the leek, carrots and celery and let them cook for 5 minutes.

2. Next put in the chicken meat and the stock and season with salt, pepper and paprika. Bring to the boil and cook for 2-3 minutes before adding the noodles.

3. Lower the heat now and let the soup simmer gently for 10 minutes before serving, garnished with the chives ∎

BRAZIL

Creme de abacate (Avocado cream)

Serves 6

The creamy-textured avocado has been a major food for people in Central America for several thousand years. Nowadays it is grown commercially in Israel, Chile, South Africa and the US. It is rich in vitamins and minerals with unsaturated fat. In many tropical parts of the world it is a basic food and has been called 'the butter of the poor'.

It is usually eaten as a vegetable, in savory dishes. Yet the inclusion of sugar, as in this recipe, does not altogether make it a dessert ... just a delicious starter or snack served with raw carrot or celery sticks, crisps or nachos.

INGREDIENTS

3 large ripe avocados

2-4 tablespoons fresh lime or lemon juice

1 tablespoon sugar

6 lime or lemon slices for garnish

1. Cut the avocados in half and remove the stones. Carefully scoop out the flesh with a spoon into a mixing bowl and mash it with a fork. Keep the skins.

2. Begin to add the lime or lemon juice and the sugar and beat the mixture until smooth. Taste, and add more juice or sugar as desired.

3. Pile some of the avocado cream into each half skin, garnish with a slice of lime or lemon, and put in the fridge to chill before serving ∎

Sopa de batata doce (Sweet potato soup)

Serves 4

Brazil's world-famous carnival takes place on the days before the Christian period of Lent. Carnival time is given over to fun and also to feasting, to build up the body reserves for the time of self-denial and fasting ahead. And the word 'carnival' helps explain this. Coming from two Latin words, *carnis* (flesh) and *levare* (to take away) it signals the fact that when the carnival is over there would be an absence of meat.

INGREDIENTS

1 pound / 450 g sweet potatoes, chopped and boiled

2 tablespoons oil

4 tomatoes, peeled and chopped or 1 can *

3 ¹/₂ cups / 825 ml stock

1 onion, finely chopped

2 tablespoons fresh cilantro / coriander or parsley, chopped

* If using canned tomatoes, drain them and keep the liquid which can be added to the soup if desired.

1. In a pan, heat the oil and sauté the onion until it is golden and soft. Now add the tomatoes and cook for another 5 minutes, stirring them round gently. Follow this with the sweet potatoes and half the stock. Sieve or mash to make a purée, or put in a blender.

2. Pour the mixture into a saucepan and stir in the rest of the stock. Season to taste and heat through before serving, garnished with the herbs ∎

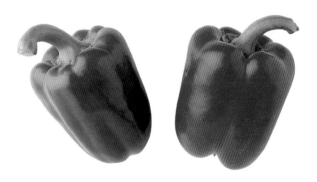

CARIBBEAN

Avocado soup

Serves 4-6

Many islanders in the Caribbean can still remember when they were ruled by the Dutch, the British, the French or the Spanish. This influence, interlaced with African, Indian and indigenous cuisine has produced a richness of cooking styles which vary from village to village as well as from island to island.

This soup has a delicate flavor and is best served chilled.

INGREDIENTS

3 avocados, very ripe

2 scallions / spring onions, sliced finely

juice of 1 lime or lemon

4 cups / 950 ml milk

salt and pepper

1. First of all slice the avocados lengthwise, remove the stones and scoop out the flesh. Put it into a bowl and mash to a purée.

2. Now put in the sliced scallions/spring onions and the lime or lemon juice and mix well.

3. Gradually add in the milk, beating constantly so that the soup is smooth. Season with salt and pepper and chill before serving ∎

CHILE

Sopa de topinambur (Jerusalem artichoke soup)

Serves 4

American indians were cultivating the Jerusalem 'artichoke' tuber long before the arrival of Colombus. It is not an artichoke however, and apparently acquired that label from the 17th century French colonialist, Samuel de Champlain, who found the flavor similar to artichokes. 'Jerusalem' is a corruption of the Italian word *girasole* (sunflower) perhaps because the tubers are related to a certain type of sunflower.

I N G R E D I E N T S

1 pound / 450 g Jerusalem artichokes

2 tablespoons oil

1 large onion, chopped finely

3$^1/_2$ cups / 825 ml stock

$^1/_2$ cup / 120 ml cream +

2 tablespoons fresh cilantro / coriander or parsley, chopped

salt and pepper

+ optional ingredient

1. To begin, scrape or peel the artichokes and cut off the most knobbly parts. Slice thickly.

2. Next heat the oil in a pan and cook the onion until golden. When that is done, add the artichokes and stock, bring the saucepan to the boil and then simmer for 25-30 minutes until the tubers are soft.

3. Purée or put the soup through a blender and then season. Return it to the saucepan and heat up, stirring in the cream (if using) before serving, with the herbs sprinkled on top ■

COLOMBIA

Banana/plantain chips

Serves 4-6

Carnations and other cut flowers are one of Colombia's most important exports and the country is the second largest producer of Arabica coffee after Brazil.

Sliced fried plantains or green bananas are a popular snack in many parts of the world, known as *Patacones* in Colombia, *Kluey chap* in Southeast Asia, *Matoke chips* in Kenya, *Plantain chips* in the Caribbean. There are many variations: paprika, pepper or salt can be used to flavor the chips or they can be served plain.

I N G R E D I E N T S

3 plantains / green bananas, peeled and cut into $^1/_2$ inch / 1 cm slices

oil for deep frying

salt

1. Using a saucepan or deep fry pan pour in enough oil to give a depth of 2-3 inches/5-7 cms. When the oil is moderately hot, put in the plantain slices and fry until tender, about 5 minutes. Then lift them out and drain. Cover with waxed (greaseproof) paper and press until each is about $^1/_4$ inch/0.5 cm thick.

2. Now raise the temperature of the oil to hot and cook the slices for a minute or so until they are brown and crispy on the outside. Lift them out, drain on paper towels and then sprinkle with salt or other flavoring. Let them cool a little before serving ■

ECUADOR

Sopa de mani (peanut soup)

Serves 4

Ecuador's main city, Quito, was the northern capital of the Inca empire. With local indians, Africans descended from slaves and Europeans as well, the country's mix of people is reflected in the types and combinations of food.

Peanuts – which are really legumes not nuts – came originally from Brazil but today they are cultivated around the world and especially in Africa and the United States.

INGREDIENTS

1 cup / 125 g peanuts, roasted and then finely ground or ¹/₂ cup / 60 g peanut butter

2 tablespoons oil

1 onion, chopped finely

1 pound / 450 g potatoes, chopped and boiled

4 cups / 950 ml stock

¹/₂ cup / 120 ml cream +

2 tablespoons chives, chopped

salt and pepper

+ optional ingredient

1. To begin with, heat the oil in a saucepan and cook the onion until it becomes transparent. Add the ground peanuts or peanut butter, potatoes and a little stock and mash well. Alternatively, put these ingredients into a blender.

2. Now pour the rest of the stock slowly into the purée, mixing well.

3. Bring the soup to the boil and then let it simmer, covered, for 5-10 minutes. After this, remove the pot from the heat, and season. Stir in the cream before serving, sprinkling the chives on top ∎

MEXICO

Carrot soup with orange

Serves 4

'Travelling around Central America for three months with very little money meant eating quite basic food – beans and eggs of course, as well as tripe in the *loncherias* (cafés) and *tortas*, filled rolls, in markets. At the end of the stay we splashed out and had a less basic meal which included a delicious carrot soup, and this is the version we make.' *Dexter Tiranti, Oxford, UK*

INGREDIENTS

1 pound / 450 g carrots, chopped

1 tablespoon oil

1 onion, sliced

¹/₄ cup / 60 ml orange juice

3 cups / 700 ml chicken stock

¹/₂ pound / 225 g potatoes, chopped

1. First put the oil in a saucepan, heat it up and then sauté the onion until it is golden. Now add the carrots and potatoes, stir them round for 1 minute and then pour in enough stock barely to cover them.

2. Put a lid on the saucepan, bring to the boil and then turn down the heat and let the vegetables simmer for 10-15 minutes until they are soft. Pour in the rest of the stock and season.

3. After this, put the soup into a blender or through a sieve until it is smooth and creamy. Return it to the pan and heat gently, adding the orange juice before serving ∎

Guacamole (Avocado dip)

Serves 6

'Mole' as in Guaca*mole* comes from the Nahuatl (Mexican indian) word *molli* meaning a sauce made from peppers or chilis, and this avocado mixture is often served as an accompaniment to meat dishes. But it also makes a delicious dip with nachos, crisps, sliced carrots or celery.

I N G R E D I E N T S

2 ripe avocados

1 small onion, sliced very finely or grated

1/2 chili, chopped or use a little chili powder or a few drops of Tabasco sauce

1 tomato, peeled and chopped finely

1 tablespoon olive oil

1 teaspoon lemon or lime juice

salt and pepper

1. To make the dip, first slice the avocados lengthwise around the center. Open them and remove the stones. Then carefully scoop out the flesh with a spoon and put it into a bowl.

2. Mash it with a fork and then add the onion, tomato, chili or Tabasco sauce, olive oil, lemon or lime juice and the salt and pepper. Mix everything until it becomes a creamy dip.

3. You can store the dip in the fridge, but cover it with cling film or a thin layer of mayonnaise to prevent discoloration ■

LEBANON

Chourba bi kousa (Zucchini/courgette and milk soup)

Serves 4-6

'Never say things cannot get worse in Lebanon, because they usually do' goes a rueful saying in this troubled state, once regarded as the jewel of the region. The war has disrupted the pattern of life and what farming remains provides some wheat, barley, maize/corn, vegetables, fruit, olives and tobacco.

Sumak used in this recipe is a ground spice which looks like chili powder but has a sour rather than hot taste. It is made from sumak berries and is widely used in Lebanese dishes. If you cannot find it in specialist grocery stores then use pieces of thinly pared lemon rind instead.

I N G R E D I E N T S

2 cups / 300 g zucchini/courgettes, cut into small chunks

2 1/2 cups / 590 ml milk or use half milk, half stock

2 tablespoons / 25 g margarine

1/4 teaspoon sumak * powder or 3 thin slices of lemon peel

1 tablespoon flour

1/2 teaspoon turmeric

handful fresh mint, chopped

1-2 tablespoons lemon juice

salt and pepper

* see above

1. First heat a little water in a pan and cook the zucchini/courgettes for a few minutes until they are soft. Drain them well and then mash and set aside.

2. Next, pour the milk or milk-and-stock mix into a saucepan and bring it to the boil. Then remove the pan from the heat.

3. While that is happening, melt the margarine in another saucepan, add the flour and turmeric and stir to make a smooth paste. Cook for 2 minutes, stirring all the time.

4. Then, with the pan off the heat, slowly add the heated milk or milk-and-stock, stirring constantly so that no lumps form. Then put the pan back on the heat and continue to stir while it thickens.

5. Next, add the zucchini/courgette purée and the sumak powder or lemon peel to the mixture, season with pepper and salt and continue stirring until the soup is hot. Pour in the lemon juice and add more liquid if necessary to achieve the consistency you prefer.

6. Sprinkle on the mint and a little turmeric before serving ■

IN ALL RECIPES
● PEPPER AND SALT ARE TO TASTE
● CHILI AND SUGAR ARE GIVEN AS GUIDE QUANTITIES ONLY. VARY TO TASTE
● MEASURES FOR BEANS AND GRAINS REFER TO DRY INGREDIENTS.

LEBANON

Hummus bi tahini (Garbanzo/chickpea dip)

Serves 4

India is the main producer of garbanzos/chickpeas, one of the legumes or pulses that are a vital part of people's diet in the South. Chickpeas probably originated in what is now Turkey and were taken overland to India. The Portuguese and Spanish slavers took the pulse to Central and South America. It was introduced into East and South Africa by the Indians who went to work there.

I N G R E D I E N T S

1¹/₂ cups / 250 g garbanzos / chickpeas, soaked and cooked

1-2 cloves garlic, crushed

1 tablespoon tahina *

a little milk

juice of 1-2 lemons

olive oil

chopped fresh parsley +

1 teaspoon sesame seeds +

salt and pepper

+ optional ingredient

* This is a paste made from sesame seeds, available from health food stores. Alternatively, you can use smooth peanut butter instead.

1. Purée the cooked garbanzos/chickpeas in a blender together with the garlic, adding the tahina paste, a little milk, lemon juice, a little oil, salt and pepper to make a smooth but not too runny mixture. You may need to do this in several batches, according to the blender's capacity.

2. Empty the mixture into a bowl and adjust the taste if necessary, adding more lemon juice, garlic or salt according to preference.

MIDDLE EAST

Beid Mahshi (Stuffed eggs)

Serves 4

Cinnamon, used with yogurt to flavor the dressing in this recipe, comes from the peeled bark of an evergreen tree native to Sri Lanka. It is best to buy it in its curled quill-shaped form if possible. Sometimes a similar-looking spice called *cassia* is sold as cinnamon; this comes from Vietnam and has a stronger flavor.

I N G R E D I E N T S

4 hard-boiled eggs, shelled

1-2 teaspoons sugar

1 inch / 2.5 cm piece of cinnamon, crushed or 1 teaspoon ground cinnamon

handful fresh parsley, finely chopped

1 cup / 240 ml yogurt

1 small onion, grated or minced

2-3 tablespoons olive oil

pinch of paprika

lettuce leaves

salt and pepper

1. To begin, pour the yogurt into a serving bowl and add the sugar, mixing well. Sprinkle half the cinnamon on top.

2. Now cut the eggs in half lengthwise, remove the yolks and put these into another bowl.

3. Mash the yolks with a fork and mix in the parsley and onion. Then add the olive oil to make a smooth mixture and season with the remainder of the cinnamon, paprika, salt and pepper.

4. Spoon some of the mixture into each of the egg white halves and place them on a plate which has the lettuce leaves arranged on it.

5. Pour or spoon a little of the yogurt-cinnamon dressing on top of the eggs and serve ■

Hab el Jose (Walnut balls)
Makes 15-20

Sesame seeds are used to garnish many dishes but in the cooking of Korea, Japan and China they are virtually a staple ingredient and a sesame seed sauce often accompanies main course foods. In the Middle East the seeds are used to make *tahina* (sesame paste), which flavor dishes including the dip, *hummus* (see p. 24).

These walnut balls, rolled in sesame seeds, are one of the specialities of the Turkish city Antakya, formerly Antioch, an early center of Christianity.

I N G R E D I E N T S

1 cup / 150 g walnuts, ground

1/2 cup / 50 g breadcrumbs

1/2 teaspoon ground cumin

1 tablespoon tahina paste *

1/2 teaspoon cayenne or chili powder

1/2 cup / 50 g sesame seeds

a little olive oil

pinch of paprika

1 tablespoon fresh mint, finely chopped +

salt and pepper

* available in health food stores

+ optional ingredient

1. Start by making a mixture with the walnuts, breadcrumbs and cumin. Put them into a bowl, and add enough tahina to make a soft paste. Flavor with the cayenne or chili powder and salt and pepper.

2. Shake the sesame seeds onto a plate. Now grease your fingers with olive oil and take up small pieces of the paste, shaping them into walnut-sized balls by rolling them between your palms. Then trail each of the walnut balls in the sesame seeds to coat them.

3. Before serving, arrange the hab el jose on a plate and sprinkle the paprika and mint over them ■

Lentil soup
Serves 4-6

Their high protein content makes lentils valuable food items. They are the customary companion of wheat and barley cultivation in the Mediterranean Arab countries and are widely grown also in India, Pakistan and Ethiopia. For this thick soup, any lentils can be used but the small red ones do not need to be pre-soaked, they cook quickly and mush down easily.

I N G R E D I E N T S

1 1/2 cups / 335 g red lentils, rinsed

2 tablespoons oil

1 onion, chopped

1 stalk celery with leaves, chopped

1 carrot, chopped

4 cups / 950 ml stock

1 teaspoon ground cumin

juice of 1 lemon

salt and pepper

1. In a large pan, heat the oil and then sauté the onion for 5 minutes or so. When it is transparent, add the celery and carrot and cook them until they begin to soften.

2. After this, put in the red lentils and the stock. Bring to the boil and skim the surface to remove any froth. Simmer gently until the lentils are soft, about 15 minutes.

3. When they are ready, add the salt, pepper, cumin and lemon juice and mix well. If a smoother soup is required you can put the mixture into the blender or through a sieve, or simply mash it with a potato masher or wooden spoon ■

25

Munazelet Banadoora (Onion and tomato soup)

Serves 6-8

The basic diet in the Middle East is wheat or rice, beans, some meat (usually lamb or goat), milk products, vegetables and fresh fruit such as dates. In this typical Arab soup – which is more like a stew – both the meat and vegetables are fried and seasoned first, before the stock is added. To make a main course meal, you can put in rice or slices of bread and use more vegetables or red lentils.

I N G R E D I E N T S

2 tablespoons / 25 g margarine	1 tablespoon tomato paste
2 onions, sliced thinly	6 cups / 1.4 liters stock
2 cloves garlic, sliced finely	1/2 teaspoon dillweed
1 pound / 450 g lamb, cut into strips, 1/4 inch / 0.5 cm thick	2 tablespoons fresh parsley, chopped
2 pounds / 900 g tomatoes, chopped	salt and pepper

1. Take a large pan and melt the margarine in it over a gentle heat. Then cook the onions and garlic until they are soft. Add the meat pieces and stir them around so that they brown on all sides. Then cover the pan and simmer very gently for 15 minutes.

2. Now add the chopped tomatoes and mix them in. Put the lid back on the pan and continue to cook slowly.

3. Using a small bowl, dilute the tomato paste in some of the stock and pour this into the pan. Add the remaining stock, dillweed, salt and pepper and bring to the boil.

4. Lower the heat and allow to simmer for 1-2 hours or until the meat is tender. Taste and adjust the seasoning before serving garnished with parsley ■

Mutabbal (Egg-plant/aubergine dip)

Serves 4-6

Egg-plant/aubergine probably originated in India and has been known in China since the fifth century BC. Taken to Africa by Arab and Persian traders, today the plant is widely grown in warm countries. It has many uses, including medicinal ones. In India its Sanskrit name implies 'anti-wind vegetable' while in the *Kama Sutra* it is included in a potion for 'enlarging the male organ for a period of one month'.

I N G R E D I E N T S

1 pound / 450 g egg-plant/aubergine	1 teaspoon ground cumin
3 cloves garlic, crushed	1 tablespoon olive oil
1-2 tablespoons tahina paste *	a few black olives
juice of 2 lemons	1 tablespoon fresh parsley, chopped
1/2 -1 teaspoon chili powder	salt

* Tahina paste is available from health food stores

Heat oven to 375°F/190°C/Gas 5

1. Make several slits in the skin of the egg-plants/aubergines and then put them in the oven for 30-40 minutes, until the skins are very dark and the flesh feels soft when squeezed. Set them aside to cool.

2. When this is done, scoop the flesh into a bowl. Mash it with a fork, adding the garlic and salt.

3. When it is pulped, spoon in the tahina, lemon juice and chili powder and mix well or put in a blender.

4. Place the mutabbal on a plate or in a shallow bowl and sprinkle the cumin on top. Then pour over the olive oil and garnish with the olives and parsley. Serve as a dip with slices of pita bread, carrot, celery and green or red bell pepper ■

IN ALL RECIPES
- **PEPPER AND SALT ARE TO TASTE**
- **CHILI AND SUGAR ARE GIVEN AS GUIDE QUANTITIES ONLY. VARY TO TASTE**
- **MEASURES FOR BEANS AND GRAINS REFER TO DRY INGREDIENTS.**

Chinese vegetable stir-fry. *Photo by: Svante Sjostedt/Camera Press.*

AFRICA

Plantains/green bananas with beans

Serves 2

More than a third of Africa's land area is desert or has dry shallow soils that cannot sustain crops. Some of the most fertile areas are in the highlands which stretch from northern Ethiopia down the Rift Valley to northern Tanzania.

Plantains – savory bananas – are grown in tropical areas of the world (see **Staple Food p.76**). In Africa as well as being an important food they are made into beer, especially in East Africa. The bananas are easier to peel if you cook them first (see step 1), and they are best served immediately after cooking.

I N G R E D I E N T S

4 plantains / green bananas

1/2 cup / 110 g black-eyed, soy or other beans, soaked and cooked

2 tablespoons / 25 g margarine

1/2 teaspoon chili powder

salt and pepper

1. Put the plantains, unpeeled, in a saucepan of boiling water and let them cook for 25-30 minutes. After that, take them out and let them cool before you peel them and chop into small pieces.

2. Mix the plantains with the cooked beans in a pan and then heat them together with a very little water until both are tender and most of the liquid has evaporated.

3. Now add the margarine, chili powder, salt and pepper and mash before serving with a sauce and vegetables ■

Cassava/manioc and corn pie

Serves 4

Originating in South America, cassava or manioc is a staple food for many people in the world. It is popular because it grows easily, requires little cultivation and is resistant to drought (see **Staple Food p.118**). In this recipe, the flavor of the toasted peanuts complements the blandness of the pie's cassava/manioc crust.

I N G R E D I E N T S

1 pound / 450 g cassava/manioc, peeled and chopped

1/4 cup / 30 g peanuts, roasted and coarsely chopped

1 cup / 240 ml milk

3 eggs

4 tablespoons / 50 g margarine

a little chili powder or paprika

2 cups / 300 g corn kernels, cooked

salt and pepper

Heat oven to 375°F/190°C/Gas 5

1. Begin by boiling the cassava/manioc for about 20 minutes until it is tender. Then drain it and mash, using a little of the milk and margarine.

2. Now melt the remaining margarine in a pan and add the corn and peanuts, mixing them with a spoon as they cook.

3. Grease a 7 inch/17.5 cm pie dish and line the base with the mashed cassava/manioc, pressing it into place with the back of a spoon. Put the corn and peanut mixture on top.

4. Break the eggs into a bowl and beat them. Pour in the milk, shake in the seasoning and mix well. Now pour the mixture over the corn and peanut pie, sprinkling some chili or paprika on top.

5. Bake for about 30 minutes until the egg mixture has set and the top is golden. Serve with spinach or salad ■

ETHIOPIA

Shiro wot (Peanut stew)

Serves 2

An Ethiopian version of peanut or groundnut stew, really a thick sauce, which is a common dish in many parts of Africa. It would normally be accompanied by the Ethiopian staple, *ingera*, which is made from a millet-like grain called *teff.* (**see Staple Foods p.160**) Try millet, rice or bulgur.

I N G R E D I E N T S

2 cups / 250 g peanuts*, ground or 1 cup / 225 g peanut butter

4 tablespoons / 50 g margarine

1 small onion, chopped

1 tablespoon tomato paste

1/2 teaspoon fresh or dried thyme

1/2 teaspoon ground mixed spice or a mixture of ground cinnamon and nutmeg

1 teaspoon paprika

2 1/2 cups / 590 ml water

salt and pepper

* If using peanuts, measure them first and then grind them.

1. To start making the stew, heat the margarine in a pan and cook the onion for about 3 minutes until it begins to turn golden. Then add the tomato paste, thyme, mixed spice and paprika, salt and pepper. Stir well to combine the ingredients.

2. When the onion is cooked, put in the finely ground peanuts or peanut butter and enough of the water to make a smooth but thick sauce. Stir constantly while you add the liquid. Check the seasoning and then let the stew heat through before serving with millet, bulgur or rice and a cucumber salad ∎

KENYA

Cassava/manioc and cheese pie

Serves 2-4

The way the cassava/manioc is used in this dish makes it similar to mashed potato, so the pie can be used as a straightforward introduction to cassava/manioc for the less adventurous palate.

I N G R E D I E N T S

1 pound / 450 g cassava/manioc, peeled and diced

1 cup / 225 g cheese, grated

2 medium carrots, sliced thinly

1/4 cup / 60 ml milk

2 tablespoons / 25 g margarine

handful fresh parsley, chopped

salt and pepper

1. First boil the diced cassava/manioc in salted water for about 30 minutes until it is tender. Then drain it and put into a bowl.

2. Cook the carrots for a few minutes in boiling water and then drain them also.

3. While they are cooking, add the milk, margarine, salt and pepper to the cooked cassava/manioc and mash it thoroughly until it is white and fluffy. Now put in most of the cheese and mix it in evenly.

4. After that, grease an oven-proof dish and spoon the mixture into it. Sprinkle the remaining cheese on top and decorate with the carrot slices. Put the pie under the broiler/grill for a few minutes until the cheese has melted and then decorate with the parsley and serve at once with vegetables ∎

IN ALL RECIPES
● **PEPPER AND SALT ARE TO TASTE**
● **CHILI AND SUGAR ARE GIVEN AS GUIDE QUANTITIES ONLY. VARY TO TASTE**
● **MEASURES FOR BEANS AND GRAINS REFER TO DRY INGREDIENTS.**

KENYA

Irio (Maize/corn and bean mash)

Serves 6

In Africa, women perform 60 to 80 per cent of the agricultural work. This contribution is often overlooked in training programs and farming credit schemes even though women take many of the most important decisions such as when to plant and which seeds to use.

Maize/corn and beans are two subsistence or food crops which are commonly grown together in many parts of the world, the beans returning to the soil the nutrients taken out by the maize/corn.

Versions of this corn and bean mash are common in Africa. It makes a substantial meal and is especially good when made with a tasty stock.

I N G R E D I E N T S

3 cups / 450 g corn kernels, cooked

1 cup / 200 g haricot, sugar or red kidney beans, soaked and cooked

1/2 pound / 225 g potatoes, chopped

2 1/2 cups / 590 ml stock or water

1 pound / 450 g pumpkin leaves or spinach, chopped

salt and pepper

1. First boil the potatoes in the stock or water for 10 minutes or until they are almost cooked. Then add in the beans, corn kernels and the spinach or pumpkin leaves.

2. Continue to cook together until the potatoes are ready, the beans and corn hot and the spinach or pumpkin leaves are cooked.

3. Then drain off most of the liquid into a bowl and keep it. Add a little margarine, salt and pepper to the bean and potato mix and mash well using a fork or a potato masher. Put in more liquid if required to make the consistency you prefer and then serve hot ■

(Opposite) Hard grind – woman (and baby) grinding millet, Burkina Faso.
Photo: Jeremy Hartley/Panos Pictures

Red kidney bean stew

Serves 2-4

Over one third of households in the world are now headed by women. In Kenya the figure is about the same. One of the reasons is that men leave the land in search of paid work in the cities, sometimes never to return. Having generally less access to land and credit than men, women end up poorer when they have to provide for their families on their own.

I N G R E D I E N T S

1 cup / 225 g red kidney beans, soaked and cooked

2-3 tablespoons / 25-40 g ghee, margarine or oil

1 onion, chopped

3 large tomatoes or 1 can tomatoes, chopped

1 1/4 cups / 300 ml milk

a little stock or water

handful fresh parsley or cilantro / coriander, chopped

salt and pepper

1. To begin, heat the ghee or oil in a heavy saucepan and add the onion, letting it cook gently until it is transparent. Then put in the tomatoes and cook for 2-3 minutes.

2. While they are cooking, mash half the beans in a bowl with a fork or potato masher.

3. Now mix the onions and tomatoes with the mashed beans. Gradually pour in enough milk to make this into a thick sauce and then return the mixture to the saucepan. Add the remaining unmashed beans. Increase the heat now and bring to the boil, stirring so that it does not stick.

4. Then lower the heat, cover, and let the stew simmer very gently for 10-15 minutes, stirring frequently to prevent it catching. The sauce should be fairly thick, but more milk or water can be added according to your preference.

5. Before you serve it, add the pepper and salt and then spoon the bean stew over rice or other cereal. Scatter the parsley or cilantro/coriander garnish on top and serve ■

STAPLE FOODS: SORGHUM

The most important food crop in Africa, drought-resistant sorghum is also cultivated in India, China, Southeast Asia and Latin America. Together with millet it forms the staple diet for some 400 million people.

Wild sorghum grasses are found in Southeast Asia, North Africa and tropical Africa. It may have been people in West Africa or the Cushite people in Ethiopia who first cultivated sorghum. The Cushites, traveling from the Middle East down to Ethiopia brought wheat and barley with them, and also the ideas and techniques of cultivating grasses for food. As long ago as 3500 BC they were developing a range of crops in the malaria-free Ethiopian highlands and out of these evolved finger-millet, sorghum and also *teff* — still a major grain in Ethiopia.

Cultivated sorghum travelled across the Sahara region (which was wetter then) towards West Africa, with improvements being made along the way and over time. Its arrival as a reliable food plant in the Upper Niger river region encouraged the Mande people there to look at their own food plants and to develop other crops such as rice, millet and cowpeas.

At some point sorghum — the Guinea type with white grains — spread down to East Africa. There it mixed with local varieties which were probably already being cultivated in what are now Kenya, Uganda and Tanzania. The Bantu people who now live in these countries came originally from the Cameroon area in West Africa, and when they reached the eastern side of the central African forests they came across sorghum. No doubt this crop gave them the means of survival and helped their expansion into the dry savannah country to the South.

India's contact with the grain goes back about 3,000 years and sorghum spikelets mixed with potting clay have been found at Ahar in Rajastan. From India the crop probably spread along the coasts of Southeast Asia and on to China at the beginning of the Christian era. Or it may have been taken much earlier to China along the ancient silk trade routes. As with so many other foods, the first grains of sorghum were probably conveyed to the Americas in the holds of the slave ships. It is grown quite widely there, especially in Central and South America — Mexico and Argentina are the world's third and fourth largest producers. The United States is the major grower but its crop is used for animal fodder. As is often the case, crop development has been geared to Western (livestock feed) priorities rather than to improving sorghum as a food for people. Some indication of sorghum's lowly status is seen in its name in South Africa, *kafir-corn*.

Sorghum is eaten as porridge and pounded into flour for bread, and it makes good beer.

Main producers (in descending order) US, India, Mexico, Argentina, China, Nigeria, Sudan, Australia, Burkina Faso, Ethiopia.

World production (1985) 75.6 million tons.

Sweet potato, cheese and onion casserole

Serves 4

Sweet potatoes featured in Columbus' chronicles of his Hispaniola expedition and they were already widely eaten in the Americas by that time. The Spanish brought sweet potatoes to Europe but they never became as popular there as the regular potato. Taken by the Portuguese to Africa, India and Southeast Asia, sweet potatoes are now widely eaten in the tropical parts of the world (see **Staple Food p. 160**).

I N G R E D I E N T S

1 pound / 450 g sweet potatoes, peeled and sliced thinly	1 large onion, sliced thinly into circles
a little water or stock	1 cup / 225 g cheese, grated
1 tablespoon margarine	1/2 teaspoon chili powder
	salt and pepper

Heat oven to 350°F/180°C/Gas 4

1. Grease an oven-proof dish and line it with the sweet potato slices. Pour in just enough water or stock to coat the base of the dish evenly and then dot margarine amongst the layers of potato.

2. Arrange the onion circles on top of the sweet potato and finish up with the cheese. Sprinkle on the chili powder, salt and pepper.

3. Cover the dish and cook for 1 hour, removing the lid for the last 15 minutes to brown. Serve hot with soybean scones (see p.148) and salad ■

LESOTHO

Mixed cereal stew

Serves 4

A few years ago, swapping his Mercedes for a Toyota was Lesotho King Moshoeshoe II's gesture to show his commitment to wealth redistribution. But it won't be easy.

Lying deep in the South African interior, the tiny state is surrounded by its powerful neighbor and dependent on it for most necessities. Hopefully the changes in South Africa will in time benefit the people of Lesotho. Since the turn of the century large numbers of Sotho men have worked in the Rand gold mines as migrant workers.

If you cannot obtain sorghum (see **Staple Food opposite**) from a health store, use millet instead. Note that the grains need to soak overnight.

I N G R E D I E N T S

1/2 cup / 110 g wheat grains, soaked overnight	1 onion, chopped
1/2 cup / 110 g sorghum or millet, soaked overnight	2 cups / 300 g mixture of potatoes, carrots and cabbage, chopped
4 cups / 950 ml stock	1/2 cup / 120 ml milk
2 tablespoons oil	salt and pepper

1. Start the stew by draining the cereals, keeping the water they were soaked in. Now put them into a pan with the stock, cover, and bring to the boil. Then turn down the heat and simmer for 45 minutes or until the grains are soft, adding some of retained soaking water if necessary to prevent them drying out.

2. Using another pan, heat up the oil and sauté the onion until it is golden. Add the potatoes and carrots and cook them for 10 minutes, stirring often so that they do not catch. Then put in the cabbage and the remaining stock and cook for a further 5-8 minutes.

3. When the vegetables are done, stir in the cooked cereals, add the milk and boil gently until the stew is the desired consistency for you. Then add the pepper and salt and serve with sliced tomatoes ■

NIGERIA

Wake-Ewa (Black-eyed beans with sauce)

Serves 4-6

Black-eyed beans, a whitish bean with a little black or yellow eye, were originally brought with slaves to America from Africa. In parts of the Caribbean black-eyed beans and rice are eaten on New Year's Day to bring good luck. In West Africa they are a staple food, often made into *akara*, bean cakes, or turned into a sauce as in this recipe.

I N G R E D I E N T S

2 cups / 450 g black-eyed beans, soaked and cooked

1 large onion

4 tablespoons oil

1 teaspoon chili powder

1 teaspoon ground cilantro / coriander

1 teaspoon thyme

3 tomatoes, chopped finely

1 teaspoon sugar

salt

1. First cut the onion in half. Grate one half and then slice the rest finely.

2. Warm the oil in a pan and soften the onion slices in it.

3. Meanwhile combine the grated onion, chili, cilantro/coriander and thyme in a bowl with the tomatoes and add this to the cooked onion slices. Continue to cook the mixture gently for 10-15 minutes, stirring constantly.

4. After this put in the beans, mash them a little with a fork and then add the sugar and salt. Mix everything well and cook for 5-10 minutes to heat all the ingredients before serving with salad and rice or fufu (see p.121) ■

SENEGAL

Vegetable mafé (Stew)

Serves 6-8

About 40 per cent of Senegal's farmland is taken up for peanuts which are the main export. This squeezes the amount of land available for growing subsistence food crops such as millet, rice, maize/corn and beans.

This tasty dish is quite peppery. Use turnips if you cannot find pumpkin, and ginger makes an acceptable alternative to chili if you prefer a less hot but still spicy flavor.

I N G R E D I E N T S

3-4 tablespoons peanut oil

2 large onions, finely chopped

1 chili, chopped or 1 teaspoon chili powder or 1 teaspoon ground ginger

1 pound / 450 g potatoes, quartered

1 small turnip, chopped coarsely

2 large carrots, sliced

1 cup / 150 g pumpkin, squash or marrow, peeled and cubed

1 cup / 240 ml water

1 cup / 240 ml tomato paste

1/2 pound / 225 g cabbage, chopped

1 cup / 225 g leafy greens (such as pumpkin leaves/ spinach)

2 large tomatoes, quartered

1 cup / 225 g peanut butter

1. Firstly heat the oil in a large pan or stew pot and then brown the onions, adding the chili or ginger when the onions are soft. Cook for 2-3 minutes.

2. Next put in the potatoes and turnip pieces and cook them for 10 minutes before adding the carrots and pumpkin. Continue cooking for a further 10 minutes.

3. Now pour the water onto the tomato paste, stirring as you do so and then add this to the vegetable pot. Cover,

bring to the boil and then reduce the heat and simmer until the vegetables are nearly done.

4. At this point add the cabbage, the other leafy vegetables and the tomatoes. Season with salt and pepper.

5. When cooked, remove about ¹/₂ cup/120 ml of the broth and mix it with the peanut butter to make a smooth paste. Put this back into the pot and stir; simmer for another 10 minutes. Serve with rice or corn/maize porridge (see p.123) ∎

TANZANIA

Beans with coconut milk

Serves 4

African peasant farmers are some of the most resourceful cultivators. Organic recycling is one aspect of this: Bukabo people in Tanzania for instance carry grasses and reeds from swamps and marshes and use them as mulch for their impoverished soils. For food, most Tanzanians grow cassava/manioc, sorghum, millet and maize/corn, with rice in the Rufiji river flood plain.

I N G R E D I E N T S

2 cups / 350 g beans or garbanzos / chickpeas, soaked and cooked

1-2 tablespoons oil

1 clove garlic, chopped finely

2 teaspoons turmeric

1-2 cloves, crushed

1 medium tomato, chopped

¹/₂ cup / 50 g creamed coconut melted in ¹/₂ cup / 120 ml hot water

salt and pepper

1. To begin, heat the oil in a pan and sauté the garlic. Then add the turmeric and cloves and cook for a further minute.

2. Next put in the cooked beans or garbanzos/chickpeas, the tomato, salt and pepper. Pour in the coconut milk and let the ingredients heat up thoroughly before serving with rice or corn porridge ∎

BANGLADESH

Sobji Bharji (Fried vegetables)

Serves 6-8

'I was taught to cook *Sobji Bharji* by Duli, one of the many single (deserted) mothers who live in the slums of Dhaka. Bangladeshis eat mainly vegetables as meat is too expensive to eat every day, and in any case 10 per cent of the population is Hindu (vegetarian). I have modified the cooking time in the recipe to keep the vegetables crunchy.' *Rachel Poulton, Dhaka, Bangladesh*

I N G R E D I E N T S

2 tablespoons oil

2 medium onions, sliced finely

1 teaspoon ground ginger

1 teaspoon ground cilantro / coriander

¹/₄ teaspoon chili powder

2 teaspoons turmeric

2 teaspoons sugar

1 teaspoon curry powder

4 medium carrots, sliced and parboiled

6 medium potatoes, cubed and parboiled

¹/₂ pound / 225 g cauliflower, cut into small pieces

1 cup / 150 g zucchini/ courgettes, squash or marrow, chopped finely

1 cup / 150 g green beans, cut into short lengths, or peas

4 tablespoons desiccated coconut, moistened in a little water, then drained

salt

NOTE: Potatoes, carrots and onions are always included but you can vary the other vegetables.

1. Begin by heating 1 tablespoon of the oil in a wok or large pan and then add the onions, cooking gently until they are transparent.

2. In a bowl, mix all the spices and sugar with the other tablespoon of oil and add this to the onions, stirring well.

3. Now put in the carrots and potatoes and cook over a medium heat for 2 minutes. After that, add the remaining vegetables and mix them well.

4. Increase the heat a little and put in the coconut, then continue to stir-fry gently for 5-10 minutes until all the vegetables are cooked. Serve hot with rice ∎

CHINA

Bean-curd/tofu with oyster sauce

Serves 4

Oyster sauce, widely used in Cantonese stir-fried foods, is made from ground oysters, soy sauce and brine. It does not give a strong fishy flavor to dishes; rather it enhances other flavors. You can usually buy it in larger supermarkets.

Bean-curd or tofu, made from soybeans, is called 'meat without bones' for its protein power. It's also low in calories and cholesterol, and it's cheap.

INGREDIENTS

1 cup / 225 g smoked
bean-curd / tofu, cut into
small cubes

2 tablespoons oil

4 cups / 200 g
mushrooms, sliced

3 stalks celery, cut into 1/2
inch / 1 cm diagonal slices

6 scallions / spring
onions, cut into 1 inch/
2.5 cm pieces

1 red or green bell pepper,
cut into chunks

1 tablespoon
cornstarch/cornflour

1/4 cup / 60 ml water

2 tablespoons oyster sauce

4 teaspoons dry sherry

4 teaspoons dark soy sauce

salt

1. First, heat 1 tablespoon of the oil in a wok or heavy pan and cook the bean-curd cubes over a high heat for about 3 minutes, stirring all the time, until they are light brown. Remove them from the pan and set to one side.

2. Now heat the rest of the oil in the wok and when it is hot add the mushrooms, celery, scallions/spring onions and bell pepper. Stir-fry for 2-3 minutes until the vegetables begin to soften.

3. Return the bean-curd to the wok and toss it lightly to mix it in.

4. Taking a small bowl, combine the cornstarch/cornflour with a little water to make a smooth paste. Then add any remaining water, the oyster sauce, sherry and soy sauce.

5. Pour this over the mixture in the wok, let it heat up while you stir until the liquid is bubbling and then cook for a further minute. Serve at once ∎

Fried rice

Serves 6

Rice cultivation was originally a haphazard business – casting the seeds into marshland and praying for a good harvest. The Chinese were the first to flood arable fields to create controlled rice paddies, with such excellent results that as long ago as 2800 BC rice was named as one of their Five Sacred Crops (the others being soybeans, wheat, millet and barley).

INGREDIENTS

2 cups / 400 g rice,
cooked and kept hot

3 tablespoons oil

2 cups / 450 g bean-curd/
tofu, cut into small cubes

1 inch / 2.5 cm fresh
ginger root, peeled and
sliced finely or 1 teaspoon
ground ginger

6-8 scallions / spring
onions, chopped finely

1/2 pound / 225 g prawns
or shrimps, shelled

1 egg, beaten

1-2 tablespoons soy
sauce

salt and pepper

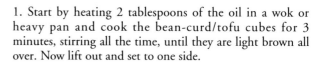

1. Start by heating 2 tablespoons of the oil in a wok or heavy pan and cook the bean-curd/tofu cubes for 3 minutes, stirring all the time, until they are light brown all over. Now lift out and set to one side.

2. When this is done, put in the ginger, scallions/spring onions, rice, prawns if using, salt and pepper, adding more oil if required, and cook gently for 10 minutes, stirring frequently. If using prawns or shrimps, put these in now. Return the bean-curd/tofu cubes and let them heat through.

3. Next, make a well in the rice mixture and pour in the beaten egg. Let it cook until set in the heat of the rice and then break it up with a fork and distribute it through the rice mixture.

4. Finally, pour in the soy sauce and mix in before serving ∎

CHINA

Prawn omelet with celery

Serves 2

China is about the same size as the United States and lies in roughly the same latitudes, with a similar climate. But the land suitable for cultivation in China only amounts to 12 per cent, whereas the US can call on nearly a quarter of its land area. Most of China's farmland requires irrigation or drainage, and management of the water supply has always been a key issue for any government.

I N G R E D I E N T S

3 eggs	1 stick celery, chopped finely
1¹/₄ cups / 300 ml milk	
2 tablespoons oil	1 cup / 50 g bean sprouts
1 cup / 100 g shelled prawns	¹/₂ teaspoon sugar
¹/₄ pound / 110 g mushrooms, sliced finely	1 teaspoon soy sauce
2 scallions / spring onions, chopped finely	salt and pepper

1. Crack the eggs into a bowl and beat them together with the milk, salt and pepper.

2. Next heat the oil in a wok or pan and add the prawns, the sliced mushrooms, scallions/spring onions, celery and bean sprouts. Sprinkle on the sugar and soy sauce. Stir-fry for 3 minutes.

3. Increase the heat if necessary and pour in the egg mixture, cooking it quickly for 2 minutes, lifting the edges to allow any uncooked mixture to flow under to the hot pan. Cut into wedges and serve immediately ■

Stir-fried vegetables with bean-curd/tofu

Serves 4-6

Water chestnuts, used in this dish, come from the tubers of marsh-growing sedges in Asia. Their crisp texture seems to survive the canning process, which is as well since fresh ones are hard to come by in the West.

Arrowroot powder is used to thicken and has less flavor than cornstarch/cornflour. Its name probably derives from the *aru* root of the South American Arucu Indian, or it could be associated with the plant's use in the treatment of wounds from poisoned arrows. In East Africa the root is eaten, boiled, as a starchy vegetable.

I N G R E D I E N T S

1¹/₂ cups / 225 g bean-curd/tofu, sliced or cubed	³/₄ cup / 110 g zucchini/ courgettes, sliced finely
4 tablespoons oil	4 cups / 200 g bean sprouts
4 scallions / spring onions, sliced finely	¹/₂ cup / 85 g peas (canned or frozen will do)
¹/₂ teaspoon ground ginger	1 cup / 150 g Chinese or white cabbage, shredded
¹/₄ pound / 110 g mushrooms, sliced finely	1 tablespoon arrowroot powder or cornstarch/ cornflour
³/₄ cup / 110 g celery, sliced finely	4 tablespoons water
¹/₂ cup / 50 g water chestnuts, sliced finely	2 tablespoons soy sauce
³/₄ cup / 110 g carrots, sliced very thinly	¹/₂ teaspoon sugar

1. The bean-curd/tofu can be cooked first in a little hot oil for about 3 minutes, stirring constantly to lightly brown all sides. Then set it aside.

2. Now put in the scallions/spring onions, ginger, mushrooms, celery, water chestnuts, carrots and zucchini/courgettes, pouring in more oil if required. Stir-fry these for 1-2 minutes.

3. After this, add the bean sprouts, peas and cabbage, again with more oil if needed, and continue to cook for 2-3 minutes, stirring all the time.

4. Now mix the arrowroot or cornstarch/cornflour with the water to make a smooth paste and pour this in, then the soy sauce, sugar, cooked bean curd and salt.

5. Simmer, covered, for 5 minutes and then remove the lid, turn up the heat and cook briskly for 1 minute. Serve at once with rice ■

HONG KONG

Omelet with bean sprouts

Serves 2

Acquired by the British in the 1840s, Hong Kong served as a trading centre between East and West. The trade was reduced in the 1950s at the time of the Korean War and a UN embargo on the export of strategic goods to China. So the colony turned to manufacturing and more recently it has become a major financial centre.

For this recipe you can use mung bean sprouts or soy bean sprouts.

INGREDIENTS

3 eggs

1 tablespoon milk

dash of soy sauce

2 cups / 100 g bean sprouts

3 scallions / spring onions, chopped finely

1 tablespoon oil

salt and pepper

1. In a bowl, beat the eggs and then mix in the milk, soy sauce, salt and pepper, scallions/spring onions and the bean sprouts.

2. When this is done, heat the oil in a pan, pour in the egg mixture and cook quickly, turning once. Serve right away ■

INDIA

Curried eggs with ginger

Serves 4

Although India's main export is pearls and precious stones, it also grows enough grains to sell some of the surplus to other countries and to save some of its people from famine. This is the up-side of the 'Green Revolution'

– the package of improved seeds, use of irrigation and chemical fertilizers which has often been seen as a blessing for richer farmers with their land and money for fertilizers, while pushing poorer ones to the brink. Despite increased grain harvests, many people in India are still too poor to buy all that they need.

INGREDIENTS

8 hard-boiled eggs, shelled

3 tablespoons ghee or margarine

1 large onion, chopped

1 clove garlic, crushed

1 medium can tomatoes, chopped

1 teaspoon ground cumin

1 teaspoon ground cilantro/ coriander

1 teaspoon ground ginger

$1/2$ teaspoon turmeric

1 cup / 240 ml water

1 tablespoon fresh cilantro/ coriander leaves, chopped

salt and pepper

Heat oven to 350°F/180°C/Gas 4

1. First of all halve the eggs lengthwise and put the yolks into a bowl.

2. Then melt the ghee or margarine in a saucepan and cook the onion until it is transparent. Add the garlic, tomatoes, spices, water, salt and pepper. Simmer gently for 20 minutes before straining or puréeing the mixture to make a sauce.

3. Next, mix the egg yolks with about 2 tablespoons of the sauce to make a soft consistency and spoon some onto each egg case.

4. Put the remaining sauce into a shallow ovenproof dish and place the stuffed egg halves on top. Cover and bake for 10 minutes, sprinkling on the cilantro/coriander before serving with rice ■

INDIA

Channa dhal (Garbanzo/chickpea curry)

Serves 6

'Many moons ago an Indian friend and his son called unexpectedly. As it was after midday I offered a light meal of stir-fried vegetables, rice and this dhal which can be quickly re-heated. The teenage lad made my day when he whispered to his dad "This dhal is better than at home".' *Rudy Montgomery, Cheshire, UK*

Channa dhal, used here, is a type of small garbanzo/chickpea. It is also called Bengal gram and is the most common Indian pulse (seed). Regular garbanzos/chickpeas can be used instead.

I N G R E D I E N T S

2 cups / 450 g Egyptian (red) lentils

²/₃ cup / 110 g channa or garbanzos / chickpeas, soaked and cooked

2 cloves garlic, crushed

2 onions, chopped

1 teaspoon ground cumin

1 teaspoon turmeric

¹/₂ - 1 teaspoon chili powder

2 tablespoons oil or ghee

a little water

salt and pepper

1. Start by heating the oil or ghee in a saucepan and then cook the onions and garlic until they are soft. Now add the cumin, turmeric, chili, pepper and salt together with 2 tablespoons of water and cook until the liquid has been taken up.

2. Next, put in the channa or garbanzos/chickpeas and the lentils and mix well. Cover with boiling water and then reduce the heat and simmer for 10 minutes, stirring from time to time.

3. When the mixture is cooked, remove the pan from the heat and mash the dhal using either a fork or a potato masher before serving ■

Dhal with tomatoes

Serves 2

'Our standard dhal, tried and tested over years, started out as a adaptation of what we had eaten in India. And although this version may not be quite how it would be made there, it's very good. Cucumber *raita* goes well with it: simply pour the yogurt into a bowl and mix in the cucumber slices.' *Chris Brazier, London, UK*

I N G R E D I E N T S

1 cup / 225 g red lentils

2 small potatoes, diced

2 tablespoons oil or ghee

1 large onion, chopped

1-2 cloves garlic, crushed

¹/₂ green bell pepper, chopped

1 teaspoon ground cumin

1 teaspoon turmeric

1 teaspoon Madras (hot) curry powder

2 teaspoons ground ginger

1 can chopped tomatoes

salt and pepper

To serve, all or some of the following:

1 banana, sliced

mango chutney

¹/₂ cup / 120 ml natural yogurt)

1 cup / 100 g cucumber, sliced thinly

1. Place the lentils and potatoes into a pan of boiling water and cook them for about 10 minutes. Drain.

2. Next heat the oil or ghee in a pan and add the onion, garlic and bell pepper. Cook these until they are soft and then put in the cumin, turmeric, curry powder, ginger, salt and pepper. Continue to cook for 1-2 minutes before adding the tomatoes.

3. After this, let the mixture cook for a further minute or so and then put in the lentils and potatoes. Simmer gently for 5-10 minutes until everything is soft and hot. Serve with rice and side dishes such as cucumber raita (see above) as desired ■

Mixed vegetable curry

Serves 4

Although India is among the world's top ten industrial countries, millions of Indians cannot afford enough to eat. Yet the largely Hindu population, as vegetarians, are among the most efficient food users in the world, eating vegetables and pulses with chapatis or rice – a more direct means of gaining nutrients than by feeding grains and pulses to animals first as we tend to do in the West.

This curry is a good way to use up vegetables from a previous meal, or it can be made from scratch using potatoes, carrots, zucchini/courgettes, peas, okra – whatever you like.

I N G R E D I E N T S

4 tablespoons / 50 g margarine or ghee

1 onion, sliced

1-2 cloves garlic, crushed

1 tablespoon curry powder

1 green bell pepper, chopped

2¼ cups / 350 g vegetables, diced and parboiled

1 tablespoon desiccated coconut

a little water or stock

½ teaspoon turmeric

salt and pepper

1. First of all, melt the margarine or ghee in a large pan and cook the onion and garlic until they are lightly browned. Sprinkle in the curry powder and turmeric; cook for 2 minutes, stirring frequently.

2. Put in the bell pepper and let it cook for a few minutes before adding the other vegetables, coconut and enough water or stock to cover the base of the pan and prevent sticking.

3. Now cover and simmer until the vegetables are tender, adding more water or stock if the mixture looks too dry. Season with pepper and salt and serve with rice, chutney and yogurt ■

Garbanzos/chickpeas and papaya/paw-paw curry

Serves 4

Garam masala, used here, is a mixture of ground spices found in many Indian foods. Pepper, coriander, cumin, cloves and cinnamon form the basic mix, but there are numerous variations. It is aromatic rather than hot and is not a substitute for curry powder.

I N G R E D I E N T S

1½ cups / 225 g garbanzos / chickpeas, soaked and cooked

2 small papayas / paw-paw, cubed or use canned (drained and rinsed)

2 medium onions, sliced

1 green chili, chopped

2 tablespoons / 50 g margarine or ghee

½ teaspoon ground cumin

½ teaspoon garam masala

3 tablespoons / 75 g desiccated coconut

salt and pepper

1. To make the curry, melt the margarine or ghee in a saucepan and sauté the onions until they are golden.

2. Then add the chili, cumin, garam masala, salt and pepper and cook for 1 minute, stirring well. After this, put in the coconut and add enough water to make a little sauce. Simmer for about 5 minutes or until the sauce thickens.

3. Add the garbanzos/chickpeas and heat them through. Then put in the papaya/paw-paw pieces and cook gently for 2 minutes before serving with plain boiled rice or chapatis ■

INDONESIA

Eggs with chili and tomato

Serves 2-4

Indonesia, location of the original Spice Islands, is now self-sufficient in rice, the main staple. Cassava/manioc, sugar, sweet potatoes, bananas and fruit are some of the other foods grown. The country has some of the world's largest reserves of tropical forests and recent laws aim to reduce the rate of felling and export of timber.

Chili and spicy flavors abound in Southeast Asian dishes, often in sauces which can be complicated to make. This meal however is very straightforward and children can make it too. To add variety, put in more vegetables such as peas or bamboo shoots.

I N G R E D I E N T S

4 eggs	4 medium tomatoes, sliced
1-2 tablespoons oil	1/2 chili, finely chopped or 1/2 teaspoon chili powder
1 small onion or 3 scallions / spring onions, chopped finely	salt and pepper

1. Using a heavy pan, heat up the oil and cook the onion for a few minutes until soft. Now add in the tomatoes and chili and simmer for 3 minutes, stirring from time to time.

2. After this break the eggs into the pan, stir the mixture well and season with salt and pepper.

3. Cook for a few more minutes more, stirring now and again and serve with a green salad and hot bread or rice ■

MALAYSIA

Dhal (Lentil curry)

Serves 4-6

'Malaysia's cooking reflects the three main groups who live in the country; the Malays, the Chinese who were brought in by the British to work in the tin mines and the Indians, mainly Tamils from South India, who came as indentured laborers on the British plantations.

'This *dhal* can use almost any firm vegetable, so don't worry if you cannot find okra (lady's fingers/gumbo). Try egg-plant/aubergine or white radish (mooli) instead – or as well.' *Joe Paul, Kuala Lumpur, Malaysia*

I N G R E D I E N T S

1 cup / 225 g red lentils	1 onion, thinly sliced
2 medium potatoes, quartered	1 clove garlic, crushed or chopped finely
2 carrots, sliced	1 red chili, sliced finely, or 1 teaspoon chili powder
3 cups / 700 ml water	
1 teaspoon turmeric	1 teaspoon mustard seeds
2 tablespoons / 25 g margarine or ghee	4 okra
	salt and pepper

1. Wash the lentils and put them, the potatoes and carrots into a pan with the water, salt and turmeric. Cover the pot, bring to the boil and then turn down the heat and cook until the ingredients are soft, about 15-20 minutes.

2. While this is cooking, melt the margarine or ghee in another pan and cook the onions, garlic, chili and mustard seeds for 5 minutes.

3. Add the lentil mixture to the onions and spices. Put in the okra and cook gently until everything is cooked and the liquid is mostly absorbed ■

IN ALL RECIPES
● **PEPPER AND SALT ARE TO TASTE**
● **CHILI AND SUGAR ARE GIVEN AS GUIDE QUANTITIES ONLY. VARY TO TASTE**
● **MEASURES FOR BEANS AND GRAINS REFER TO DRY INGREDIENTS.**

MALAYSIA

Gado-Gado (Vegetable salad with peanut sauce)

Serves 4

Gado-Gado is eaten throughout Southeast Asia using a variety of crunchy vegetables which contrast well with the peanut sauce. Less spicy than many dishes of this region, *Gado-Gado* is a good starting point for people experimenting with new tastes.

The vegetables given here can be altered according to availability and preference. The secret is not to cook them for long so they retain their crispness.

I N G R E D I E N T S

THE SALAD	THE SAUCE
2 carrots, finely sliced	1 tablespoon oil
2 medium potatoes, sliced	1-2 cloves garlic, crushed
1 cup / 150 g shredded cabbage	1 small onion, grated
2 cups / 100 g bean sprouts	1 green chili, finely chopped or 1 teaspoon chili powder
1 tablespoon oil	
1 cup / 150 g bean-curd/ tofu, cut in 1 inch / 2.5 cm cubes	$^1/_2$ cup / 110 g crunchy peanut butter
1 cup / 100 g sliced cucumber	1 teaspoon lemon juice or vinegar
2 medium tomatoes, sliced	$^1/_2$ cup / 50 g creamed coconut melted in $^1/_2$ cup/ 120 ml hot water
2 hard-boiled eggs, sliced	
1 scallion / spring onion, sliced	salt

1. Steam or parboil the carrots and potato slices for 5 minutes. Then cook the cabbage, bean sprouts and cucumber for 1-2 minutes. Drain the vegetables and leave them to cool.

2. If using bean-curd/tofu, heat 1 tablespoon of oil in a wok or pan and cook it for 3-5 minutes, turning from time to time so that it is golden all over.

3. Now arrange the steamed vegetables in layers on a flat slices, then bean sprouts, carrots and cucumber. Put the tomatoes, sliced eggs and tofu on top.

4. For the sauce, heat the oil in a wok or large pan. Stir-fry the garlic, onion and chili for 2-3 minutes.

5. Add the peanut butter, lemon juice or vinegar and coconut milk and simmer for 2-3 minutes. The sauce should be thick but pourable, so add more lemon juice and/or milk if necessary.

6. To serve, pour the hot sauce over the vegetables and garnish with the scallion/spring onion slices ∎

PAKISTAN

Nauratan pullao (Mixed vegetable pillau)

Serves 2-4

*B*asmati rice grows in the foothills of the Himalayas. It is thought the best of the aromatic varieties, and Indians believed the fragrance was a gift of the God Veda. And it may well be so, although more secular research shows that the aromatic characteristic derives from a chemical present in all rice. The higher concentration of this substance in Basmati rice gives it the distinctive aroma. The US has recently produced its own version known as 'Texmati' rice (see Staple Food p.88).

I N G R E D I E N T S

2 cups / 450 g Basmati or other long-grain rice, soaked for 30 minutes in cold water	half a stick of cinnamon, crushed or $^1/_2$ teaspoon ground cinnamon
	4 cloves
4-8 tablespoons / 50-100 g margarine or ghee	2 cups / 300 g mixed vegetables, diced into small pieces of similar size *
$^1/_2$ teaspoon cumin seeds	
1 medium onion, finely sliced	$^1/_2$ teaspoon chili powder
8 whole black peppercorns	salt and pepper
4 cardamom pods	
2 bayleaves	

* You can use cauliflower, carrots, peas, okra, tomatoes, beans, turnips or whatever you like – frozen mixed vegetables will do.

1. To begin, heat the margarine or ghee in a large heavy pan. When it has melted add the cumin seeds and cook them for a few seconds before putting in the onions. Stir for 3-5 minutes until the onions are soft.

2. Now add the peppercorns, cardamom pods, bayleaves, cinnamon and cloves and cook for about 3 minutes, stirring from time to time.

3. Put in the vegetables next, and the salt, pepper and chili powder. Stir to mix them and then reduce the heat, cover and simmer gently for 2 minutes.

4. When this is done add the drained rice and stir it into the other ingredients. Pour in enough water to cover the rice mixture by 1 inch/2.5 cm. Cover the pan, bring to the boil and then reduce the heat and simmer undisturbed for 20 minutes or until the water has been absorbed. Serve at once ■

Samosas

Serves 2-4

More than a quarter of Pakistan's land is cultivated for arable crops and one of these is sorghum. In the West sorghum is mainly grown to feed cattle, but in parts of the Third World together with bulrush millet it is a staple food for 400,000 million people – nearly double the US population (see **Staple Food p.32**).

INGREDIENTS

1 small onion, chopped finely

2 cloves garlic, crushed

1 tablespoon oil

$^1/_2$ cup / 85 g peas

1 medium potato, parboiled and diced

1 carrot, diced finely

$^1/_2$ teaspoon garam masala

$^1/_2$ teaspoon chili powder

small handful fresh cilantro / coriander leaves, chopped

salt and pepper

PASTRY

1 cup / 125 g plain flour

$^1/_4$ cup / 60 ml water

2 teaspoons oil

} or use $^1/_2$ pound / 225 g frozen plain pastry, thawed

1. First of all, make the pastry by mixing the flour with the water and oil. Leave it to stand for 30 minutes.

2. For the filling, sauté the onion and garlic in the oil and then add the spices and cook for 2 minutes. Now put in the other vegetables and cilantro/coriander and cook them until they are soft. Leave to cool.

3. After that divide the pastry into 2 pieces and roll each portion out on a floured board into a thin rectangular shape, roughly 12 x 6 inches/30 x 15 cms. The pastry should not be too thick.

4. Cut the pastry into strips measuring 2 x 6 inches/5 x 15 cms. Put a small amount of the filling in the center of each strip and fold up into the shape of a triangle. Seal the edges with a little water.

5. Cook the samosas in shallow oil over a medium heat until they are golden brown, or alternatively place them on a oiled broiling/grill pan and dot each with a little margarine. Broil/grill under a medium heat, turning a few times so they do not catch ■

THAILAND

Kao pad supparot (Pineapple rice)

Serves 4-6

'During a visit to rural Thailand, arranged by a development group who wanted to show us a view of the country that was different from the fleshpots of the cities, we went to a school for Bangkok street children by the River Kwai. On the way we visited Nakhon Pathom with its huge temple, and nearby found a shop selling Thai wine and a restaurant serving this meal. It was a winning combination, and the pineapple-rice dish at least is replicable, even if the wine and the setting are not …'
Andrew Herxheimer, London, UK

INGREDIENTS

1 large pineapple

1 pound / 450 g rice, cooked and kept warm

3 tablespoons oil

1 egg, beaten

1 medium onion, sliced finely

1 tablespoon soy sauce

1 cup / 100 g shrimps or tuna

3/4 cup / 100 g cashewnuts

1 fresh red chili, sliced thinly

1 tablespoon fresh cilantro / coriander or parsley, chopped

salt and pepper

1. Cut a thin lengthwise slice off the pineapple to enable you to scoop out the flesh while keeping the shell intact to serve the meal in. Cut the fruit into chunks, keeping any juice.

2. Next, heat the oil in a wok or pan and then pour in the beaten egg, circling the wok to distribute the mixture evenly. Cook the egg for a few minutes on one side, then turn it over and cook the other side. Remove the omelet from the pan and cut it into thin strips.

3. Then, using more oil if necessary, stir-fry the onion for 2-3 minutes until it is golden and soft. Add the soy sauce and the rice and cook for 3 minutes. Now put in the pineapple pieces and juice, shrimps/tuna, nuts and strips of egg. Cook for 2 minutes, stirring well. Season with salt and pepper.

4. Fill the scooped-out pineapple with the mixture and decorate with chili slices and the cilantro/coriander or parsley. Place on a flat dish and spoon any remaining mixture around the pineapple before serving ■

AMERICA

Succotash (Corn/maize and beans)

Serves 4

Indians in America were eating succotash (from an indian word *m'sickquatash* meaning boiled corn) of corn kernels and lima beans before the Europeans came. The indians enriched it with molasses, bear fat and threw in game or fish when they had been lucky on the hunt. Many variations of succotash exist; try adding tomatoes, onions, bell pepper, mustard and bacon (for meat eaters) and/or grated cheese.

INGREDIENTS

2 tablespoons oil

1 onion, sliced

2 tomatoes, sliced

1 cup / 225 g lima beans, soaked and cooked

1 cup / 225 g sweetcorn, cooked

1 teaspoon molasses, honey or sugar

1/2 teaspoon paprika

salt and pepper

1. In a pan, heat the oil and sauté the onion. Then add the beans and corn, and the tomatoes or any other ingredients you are using (see note above).

2. Next put in the molasses and stir until it has melted. When everything has heated through, season with salt, pepper and paprika and serve right away. ■

CARIBBEAN

Rice and peas

Serves 4-6

*G*unga or *pigeon* peas are used here. Together with rice they form the staple diet in many Caribbean households. The peas are usually grown on poor land by small farmers. India is the main producer, but pigeon peas are also grown in the Caribbean, Southeast Asia, Pakistan, Malawi and Uganda.

You can find pigeon peas in West Indian shops, or else substitute black-eyed beans, cowpeas or red kidney beans.

I N G R E D I E N T S

1 cup / 225 g pigeon peas*, soaked

1 onion, sliced finely

1 pound / 450 g rice

$^1/_2$ cup / 50 g creamed coconut

$^1/_4$ teaspoon thyme

$^1/_4$ teaspoon oregano

$^1/_2$ teaspoon chili powder

salt

* A quicker version is to use canned red kidney beans. Simply add them to the rice which has been cooked with the other ingredients.

1. To begin with, put the peas in a pan with the onion and enough water to cover. Bring this to the boil and then add 2 cups/470 ml water. Cover with a lid, bring to the boil again; this time allow it to simmer until the gunga are tender, about 1 hour.

2. After this, add the coconut cream, herbs, chili powder and salt, stirring well to mix them.

3. Put in the rice, adding more water if necessary and bring to the boil. Then reduce the heat and cook the rice until it is done, about 20-30 minutes. Season and serve ∎

Plantains/green banana pie

Serves 4

Plantains or green bananas are a basic food in the Caribbean as they are in some parts of Africa, and one of the first things children are taught when they start to help at home is how to peel plantains. It certainly needs some skill. Cut off both ends of the plantain, then halve it and make a lengthwise slit along each piece. You can now remove the peel – if not, follow the directions below and cook the plantains in their skins as they peel more easily when cooked.

I N G R E D I E N T S

2 pounds / 900 g green bananas

3 eggs

juice of 1 lime or lemon

$^1/_4$ cup / 25 g breadcrumbs

1 tablespoon margarine

red and green bell pepper slices for garnish

salt

Heat oven to 300°F/150°C/Gas 2

1. Heat the water in a pan, adding a little salt. When boiling, put in the bananas and cook them for 20-30 minutes. Drain and allow them to cool a little before peeling.

2. Now, in a bowl, beat the eggs until they are frothy and then add the lime or lemon juice.

3. Cut the bananas into circles and add them to the bowl containing the eggs. Stir well.

4. Pour the mixture into a greased oven-proof dish, sprinkle on the breadcrumbs, decorate with bell pepper slices and dot with margarine. Cook for 20 minutes or until eggs have set and the breadcrumbs have browned. Serve with rice ∎

CHILE

Empanadas (Turnovers)

Serves 6

Copper, fishmeal, fruit and timber are some of Chile's main exports. And the country, with its long coastline, is the most important fish-producing nation in Latin America – hake, mackerel, sardines and anchovies fill the nets. Along with fish, lentils and beans provide the protein for most Chileans.

INGREDIENTS

1/2 pound / 225 g frozen flaky pastry, thawed

FILLING 1 – lentils

1 cup / 225 g red lentils, cooked

1 onion, chopped

1 clove garlic, chopped or crushed

1 tablespoon oil

1/2 teaspoon chili powder

1/2 cup / 50 g raisins or sultanas

1/4 teaspoon paprika

1/4 teaspoon marjoram

2 tablespoons tomato paste

1-2 tablespoons lemon juice

salt and pepper

FILLING 2 – cheese

1 cup / 110 g strong cheese, grated

1 hard-boiled egg, chopped finely

seeds of 2 cardamom pods, crushed

salt and pepper

Heat oven to 400°F/200°C/Gas 6

1. For the lentil filling, heat the oil in a pan and cook the onion and garlic until they are soft. Then add the chili powder and the cooked lentils, tomato paste and raisins or sultanas. Sprinkle in the paprika and marjoram, add the lemon juice and continue to cook over a low heat until everything is well combined. Season.

2. Allow the mixture to cool while you prepare the pastry cases.

3. For the cheese filling, simply mix together all the ingredients in a bowl and proceed as below.

4. Roll out the pastry on a floured board and then cut it into circles approximately 4 inches/10 cms across, using a saucer or small bowl. How many you make depends on how thin you like the pastry.

5. Now cover one half of each circle with some of the filling. Then brush the edges with a little water, and fold the empanada together, pressing the sides closed with a fork.

6. Place the empanadas in a shallow baking tin and put them into the oven for about 35 minutes or until the pastry is golden brown. Serve with a salad ■

MEXICO

Avocado and bean salad

Serves 4

For thousands of years beans have provided the people of North, Central and South America with most of their protein. The Mohicans and other indians of the northeast US ate the large green lima beans from Peru and introduced them and other beans to the Massachusetts settlers; and trade between Old and New Worlds was bolstered by beans giving sustenance to sailors (and no doubt slaves) on long sea voyages.

INGREDIENTS

1 cup / 100 g red kidney beans, soaked, cooked and cooled

1 large avocado

1 clove garlic, crushed

1/4 teaspoon chili powder

1 tablespoon olive oil

1 tablespoon lemon juice or vinegar

a few lettuce leaves, washed and dried

1 small onion, sliced finely into circles

1 small red or green bell pepper, sliced in rounds

4 hard-boiled eggs, sliced

1/4 teaspoon paprika

salt and pepper

1. First make a lengthwise slit round the avocado to open it. Then, using a spoon, scoop the flesh into a bowl and

mash. Add the garlic, chili powder, oil, lemon juice or vinegar, salt and pepper and mix to a creamy consistency.

2. Now partially mash the beans with a fork.

3. Place the lettuce leaves on a large plate, spoon on the beans and then the avocado mixture. Top with the onion circles, pepper and egg slices and sprinkle on the paprika before serving ∎

Frijoles refritos (Re-heated beans)
Serves 4

Nearly three-quarters of Mexico's 85 million people live in towns. The capital, Mexico City, is on track to become the world's biggest city of over 25 million people by the year 2000. Emphasis on industrial development has meant fewer resources going into agriculture, and this neglect is one of the spurs for the move into towns.

I N G R E D I E N T S

1 cup / 225 g pink or red kidney beans, soaked	1 cup / 110 g grated cheddar cheese +
2 teaspoons ground cumin	2 tomatoes, sliced
1 tablespoon oil	4 eggs
1/2 - 1 teaspoon chili powder	salt and pepper

+ optional ingredient

Note: Meat-eaters can add 1/2 pound / 225 g bacon, cut into pieces and put in at the same time as the beans

1. Start by putting the beans into a heavy pot and then sprinkle on the cumin. Add enough water to cover the beans by 1 inch/2.5 cm.

2. Bring the saucepan to the boil, cover and simmer for 2-3 hours until the beans are tender, or use a pressure cooker. Drain.

3. Heat the oil in a pan and fry the beans, mashing some with a fork and leaving others intact. Add the chili powder, salt and pepper.

4. Turn the beans out onto a flat heat-proof plate. Lay the tomato slices on top and sprinkle the cheese over. Place the dish under the broiler/grill until the cheese melts.

5. While this is happening poach, fry or scramble the eggs and serve them with the beans ∎

PERU

Papas à la Huancaina (Huancaina-style potatoes)
Serves 4-6

Potatoes are a staple food in parts of Latin America, especially up in the *Altiplano* region of Peru. There, potatoes are literally freeze-dried by leaving them out in the icy winds at night and then squeezing out the moisture each day for about a week until they are dried. After that the *chuño* – dried potatoes – will keep for a long time.

I N G R E D I E N T S

10 medium potatoes, cooked and sliced	2 tablespoons single cream or evaporated milk
1 small onion, finely chopped	3 tablespoons oil
4 hard-boiled eggs	juice of half a lemon
1/2 cup / 100 g ricotta or cottage cheese, sieved	10 black or green olives
2 teaspoons chili powder	handful fresh parsley, chopped
	salt and pepper

1. Boil a little water in a pan and cook the onion in it for a few minutes, and then drain.

2. Take out the yolks from 2 of the eggs and mash them in a bowl, using a fork. Then add the ricotta or cottage cheese and season with the chili powder, salt and pepper. When this is done, stir in the cream or evaporated milk and mix well before adding the oil, lemon juice and cooked onion.

3. Arrange the potato slices on a flat dish. Cover them with the cheese sauce and then garnish with the olives, slices of hard-boiled egg and parsley ∎

EGYPT

Falafel or Ta'amia (Spicy cakes)

Makes 20

Ta'amia is an Egyptian national dish associated with the Christian Copts who eat these patties made of white broad beans (*ful nabed*) during Lent when they are not allowed to eat meat. In Israel, Lebanon, Syria and Jordan the variation, *falafel*, uses garbanzos/chickpeas. They are commonly sold as 'fast food'.

I N G R E D I E N T S

2 ¹/₂ cups / 450 g garbanzos/chickpeas or white broad beans*, soaked and cooked

2 cloves garlic, crushed

1 medium onion, grated

handful fresh cilantro/coriander leaves or parsley, chopped

1 teaspoon ground cumin

1 teaspoon ground coriander

+ optional ingredient

¹/₂ teaspoon cayenne pepper

¹/₂ teaspoon turmeric

¹/₂ teaspoon baking powder

lemon juice

sesame seeds +

a little flour

oil for cooking

water

salt and pepper

* The white broad beans (*ful nabed*) can be bought in Greek stores and some delicatessen stores. Buy them already skinned if possible; if not, remove the skins after soaking. Dried green broad beans can also be used.

1. First of all, mince, pound or put the beans/chickpeas through a blender until they are very smooth. Making a smooth mixture is important since the falafel will not bind well otherwise.

2. Now put in all the other ingredients except the sesame seeds, flour and oil. Leave to stand for at least 15 minutes; 1 hour if possible.

3. Now take small amounts of the mixture and make round cakes about 2 inches/5 cms in diameter and ³/₄ inch/1.5 cm thick. Add a little flour and water if they are not binding well.

4. Leave them to rest for 15 minutes and then press a few sesame seeds on top of each one.

5. Next, heat the oil in a pan and brown the falafel for a few minutes on each side, until golden brown. Drain on absorbent paper and serve hot with pita bread, yogurt and slices of tomato or salad ■

Ful Medames (Egyptian brown bean stew)

Serves 4

Ful is the Egyptian word for bean and *Medames* describes the variety used: a brown, round broad bean. This is a popular meal with both rich and poor in Egypt, eaten in the fields, sold in bazaars and Ful cafes, even served in luxury hotels and restaurants. The eggs, onions, oil and lemon are served separately for people to help themselves.

I N G R E D I E N T S

1 pound / 450 g ful beans*, soaked

1 tablespoon ground cumin

4 cloves garlic, crushed

4 hard-boiled eggs, shelled, and chopped coarsely

handful fresh parsley, chopped

2 lemons, quartered

1 medium onion, sliced thinly in circles

olive oil

salt and pepper

* Dried Ful Medames can be found in specialist Asian stores and delicatessens.

NOTE: The ful can be eaten cold as a salad – mix with chopped parsley, and add yogurt, oil and vinegar as a dressing.

Heat oven to 300°F/150°C/Gas 2

1. Put the soaked beans in an oven-proof dish which has a cover and pour in enough water to cover them by 2 inches/5 cms. Add the cumin, pepper and garlic and put the dish into the oven. Let the beans cook slowly for 3-4 hours so that they become very soft but not broken up, and the juice is quite thick.

2. When the beans are ready, put the eggs, parsley, lemon quarters and sliced onion into separate dishes on the table as well as a bottle of olive oil.

3. Add the salt to the cooked beans, stir them carefully, and then bring the dish to the table. Serve the ful and invite people to add their own eggs crumbled on top, parsley and lemon juice, and then pour on enough oil to give a smooth consistency.

4. Tomato and onion salad (see p.141) goes well with this dish as well as hot pita bread ■

IRAN

Kukuye Sabzi (Vegetable and walnut bake)
Serves 4

Iran's economy has suffered from the war with Iraq, although its agriculture was already neglected in the Shah's time. Wheat, barley and rice are the three main cereal crops but continuing disputes over land ownership, arising from differing interpretations of Islamic law, have prevented full use of the best land.

'We ate this delicious dish as guests in a private house in Teheran, before the fall of the Shah.'
Angeline Hampton, Lymington, UK

INGREDIENTS

2 cups / 200 g leeks, chopped finely

1 cup / 150 g lettuce, chopped finely

1 tablespoon fresh parsley, chopped

1 cup / 100 g spinach, chopped finely

3 scallions / spring onions, sliced finely

1 tablespoon flour

1/2 cup / 60 g walnuts, chopped

8 eggs

4 tablespoons / 50 g margarine

salt and pepper

Heat oven to 325°F/160°C/Gas 3

1. Put all the vegetables into a large bowl, shake on the flour and seasoning. Mix well and then add the walnuts.

2. Next, beat the eggs and pour them into the vegetable mixture. Stir so that the egg coats the other ingredients to bind them.

3. Using a loaf tin, melt the margarine gently over a low heat and swirl it around the pan to coat the sides. Then transfer the vegetable mixture to the tin and cook in the oven for about 1 hour or until the top is crisp and brown. Turn out onto a dish and serve with rice and yogurt ■

STAPLE FOODS: MILLET

In the Bible, millet is made into the *'gruel of endurance'*, its own resilience as a plant that withstands climatic privations being thought to endow people with strength. It has been grown and eaten for about 3,000 years in China and India. Etruscans, Greeks, Romans, Gauls, Persians, Assyrians, Tartars and Visigoths — warriors all — consumed it avidly as food fit for fighting men, keeping them sound of body and clear of mind.

Millet is probably the most ancient of the grains grown today, evolving from grasses that the brontosaurus may have browsed upon. One of millet's related grasses, *teff*, was used as straw in the bricks made around 3300 BC for the Egyptian pyramids.

In drought regions millet is a bulwark against famine: it can grow in poor soils with little rainfall. If there should be no rain the plant waits, hibernates, until the next drops fall. And

then, once harvested, millet can be stored for several years.

Finger millet and bulrush millet, the two main types, probably originated in Africa. Finger millet has long been cultivated in what is now Uganda and features in ceremonies there. It is a staple food, feeding people from Uganda in East Africa south to Zambia, Natal and Namibia; north to Eritrea and west across to Nigeria. This kind of millet probably went over to India at the same time as the bulrush variety, and sorghum too, in the *dhows* (ships) of Arab traders.

Known as *ragi* in India, finger millet grows mainly in the area around Mysore. In Rajastan they cultivate bulrush millet, called *bajra*. This cereal is India's fourth main food crop after rice, sorghum and wheat. For many Africans too, in the dry Sahel zone, bulrush millet is a major food. It needs even less water than sorghum and is nutritious — high in vitamins and only just lower than wheat in its protein.

Aside from the two main types above, a variety of millet appears in Southeast Asia and Brazil known as *adlay* or Jacob's Tears. This type provides grass for animals and its tiny seeds are eaten like rice or brewed into beer, some are used for ornamentation. Other strains are Japanese barnyard millet (which however is not as common as another type, Fox-tail millet, in that country), common millet and little millet which is chiefly found in India's Madhya Pradesh and Uttar Pradesh states.

Millet is usually cooked into porridge, made into flat bread or fermented into beer. Its adaptable flavor makes it versatile: in Rajasthan street vendors sell slices of *raj halwah*, a millet, prune and almond tart made specially for the day that marks the coming of Spring.

Linking millet with the arrival of the growing season in this way acknowledges the plant's importance — after all, together with sorghum, it is the basic food relied upon by 400 million people or so in India, Africa and China. In the West by contrast it is mainly used to make hay and silage for animals — and as birdseed for caged budgerigars and canaries.

Main producers (in descending order) India, China, Nigeria, Soviet Union, Niger, Mali, Senegal, Chad and Egypt.

World production (1985) 29 million tons.

IRAN

Millet and lentil bake

Serves 4-6

Dishes with millet and lentils in the Middle East, or with maize/corn and beans in Central and South America, have been eaten for centuries. They are a good example of how people have combined two of their basic foods, which are incomplete in protein on their own, to provide a balanced meal – without the guidance of modern nutritional science.

INGREDIENTS

1 cup / 225 g red lentils	6 cloves
1 cup / 225 g millet, soaked	seeds from 3 cardamom pods, crushed
2 tablespoons oil	$1/2$ teaspoon ground cinnamon
3 cloves garlic, crushed	
1 onion, chopped	2 bayleaves
6 cups / 1.4 liters stock	salt and pepper

Heat oven to 300°F/150°C/Gas 2 (after step 2 below)

1. For this you need to use a large cooking pot that is suitable both for cooking with on top of the cooker and inside the oven too. Start by heating the oil in the pot and then soften the garlic and onion in it.

2. After that, add the millet together with the stock, cloves, cardamom seeds, cinnamon, bayleaves and bring to the boil. Turn down the heat, cover the pan and simmer very gently for 1 hour or until the millet is cooked.

3. Put in the lentils now and cook for a further 15 minutes until they and the millet are ready.

4. When this is done, pour off any remaining liquid. Replace the cover, put the dish into the oven and let it cook for 10-20 minutes until the moisture has been absorbed. This should be a fairly dry mixture and green salad makes a good accompaniment together with cucumber raita – simply dice some cucumber and mix it with plain yogurt (see p. 39) ■

ISRAEL

Nezid adashim (Lentil and cheese bake)

Serves 4

Israel is more or less self-sufficient in food, needing to import only some cereals. Farms are small but they are usually part of larger co-operatives, *kibbutzim*, or small-holder villages – *moshavim*, growing citrus fruits, melons, avocados, tomatoes, melons and peanuts.

INGREDIENTS

$3^1/2$ cups / 830 ml water	2 tablespoons / 25 g margarine
2 cups / 225 g red lentils	2 tablespoons flour
1 medium onion, finely sliced	2 tablespoons tomato paste
1 tablespoon fresh parsley, finely chopped	2 cups / 225 g cheddar cheese, grated
1 clove garlic, crushed	salt and pepper
1 stalk celery, cut into small pieces	

Heat oven to 350°F/180°C/Gas 3

1. Put the water in a saucepan and bring it to the boil. Add the lentils, onion, parsley, garlic and celery. Cover the pan, reduce the heat and let it simmer until everything is tender, about 15 minutes. Pour off any liquid into a container and keep it to use in the next step.

2. Now grease an oven dish and spoon in the lentil mixture. Make up the retained liquid to $1^1/4$ cups/300 ml.

3. Next, melt the margarine in a pan. Gradually sieve in the flour and mix well before pouring in the liquid, little by little. Stirring all the time to prevent lumps, cook the sauce until it thickens. Season with salt and pepper.

4. When ready, pour the sauce over the lentil mixture and cover with the tomato paste, spreading this as evenly as possible.

5. Sprinkle the grated cheese on top and bake for 10-15 minutes until the cheese is melted and bubbling ■

JORDAN

Basal badawi (Onions with lentils, nuts and fruit)

Serves 4

Jordan has become a net importer of food now that its main growing areas on the West Bank are controlled by Israel. Local foods raised include wheat, barley, fruit, vegetables, olives and lentils.

This is a vegetarian version of a Bedouin dish. If you serve it with rice, try adding saffron or turmeric to the rice before cooking. It adds a distinctive flavor as well as color, creating 'red' rice.

I N G R E D I E N T S

4 large onions

$^1/_2$ cup / 100 g red lentils, cooked

$^3/_4$ cup / 150 ml plain yogurt

2 tablespoons dates, stoned and finely chopped

2 tablespoons walnuts, chopped

1 tablespoon raisins or sultanas

2 tablespoons breadcrumbs

handful fresh parsley, chopped

salt and pepper

1. Peel the onions and place them in a large pan of boiling water. Reduce the heat and let them simmer for 15-20 minutes, covered, until they are fairly tender. When they are ready, take them out and set aside to cool.

2. Now remove the center section of each onion to leave a shell about $^3/_4$ inch/1.5 cm thick.

3. In a bowl mix together the lentils, pepper, salt, yogurt, dates, walnuts, raisins or sultanas and breadcrumbs.

4. Fill the onions with this mixture. Keep any that remains and mix it with the chopped discarded onion centers.

5. Place the filled onions in an oven-proof dish, spoon any remaining mixture around them and cook for about 20 minutes. Garnish with parsley and serve with bulgur or red rice (see note above) ■

(Opposite) Baking bread in traditional oven, Egypt.
Photo: Jørgen Schytte/Still Pictures

MIDDLE EAST

Maraga bil-tomatich (Tomato and lentil sauce)

Serves 4

People in the Middle East lead very different lives, some in modern cities, others as nomadic Bedouin and some farming in river valleys. For example, 95 per cent of Kuwaitis live in towns, compared with less than half of Egypt's people.

Maraga is a tomato and lentil sauce that goes well with cracked wheat or bulgur.

I N G R E D I E N T S

1 cup / 225 g red lentils

6 large tomatoes, chopped

1 teaspoon tomato paste

3 tablespoons water

2-4 cloves garlic, sliced finely or crushed

handful fresh parsley, chopped

1 large onion, grated

2 tablespoons margarine

1 teaspoon sugar

$^1/_2$ teaspoon thyme

1 bayleaf, crushed

lemon juice

salt and pepper

1. First, mix the tomato paste with the water. Then pour it into into a large pan containing the lentils and rest of the ingredients.

2. Cover the saucepan and cook very gently for 20 minutes, stirring regularly to prevent sticking.

3. After this, remove the pan from the heat and leave it to cool. Mash the ingredients with a wooden spoon adding lemon juice and a little water to make a moist mixture.

4. Return the mixture to the pan and boil for a few minutes. Serve with rice or bulgur and salad ■

MIDDLE EAST

Reuchta mubowakh (Noodles with garbanzos/chickpeas and tomatoes)
Serves 4

Reuchta or *rishta* means 'thread' in Farsi (Persian) and you can use spaghetti, macaroni or tagliatelle in this recipe. The repeated ladling of the sauce over the noodles while they are cooking adds to the flavor and alters their texture in an interesting way. But of course you can simply cook the noodles in the usual way, in boiling water, and pour on the sauce at the end. Meat can also be used – cook it first with the onion.

INGREDIENTS

1 pound / 450 g noodles

1 tablespoon / 25 g margarine

1 large onion, chopped

2 large tomatoes, chopped

2 tablespoons tomato paste

1 cup / 175 g garbanzos/chickpeas, soaked and cooked

1/4 teaspoon saffron, soaked in 4 tablespoons water +

1/2 teaspoon paprika

4 cups / 950 ml water

salt and pepper

+ optional ingredient or use 1/2 teaspoon turmeric

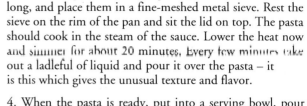

1. Melt the margarine in a pan and cook the onion until it is soft. Add the chopped tomatoes, and the tomato paste diluted in 5 tablespoons of the water. Cook for 5 minutes.

2. Next put in the garbanzos/chickpeas, spices and remaining water and bring to the boil, stirring frequently. After this, reduce the heat, season and let the sauce bubble very slowly while you cook the pasta.

3. Break the pasta into small pieces, about 2 inches/5 cms long, and place them in a fine-meshed metal sieve. Rest the sieve on the rim of the pan and sit the lid on top. The pasta should cook in the steam of the sauce. Lower the heat now and simmer for about 20 minutes. Every few minutes take out a ladleful of liquid and pour it over the pasta – it is this which gives the unusual texture and flavor.

4. When the pasta is ready, put into a serving bowl, pour the sauce over and serve with a green salad ■

MOROCCO

Khboz (Spicy spinach and cheese pastries)
Serves 4

Morocco is the world's third largest exporter of phosphates which are used in fertilizers. Apart from this mining and processing work, farming is the other major activity.

'I was involved in making and selling *khboz* – wonderful, spicy goodies at a local fair for several summers and they were certainly popular. Instead of baking them, you can cook them on a griddle or in a pan with a little oil, turning them frequently until browned.' *Valerie Sherriff, British Columbia, Canada*

INGREDIENTS

1 tablespoon dried yeast

2/3 cup / 160 ml lukewarm water

2 cups / 250 g flour

3 tablespoons / 40 g margarine, melted

1/2 teaspoon cumin

1 tablespoon paprika

1/2 teaspoon chili powder

2 cloves garlic, crushed

2 cups / 200 g spinach or parsley, chopped finely

2 onions, chopped finely

2 cups / 225 g feta or other crumbly cheese

salt and pepper

Heat oven to 375°F/190°C/Gas 5

1. First soften the yeast by soaking it in the lukewarm water in a large bowl. Then stir in the flour and a pinch of salt and pull the mixture together into a ball. Knead it thoroughly and then place the dough in an oiled bowl or plastic bag and set it to rise in a warm place for 30 minutes.

2. Meanwhile, combine the melted margarine, cumin, paprika, chili powder, garlic, spinach or parsley and the onions. Add the seasoning.

3. When the dough has risen, divide it into 8 pieces and knead each one well. Then, on a floured surface, roll each piece out into a rectangle approximately 8 x 6 inches/20 x 15 cms.

4. Divide the filling equally between the portions and spread it nearly to the edges. Crumble some of the cheese on each.

5. Fold the two short sides of the pastry rectangle into the middle so they just meet over the filling. Then roll the cake up, beginning with one of the long sides. Seal each end with water and press together with a fork.

6. Put the khboz on a baking sheet and bake for 35 minutes or until slightly browned. Serve hot with salad ■

SYRIA

Badenjan wya choban (Egg-plant/aubergine casserole)

Serves 4-6

If you can find it in a specialist grocery store, the Greek *kefalotiri* cheese is best with this dish. The name of this cheese comes from the fact that it is shaped like a head – *kefali* is the Greek word for head (*cephalo* in Latin). Parmesan or cheddar cheese can be used instead.

INGREDIENTS

3 tablespoons olive oil

2 eggs

1 tablespoon milk

1 cup / 110 g kefalotiri, parmesan or cheddar cheese, finely grated

2 medium egg-plants/ aubergines, cut crosswise into thin slices

6 large tomatoes, sliced thinly

2 handfuls fresh parsley, chopped finely

pepper and salt to taste

SAUCE

1 egg

1 small onion, minced or grated

$^1/_2$ teaspoon marjoram

2 tablespoons tomato paste

3 tablespoons water

pepper and salt

Heat oven to 350°F/180°C/Gas 4

1. Pour the oil into a large shallow pan and let it heat gently while you prepare the next step.

2. In a bowl, beat the eggs with the milk, salt and pepper.

3. Dip each egg-plant/aubergine slice into the egg mixture and then cook them in the hot oil, turning once so they are soft and golden. Drain the cooked slices on paper towels.

4. Now place half the slices over the base of a greased shallow oven-proof dish. Arrange a layer of tomato slices on top, and then sprinkle some of the grated cheese and a little of the parsley over them.

5. Repeat this until the remaining egg-plant/aubergine, tomato, cheese and parsley have been used up.

6. Now put the ingredients for the sauce into a bowl and mix them together, adding enough water to make a smooth, pouring sauce. You can use a blender or liquidizer if preferred.

7. When the sauce is ready, pour it evenly over the surface of the egg-plant/aubergine mixture, place the dish in the oven and cook it, covered, for 30 minutes. Then remove the lid and continue to cook for another 15 minutes so that the top is golden. Serve hot with rice or bulgur ■

SYRIA

Herb eggeh

Serves 4-6

Here is an egg dish which can be made with many different fillings. It is popular for picnics in Arab countries, and can be used itself as a filling for sandwiches. You can make individual *eggeh* by using a tin for small cakes, or make one big one and cut it up as in this recipe.

INGREDIENTS

2 handfuls fresh parsley, chopped

2 handfuls fresh mint, chopped

1 medium potato, cooked and diced

1 medium onion, chopped finely

6 eggs, beaten

1 tablespoon self-raising flour

2 cloves garlic, crushed

1-2 tablespoons oil

salt and pepper

1. Take a large bowl and mix all the ingredients together, except the oil. The mixture should be thick.

2. Then heat the oil in a large flat pan. When it is hot, spoon in the eggeh, moving the pan around so that the mixture is evenly distributed. Cook for a few minutes on one side and then the other. Serve hot or cold ■

(Opposite) Trading place – market steps in Mexico.
Photo: The Hutchison Library

TUNISIA

Baked eggs with zucchini/courgettes

Serves 4

'Don't enter other people's houses, except with permission and good manners', exhorts the Koran. Once inside, rigorous customs guide the pattern of hospitality with host and guest almost vying with one another to show warmth and politeness. An extra place is often laid at mealtimes in case an unexpected visitor arrives. No growling if that occurs: food and drink must cheerfully be offered and, after the requisite number of demurrals, consumed by the guest.

INGREDIENTS

4 tablespoons olive oil

1-2 cloves garlic, crushed

1 medium onion, chopped finely

2 medium zucchini/courgettes, sliced finely

2 medium green or red bell peppers, sliced

4 large tomatoes, chopped

1/2 teaspoon ground cumin

1/2 teaspoon ground cilantro / coriander

1/2 teaspoon ground cinnamon

pinch ground nutmeg

6 eggs, lightly beaten

salt and pepper

Heat oven to 350°F/180°C/Gas 4

1. First sauté the garlic and onion in the olive oil for about 5 minutes until the onion is transparent and then add the zucchini/courgettes. Cook for a few minutes more before adding the bell peppers, tomatoes, spices, salt and pepper. Stir gently and continue to cook for 2 to 3 minutes.

2. Now add just enough water to cover and cook over a low heat for 20 minutes or until most of the liquid has evaporated.

3. Transfer the mixture to a lightly greased baking dish which has a lid and stir in the beaten eggs. Adjust the seasoning, cover, and bake for 40-45 minutes. Remove the cover for the last 15 minutes so that the top can brown. Serve with hot bread and salad ■

TURKEY

Pilaff with apricots and almonds

Serves 6-8

Over half Turkey's workforce is involved in farming, the mainstay of the economy. Another source of wealth comes from the five per cent, or about 600,000 people, who have made their way to West Germany as 'Gast-Arbeiten' (guest workers), sending some of their wages home to their families.

'This dish shows the characteristic Middle Eastern use of dried fruit and nuts to give a sweet and savory taste.' *Pat Tope, London, UK*

INGREDIENTS

3-4 tablespoons oil

2 medium onions, finely chopped

3 cloves garlic, crushed

1 pound / 450 g brown rice

3 bayleaves

1 can tomatoes, chopped

2 tablespoons tomato paste

1 cup / 100 g dried apricots

1/2 cup / 50 g raisins or sultanas

1/2 cup / 60 g flaked almonds

2 1/2 cups / 590 ml stock

1 tablespoon fresh cilantro/ coriander leaves, chopped

salt and pepper

1. To start, first heat the oil and then soften the onions and garlic in it.

2. Add the rice and fry it for 3 minutes, stirring frequently so that each grain is lightly coated with oil.

3. When this is done, put in the bayleaves, tomatoes and tomato paste, dried fruit, nuts, stock and seasoning.

4. Bring the pan to the boil and then reduce the heat and simmer, covered, for 45 minutes until the rice is cooked and most of the moisture has been absorbed. Serve garnished with chopped coriander leaves ■

African lamb and olive casserole. *Photo by: IMS UGGLA/Camera Press.*

AFRICA

Lamb and chili casserole

Serves 6-8

Strolling near Lake Victoria in Kenya at the end of the day, you might come across a scattering of smooth-coated sheep being brought home after grazing. The boy herders strut past waving their switches menacingly at errant lambs. Some people keep fat-tailed sheep; the tail is a delicacy served to guests and men.

INGREDIENTS

4 pounds / 2 kg lamb shoulder

salt and pepper

2 large onions, sliced

2 tablespoons / 25 g margarine

1 tablespoon oil

6 cloves, crushed

1 teaspoon ground cumin

¹/2 teaspoon curry powder

4 cloves garlic, crushed

1 can tomatoes

1¹/4 cups / 300 ml water

1 tablespoon ground coriander

¹/2 teaspoon ground cinnamon

1 teaspoon chili powder

4 large potatoes, halved lengthwise

¹/2 cup / 75 g black olives, stoned

1. To start, season the lamb with a little salt and pepper. Then, using a large heavy pan with a lid, brown the meat in the heated margarine and oil. When it is ready, remove it and set to one side while you cook the onions.

2. Next add the crushed cloves, cumin, curry powder and garlic and stir them round with the onions for 1 minute. Put in the canned tomatoes and their juice.

3. Sprinkle on the coriander, cinnamon, chili powder and salt and pepper. Mix well.

4. Now put the meat back in, place the potatoes around it and spoon some of the spicy onion mixture on top. Add enough water to cover the bottom of the pan by 1 inch/2.5 cm; cover and cook over a low heat for 1¹/2 - 2 hours until the meat comes easily off the bone. Baste the meat from time to time and add more liquid if necessary.

5. Transfer the meat pieces to a warm serving dish and mix them with the onions and juices from the cooking pan, and the olives ∎

BURKINA FASO

Fish stew with okra

Serves 4-6

Despite former President Thomas Sankara's wish to see men *'au marché, au ménage et au foyer'*, (shopping, doing housework and helping at home) women still bear the brunt of the work in Burkina. The food crops they raise are sorghum, millet, yams, maize/corn, rice and beans.

INGREDIENTS

1¹/2 pounds / 675 g fresh-water fish, cut into pieces, or equivalent amount of frozen white fish

3 tablespoons peanut or other oil

1 onion, sliced

3 carrots, sliced in rounds

6-8 okra, halved lengthwise

¹/2 teaspoon chili powder

1 cup / 100 g tomato paste

1 cup / 225 g cabbage or spinach, sliced

²/3 cup / 100 g green beans *

a little water

1 cup / 200 g rice

2 cups / 470 ml stock

salt

* Use French beans or string/runner beans.

1. First heat the oil and cook the onion, carrots, okra, chili powder, salt and tomato paste for 5-10 minutes.

2. Then put in the fish, cabbage or spinach, beans and a little water to provide some moisture for cooking the vegetables. Cover and cook gently for 5 minutes.

3. Now add the rice, pour in the stock, bring to the boil and cook for 20 minutes or until the rice is cooked as you like it, adding more stock or water as necessary to prevent the rice from drying out ■

CAMEROON

Fish stew with chili

Serves 4

Cameroon exports oil, coffee, cocoa, aluminium and timber and so it is greatly affected by the ups and downs in prices for these commodities. But thankfully it also has a steady farming base providing millet, cassava, maize/corn and plantains (bananas) as staples; livestock and fishing are also important.

I N G R E D I E N T S

1 pound / 450 g fish fillets (haddock or cod), cut into pieces

¹/₂ cup / 60 g flour

2 tablespoons / 25g margarine

2 tablespoons oil

1 onion, chopped

2 tomatoes, chopped finely

1 cup / 240 ml water

$^{1}/_{2}$ teaspoon chili powder

2 bayleaves

salt and pepper

1. On a large flat plate, mix the flour with a little salt and pepper and dredge the fish pieces in it.

2. Then melt the margarine in a pan and cook the fish until it is golden brown. After that, take out the fillets, add the oil and sauté the onion. When that is done, put in the chopped tomatoes.

3. Now return the fish to the pan and season with pepper and salt. Add the water, chili powder and bayleaves.

4. Bring the pan to the boil and then cover it, reduce the heat and cook gently for about 15 minutes without stirring, taking care that it does not catch. Serve with rice, macaroni or plantains ■

Zom (Spinach with meat)

Serves 6-8

'Africa in miniature' is how Cameroon has been described: its geographical, social and political features reflect the mix of the continent. More than 150 ethnic groups live there, the result of migrations from the Congo River basin, from Nigeria and from Sudan. 'Cameroon' comes from the Portuguese name for the Sanaga river, *Rio dos Camaroes* (Shrimp River) although what the Portuguese caught apparently was crayfish, a river crustacean, not shrimp, a sea-water related species.

I N G R E D I E N T S

2 pounds / 900 g stewing beef, cut into small chunks

water

4 tablespoons oil

1 large onion, chopped

2 pounds / 900 g fresh spinach, chopped

2 tomatoes, chopped finely

1 tablespoon tomato paste

2 tablespoons peanut butter

salt and pepper

1. Put the beef in a saucepan with a little salt and enough water to cover. Bring to the boil, covered, and simmer for 1¹/₂ - 2 hours or until the meat is just tender (it will cook for 30 minutes later on: see step 3). The length of time will vary according to the cut of meat you are using and the size of the pieces. Take the meat out and keep the liquid.

2. Using a large pan, now heat the oil and soften the onion in it. Add the meat pieces and cook for 2 minutes.

3. Taking the liquid used for cooking the beef in, add water to make up to 2 cups/470 ml and then pour this into the pan containing the onion and meat. Add the spinach, tomatoes, tomato paste, peanut butter, pepper and salt. Bring it to the boil and then cover, lower the heat and cook for 30 minutes, stirring regularly ■

> **IN ALL RECIPES**
> ● **PEPPER AND SALT ARE TO TASTE**
> ● **CHILI AND SUGAR ARE GIVEN AS GUIDE QUANTITIES ONLY. VARY TO TASTE**
> ● **MEASURES FOR BEANS AND GRAINS REFER TO DRY INGREDIENTS.**

CONGO

Mbisi ye kalou na loso (Fish and kale)

Serves 6

Film buffs will recall that at the end of *Casablanca* Humphrey Bogart goes off to join the Free French in Brazzaville, today the capital of Congo. Less famous or infamous than its big neighbor across the river, Zaire, Congo is about the size of Japan and is still quite well covered with rainforest.

Fish, greens and rice – as in this recipe – make a nutritious combination; this version is spiced up with chili.

INGREDIENTS

1¹/₂ pounds / 675 g fish fillets, cut into pieces

1 large onion, chopped

1 green bell pepper, sliced

3 tablespoons oil

¹/₂ teaspoon paprika

¹/₂ teaspoon chili powder

1¹/₂ cups / 040 g kale or spinach, chopped

1¹/₄ cups / 300 ml water

2-3 tablespoons / 25-40 g margarine

salt and pepper

1. Start by cooking the onion and bell pepper in the oil for about for 5 minutes until they are soft. Then add the paprika, chili, kale or spinach and water. Cover and simmer for 5 minutes.

2. Now put in the margarine and, when it has melted, add the pieces of fish. Cover and simmer for 10 minutes and then remove the lid and continue to simmer for a further 10 minutes or until the fish is tender. Serve with yams, sweet potatoes or rice ■

GABON

Poulet au gnemboue (Chicken with nuts)

Serves 4-6

By World Bank figures, Gabon is richer than South Africa, Hungary and Yugoslavia. Formerly a French colony, it became independent in 1960 but its major income-earners – petroleum, uranium and manganese – are still linked with French companies. Ordinary people remain poor and around 65 per cent of food has to be imported.

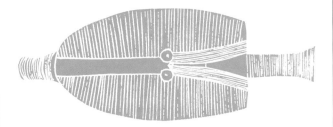

INGREDIENTS

3 pound / 1.5 kg chicken, skinned and cut into portions

1 cup / 125 g macadamia or hazelnuts, roasted lightly

2 cups / 470 ml stock

¹/₂ teaspoon chili powder

1 clove garlic, crushed

3 scallions / spring onions, thinly sliced

salt and pepper

1. Start by putting the roasted nuts into a blender with a little of the stock. Mix well, making sure the nuts are crushed into a paste and then adding more stock as required to make a sauce.

2. Pour the sauce into a large pan and place over a gentle heat. Now add the chili powder, garlic, scallions/spring onions, salt and pepper, mixing with a spoon.

3. Next put in the chicken pieces and turn them round to coat them all over with the nut sauce. Cover the pot and cook over a very low heat for 1 hour or until the meat is cooked. Check often and stir to prevent sticking, adding more stock or water if necessary ■

THE GAMBIA

Benachin or Wolof Rice

Serves 4-6

Local fishing has long been a mainstay in The Gambia but poaching by foreign trawlers has depleted the stocks. Peanuts provide half of all export earnings and food crops include rice, maize/corn as well as those mainstays of drought-prone countries – millet, sorghum and cassava/manioc.

'The Senegambia Restaurant in Basse makes memorable *benachin* which is often served up on festive occasions. You can leave out the meat and eat it as a vegetarian dish if you prefer.' *Rosemarie Daly, London, UK*

I N G R E D I E N T S

¹/₂ pound / 225 g meat or white fish, cut into 1 inch/ 2.5 cm pieces

Some or all of the following vegetables:

1 egg-plant / aubergine, diced

¹/₂ pound / 225 g white cabbage, chopped

1¹/₂ cups / 225 g pumpkin, squash or turnip, diced

1¹/₂ cups / 225 g zucchini/ courgettes or marrow, sliced

4 okra, sliced

1-2 tablespoons peanut oil

2 medium onions, finely chopped

1-2 cloves garlic, crushed

12 peppercorns, crushed

1 tablespoon tomato paste

1 cup / 240 ml chicken stock

1 chili or 1 teaspoon chili powder or a few drops of Tabasco sauce

1 cup / 225 g rice

2 cups / 470 ml water

juice of 1 lemon

salt

1. Using a large pan, heat the oil and cook the onions and garlic together with the peppercorns for a few minutes until the onions are golden. Then add the meat or fish and the vegetables.

2. Now put in the tomato paste, salt, stock and chili powder or Tabasco sauce.

3. Cook the meat or fish and vegetables until they are done. If using fish this will take about 10-20 minutes with the vegetables, but if you are using meat you will need to allow up to 2 hours, depending on what cut you are using. In this case, cook the meat without the vegetables until it is almost ready and then put the vegetables in to cook for the last 20 minutes or so.

4. When this is ready, remove the vegetables and meat or fish from the pan and keep them warm.

5. Let the sauce that remains in the pan cool a little and then add the rice and water.

6. Cover the pan, bring to the boil and cook the rice for 20-30 minutes. Add more water if necessary. When cooked, the rice should have absorbed all the water.

7. Turn the rice out onto a serving plate and garnish it with the hot vegetables and meat or fish. Squeeze the lemon juice over and serve the food right away ∎

GHANA

Beef palava (Stew)

Serves 4-6

'Palava: conference, (prolonged) discussion, esp. between savages (sic) *and traders etc; empty words, talk, cajolery. From Portuguese palavra, from Latin (parable).' Oxford Dictionary 1976.* Otherwise it means the mixture of distinctive-tasting vegetables such as egg-plant/aubergine, or spinach as below. It is a common dish, with variations, in several West African countries.

I N G R E D I E N T S

2 pounds / 900 g beef, cut into small chunks

1 large onion, chopped

4 cups / 950 ml stock

2 cups / 450 g spinach, chopped

1¹/₂ cups / 225 g okra, sliced

3 tablespoons oil

1 teaspoon chili powder

1 tablespoon lemon juice

salt

1. First put the meat pieces and onion into a pot and pour in the stock. Then put the lid on and bring to the boil. Now turn down the heat and simmer for 1-2 hours, until the meat is almost done.

2. Mix in the spinach and okra and cook for 5 minutes over a medium heat, stirring occasionally. Pour in the oil and season with chili powder and salt.

3. Reduce the heat at this point, add the lemon juice and cook gently for about 30 minutes until the meat is tender and the mixture fairly dry ■

IVORY COAST

Chicken à la n'gatietro (Chicken with peanut sauce)

Serves 6

Ivory Coast is the world's main cocoa producer and also grows coffee, sugar and pineapples for export. Peanuts, used in this recipe, are grown widely in Africa where they were taken from South America by the Portuguese in the 16th century. Also known as groundnuts and earthnuts, they develop as pods from the plant's yellow flowers. The pods bury themselves in the ground and are dug up at harvest time.

I N G R E D I E N T S

3 pound / 1.5 kg chicken, skinned and cut into joints

3 tablespoons oil

1 medium onion, chopped

3 scallions / spring onions, sliced

1 large tomato, chopped

1 tablespoon tomato paste

1 teaspoon paprika

1 bayleaf

2 cups / 470 ml stock or water

1 cup / 225 g peanut butter

salt and pepper

1. To start, heat the oil in a pan and brown the chicken joints. After that, remove the pieces and then cook the onion, scallions/spring onions, tomato, tomato paste, paprika, bayleaf and seasoning. Mix well.

2. Return the chicken pieces, cover the pan and simmer for 5 minutes. Now add the stock and cook for a further 30 minutes or until the chicken is almost ready.

3. Put the peanut butter into a bowl and slowly add the drained liquid from the cooking pan. Mix the sauce well and then pour it back over the chicken and heat for a further 5-10 minutes or until the chicken is cooked ■

KENYA

Grilled chicken with honey barbecue sauce

Serves 2

'Bees don't need constant attention like cows' says Milka Kathou, a member of Kibwezi women's group in Kenya who have found selling honey to Nairobi supermarkets brings them vital income. 'Harvests from five hives will pay for two terms of schooling for each of my five children. And we use the honey as well to soothe coughs and to ease stomach-aches.'
'Honey is delicious cooked with chicken, as in this recipe.'
Jane Nash, Ashford, UK

I N G R E D I E N T S

6 chicken drumsticks	2 tablespoons Worcestershire sauce
1 small onion, finely sliced	1 tablespoon honey
1 clove garlic, finely chopped	1 cup / 225 g rice
2 tablespoons oil	a few grilled mushrooms for garnish
1 medium can tomatoes, chopped	1 tomato, sliced, for garnish
	salt and pepper

1. Gently cook the onion and garlic in the heated oil. Then add the tomatoes, honey, Worcestershire sauce, pepper and salt. Cook gently for 20-30 minutes, until the sauce is quite thick.

2. While that is cooking, boil the rice in a separate saucepan and keep it hot.

3. Now place the chicken drumsticks in the broiler/grill pan and coat them well with the honey sauce. Grill for 10-15 minutes on each side or until they are cooked, brushing frequently with the sauce.

4. Serve the chicken on a bed of rice garnished with the grilled mushrooms and slices of tomato and hand round the remaining sauce separately ∎

Lamb and pumpkin stew

Serves 4-6

Livestock farming is a major source of food supply in Kenya, especially goats, fat-tailed sheep and cattle. Cattle are kept as a source of wealth on the hoof, providing food through their milk and blood.

I N G R E D I E N T S

1 1/2 pounds / 675 g shoulder of lamb, cut into 1 inch / 2.5 cm cubes	
4 tablespoons / 50 g ghee or margarine	
2 onions, sliced	
3 cloves garlic, chopped finely	
1 green chili, finely chopped +	
1 inch / 2.5 cm fresh root ginger, peeled and chopped finely or 2 teaspoons ground ginger	3/4 cup / 180 ml water
4 large tomatoes, chopped or canned tomatoes	1/2 pound / 225 g pumpkin, squash or marrow, peeled and cubed
+ optional ingredient	salt and pepper

1. Melt half the ghee or margarine in a heavy pan and add the lamb chunks, turning them so that they brown on all sides. Then season with salt and pepper and when this is done, take out the meat and keep it warm.

2. Put the rest of the ghee or margarine into the pan and cook the onions, garlic, chili, ginger and tomatoes for about 7-8 minutes. Now put the lamb pieces back in.

3. Cover the saucepan and cook for 40 minutes or so, stirring occasionally to prevent sticking. After that time add the water and pumpkin, squash or marrow, cover again and cook for a further 30 minutes or until the lamb is tender. Check the seasoning; serve with potatoes and vegetables ∎

65

KENYA

Roast chicken with peanut sauce

Serves 4-6

Coffee, tea, fruit and vegetables – mostly grown around Mount Kenya – are some of the country's prime exports. Falling prices for tea and coffee have meant less foreign exchange to buy oil and other necessities.

'In this recipe the peanut sauce is handed round separately. Serve the chicken with sweet potatoes or rice.' *Jane Nash, Ashford, UK*

I N G R E D I E N T S

3 pound / 1.5 kg chicken

3 tablespoons / 40 g margarine or ghee

2 medium onions, finely chopped

1 tomato, finely chopped

$^{1}/_{2}$ cup / 110 g crunchy peanut butter

1 cup / 240 ml milk

salt and pepper

Heat the oven to 325°F/160°C/Gas 3

1. Sprinkle some salt and pepper over the chicken and dot it with the margarine, keeping 1 tablespoon back for later use. Then bake it in the oven for about 1$^{1}/_{2}$ - 2 hours until done, spooning the margarine and juices over from time to time.

2. About half an hour before the chicken is ready, melt the remaining margarine in a saucepan and sauté the onions until golden. Stir in the chopped tomato and cook for 5 minutes.

3. Add the peanut butter and blend it well. Now gradually stir in the milk and seasoning. Then cover the saucepan and simmer for about 20-30 minutes, stirring occasionally. Pour this sauce into a dish and then serve the chicken, handing the sauce separately ■

Spring chicken in mango sauce

Serves 4

'Mangoes, a tropical fruit native to India, are now found in many parts of the world. India is the world's largest commercial producer of these fruits which come in all shapes and sizes. If you want to eat them raw look for ones which are beginning to go yellow and pink. Canned mango is an acceptable alternative for this recipe if you drain off the syrup first.' *Jane Nash, Ashford, UK*

I N G R E D I E N T S

3 pound / 1.5 kg chicken, skinned, boned and cut into pieces *

2 tablespoons oil

1 cup / 240 ml chicken stock

1 cup / 240 ml fresh double or whipping cream

$^{1}/_{2}$ cup / 60 ml sherry

1 tablespoon margarine

$^{1}/_{2}$ cup / 60 g broken or chopped, unsalted cashewnuts

2 medium mangoes, peeled and cut into slices

salt and pepper

* Keep the bones to make the stock

1. To start, season the pieces of chicken with pepper and salt. Heat the oil in a pan and brown them on all sides.

2. After this, carefully pour off the oil and then add the stock. Cook the chicken, covered, for about 25 minutes until tender. Then remove the pieces and keep them hot.

3. Now whip the cream and then spoon it into the pan containing the stock. Stir it in gently and let it heat slowly, without boiling, for a few minutes until the sauce thickens. Remove from the heat and add all the sherry except 1 tablespoonful, mixing it in well.

4. In a small pan, melt the margarine and roast the cashewnuts until they are lightly brown. When this is done, keep some for the garnish and add the rest to the sherry sauce.

5. Keeping a few of the mango slices aside for the garnish, warm the other pieces in a pan with the remaining tablespoon of sherry and then add them to the sauce. Gently re-heat the sauce without boiling. Pour it over the hot chicken and sprinkle on the garnish of cashewnuts and mango cubes. Serve with fresh vegetables and potatoes or rice ■

LIBERIA

Egg-plant/aubergine stew with ham and fish

Serves 6-8

The idea of Liberia ('land of liberation') was born in the USA in the 1820s when the cotton gin reduced the need for slaves. Sending them 'home' seemed the solution, even though West Africa was hardly home after more than 100 years in America. The American influence in Liberia is still strong, and hamburgers are as much part of the city diet as dishes like this one.

I N G R E D I E N T S

2 pounds / 900 g egg-plants/
aubergines, sliced thinly

4-6 tablespoons oil

1 pound / 450 g white fish
fillets, cut into pieces

1 onion, chopped finely

$^1/_2$ pound / 225 g bacon or
ham, chopped

$2^1/_2$ cups / 590 ml water

salt and pepper

1. In a flat pan with a lid, heat 2 tablespoons of the oil and gently cook the fish fillets until they are golden brown. Then take them out of the pan and set aside.

2. Adding more oil if necessary, cook the onion for a few minutes and then put in the bacon or ham.

3. After this, replace the fish and add the water, salt and pepper. Bring to the boil and then toss in the egg-plant/aubergine slices.

4. Cover the pan now and turn down the heat, cooking for 20-30 minutes until the egg-plant/aubergine is soft ■

Fish with spicy sauce

Serves 4-6

Nutmeg, one of the ingredients used in this dish, is the aromatic seed of a tree found in the Moluccas and Indonesia; mace comes from the same plant. In the 12th century Arab traders brought the spices to Europe. Later it was the Portuguese and then the Dutch who held the monopoly on the 'Spice Islands'. Today, Grenada in the Caribbean is the other main producer.

I N G R E D I E N T S

6 mackerel or herring fillets
(or similar fish)

$^1/_2$ cup / 60 g flour

2 medium onions, chopped

4-5 tablespoons / 50-60 g
margarine

1 pound / 450 g tomatoes,
chopped

1 teaspoon cayenne
pepper or chili powder

$^1/_2$ teaspoon grated or
ground nutmeg

handful fresh parsley,
chopped

salt and pepper

1. Sprinkle the salt and pepper into the flour in a bowl and then shake the mixture evenly onto a plate. Coat the fish fillets with it.

2. Then soften the onion in 2 tablespoons of margarine in a pan and after that add the tomatoes and cayenne or chili powder. Cook over a low heat for 20 minutes.

3. Now stir in the nutmeg and more seasoning if required.

4. While this is cooking, heat the remaining margarine in another pan and place the fish fillets in it, cooking them until they are brown on both sides.

5. Place the fish on a hot serving dish and pour over the sauce, scattering the parsley on top to garnish. Serve with rice ■

MALI

Chicken Ramatoulaye

Serves 4-6

Nearly all the people in Mali are involved in subsistence farming and herding of sheep and cattle. Food crops can only be grown along the Senegal River and 90 per cent of food is imported.

'This is how Ramatoulaye, who is a primary-school teacher in Donentza, Mali, cooks chickens … very tasty.' *Rosemarie Daly, London, UK*

I N G R E D I E N T S

3 pound / 1.5 kg chicken

3 cloves garlic

juice of 1 lemon

2 tablespoons oil

4 small onions, peeled but left whole or use 1 large onion cut into quarters

8 mushrooms +

2 celery stalks, cut into 1 inch / 2.5 cm pieces +

3 tablespoons tomato paste

1 chili, sliced finely or 1-2 teaspoons chili powder

10 peppercorns, crushed

1/2 cup / 120 ml water

salt

+ optional ingredients: you can use other vegetables such as carrots and also cook potatoes around the chicken.

Heat oven to 375°F/190°C/Gas 5

1. First pierce the chicken with the point of a knife in several places and then cut one of the cloves of garlic into slivers. Insert the slivers into the slits in the chicken.

2. Using a large pot with a lid, place the chicken inside and pour half of the lemon juice over it.

3. Then crush the 2 remaining cloves of garlic and put them with all the other ingredients, except the remaining lemon juice, into the pot with the chicken. Pour in a little water to prevent the chicken from drying out.

4. Cover the dish and put it in the middle of the oven to cook for 1¹/₂ - 2 hours according to how well done you like the chicken. Baste frequently and pour the rest of the lemon juice over before serving ■

NIGER

Chicken Djerma

Serves 4-6

Land-locked Niger has the world's largest underground uranium mine, with plenty of the mineral in it. Most goes to the former colonizing power, France. But falling world demand for uranium has hit Niger badly, as have the droughts which have rocked food and livestock production.

This plain dish is good served with baked potatoes or rice and a salad. Hot toasted chopped almonds or sesame seeds can be handed round separately to sprinkle on top.

I N G R E D I E N T S

3 pound / 1.5 kg chicken, portions, skinned

1 clove garlic, crushed

a little flour

1 egg, beaten

margarine for cooking

some chopped almonds or sesame seeds, toasted, for garnish

salt and pepper

1. Cut the chicken meat from the bone and grind, chop or mince it very finely. Add the garlic, salt and pepper and mix well, adding enough flour and beaten egg to bind.

2. Take up equal amounts of the mixture and shape into burgers. Melt the margarine in a pan and cook them for a few minutes on each side, until they are golden. Scatter the nuts on top and serve ■

Tabshe (Beef stew)

Serves 6

Niger's six million people are mostly subsistence farmers, growing millet, sorghum, green beans, rice and cowpeas. Cowpeas, also known as black-eyed peas or yellow-eyed peas, were taken from Africa with the slaves to America. They are widely eaten in the southern states of the US, in dishes such as Hopping John – beans with rice, eaten especially at New Year. They are called 'cowpeas' because of their original use as animal fodder.

I N G R E D I E N T S

2 pounds / 900 g stewing beef, cut into 1 inch / 2.5 cm cubes

1 large onion, chopped

1$\frac{1}{4}$ cups / 300 ml water

2 tablespoons peanut or other oil

1 tomato, diced

3 tablespoons tomato paste

$\frac{1}{2}$ pound / 225 g pumpkin, squash or marrow, chopped

1 pound / 450 g spinach, chopped

2 tablespoons peanut butter

salt and pepper

1. To start, place the beef and onion in a pan with $\frac{1}{2}$ cup/120 ml water and a little salt. Add the oil, tomato and tomato paste. Cover and cook for about 1$\frac{1}{4}$ hours or until the meat is tender.

2. Now add the remaining water and the pumpkin and cook uncovered for 10 minutes. Put the spinach in and bring to the boil.

3. Mix the peanut butter with a little water in a bowl and add it to the stew. Season with salt and pepper and cook, covered, for 10 minutes or longer until the meat is cooked. Serve with boiled rice or mashed yams ■

NIGERIA

Jollof rice with beef and prawns

Serves 6

Unlike many African countries, Nigeria has not been devastated by the famine and drought of recent years, and production of the main food crops (sorghum, maize/corn, cassava/manioc, yams, rice and millet) is increasing – though not rapidly enough to fulfil the country's needs. The main export is oil and petroleum products.

'Jollof' rice is like paella and crops up in many West African countries, though the actual ingredients vary from place to place.

I N G R E D I E N T S

1 pound / 450 g stewing beef, cut into small pieces

4 tablespoons oil

1 medium onion, sliced finely

2 large green bell peppers, sliced finely

2 cups / 400 g rice

$\frac{1}{2}$ pound / 225 g shrimps / prawns, shelled

4 tablespoons tomato paste

2 tablespoons / 25 g margarine

salt and pepper

1. Begin by browning the meat on all sides in the hot oil. Then add the onion and bell peppers and cook for 3 minutes. Now pour in 1$\frac{1}{4}$ cups/300 ml water and simmer for about 2 hours or until the meat is tender.

2. Next, put the rice in a saucepan of salted boiling water and cook for 20-30 minutes. Drain off any surplus liquid and then add all the other ingredients to the rice, season and mix everything well. Cook for a further 10 minutes, stirring from time to time, before serving ■

> **IN ALL RECIPES**
> ● PEPPER AND SALT ARE TO TASTE
> ● CHILI AND SUGAR ARE GIVEN AS GUIDE QUANTITIES ONLY. VARY TO TASTE
> ● MEASURES FOR BEANS AND GRAINS REFER TO DRY INGREDIENTS.

SENEGAL

Ceeb ak Jen (Rice and fish)

Serves 8-10

Drought-prone Senegal needs to import food but it is trying to grow more of its staples, millet and rice. Fishing is also being developed with tuna, prawns and lobsters among the catch. Oysters, too, are gathered but no doubt they are mostly destined for the former colonizer, France and wealthy locals.

'This national dish of Senegal is also eaten in many other West African countries. Ideally it uses sea bream, West African rice ("Ceeb"), the complete range of ingredients and is cooked over a charcoal fire – but even if you don't manage all these requirements the result will be good, with the fish, peanut and sweet potato tastes predominating.' *Albert Stol, Dakar, Senegal*

I N G R E D I E N T S

3 pounds / 1.5 kg sea bream or cod, filleted and cut into pieces. If using whole fish, keep the heads.

3 quarts / 2.75 liters water

1 cup / 240 ml peanut or vegetable oil

2 large onions, finely sliced

small packet frozen prawns or canned prawns

6-8 tablespoons tomato paste

handful fresh parsley, chopped

2 cloves garlic, crushed

4 carrots, chopped

1 small turnip, chopped

2 cups / 300 g cassava/ manioc, chopped +

2 egg-plants / aubergines, sliced +

2 sweet potatoes, chopped

6 okra, sliced +

handful fresh sorrel or 1 tablespoon dried

1 pound / 450 g cabbage, chopped

2 cups / 300 g pumpkin, squash or zucchini / courgettes

2 pounds / 900 g rice

2 chilis, sliced finely

juice of 2 lemons

salt and pepper

+ optional ingredients

1. If using whole fish, take off the heads and put them into a pan with some water, bring to the boil and simmer for 20 minutes to make a stock. Make this up to 3 quarts/2.75 liters with water and use as directed in the recipe.

2. In a large pan, heat the oil and cook one of the onions till golden. Then add the prawns and the tomato paste mixed with a little water.

3. Now put the parsley, garlic, a little salt and the other onion into a mortar, mixing bowl or blender and grind them together.

4. Put this mixture into the pan containing the onions and prawns. Add the fish and cook gently for 3 minutes.

5. Now pour in the stock, add some salt and all the other ingredients except chilis, rice, lemon juice and the shorter-cooking vegetables (eg the cabbage and zucchini/courgettes).

6. After about 20 minutes or when the fish is cooked, remove it from the pot and place the pieces in the center of a dish which will be large enough to hold the vegetables as well. Pour a little of the liquid over the fish to keep it moist and set aside to keep warm.

7. Put the remaining vegetables into the pot and continue to cook the rest of the ingredients until they are all ready, about another 10-20 minutes. Now remove the vegetables from the pot, but keep both pot and the remaining liquid for later use. Arrange the vegetables around the fish and keep this dish warm.

8. Pour out 4 cups/940 ml of the liquid the fish and vegetables were cooked in and put 1 cup/240 ml of it into a small saucepan, and the remainder into another pan. This is for two sauces, see (10) below.

9. Now add the rice to the pot containing the vegetable liquid, bring it to the boil and cook for 20-30 minutes until the moisture is absorbed and the rice cooked.

10. Next put the finely sliced chilis into the saucepan with the 1 cup/240 ml of sauce; bring to the boil and cook for 3 minutes. Heat up the 4 cups/940 ml of sauce in the other pan also.

11. Pour the mild sauce over the fish and vegetables, squeeze the lemon juice over the top and serve the chili sauce separately ■

Fishballs

Serves 8

'The *Ile de Goree* where I am living lies just off the Senegalese coast. It used to be a collecting point for slaves, where they were assembled for transit to America.

'In this recipe, the fishballs can be eaten on their own although sometimes they are served with a dish called *ceeb ak jen* (fish with rice, see opposite). Usually in Senegal there is just one course and no appetizers or desserts.'
Albert Stol, Dakar, Senegal

I N G R E D I E N T S

2 pounds / 900 g brown rice

3 pounds / 1.5 kg sea bream or cod, filleted and cut into pieces

1 cup / 100 g breadcrumbs

1/2 cup / 120 ml milk

1 large onion, chopped finely

1 clove garlic, crushed

1 green bell pepper, sliced

handful fresh parsley, chopped

2 scallions / spring onions

4-5 tablespoons oil, preferably peanut

a little flour

SAUCE

2 onions, chopped

1 tablespoon oil, preferably peanut

8 tablespoons tomato paste

1 1/4 cups / 300 ml water

1 teaspoon thyme

1 bayleaf

3 sweet potatoes, chopped

4 carrots, chopped

1 small turnip, chopped

1/2 pound / 225 g cabbage or spinach, chopped

salt and pepper

1. To begin, soak the breadcrumbs in the milk for 30 minutes.

2. During that time, put one onion, the garlic, bell pepper, parsley, scallions/spring onions, a little oil, salt and pepper in a bowl and mix them well together, or use a blender.

3. Now add the fish and crumble it with a fork. Squeeze the milk from the breadcrumbs next and add them to the mixture, adding a little flour and some more oil if necessary to help it bind.

4. Put a little oil on your hands, take out equal amounts of the fish mixture and roll it into balls on a floured surface.

5. Then heat the oil in a pan and cook the fishballs until golden brown all over. Remove them and keep warm.

6. To make the sauce, cook the two remaining onions in the oil. Mix the tomato paste with a little water and pour this in slowly, stirring all the time.

7. Put the fishballs back into the pan with the onions and tomato paste and pour in the remaining water. When it boils, add the thyme, the bayleaf, the sweet potatoes, carrots and turnip. Season with pepper and salt. Simmer for 30-40 minutes, adding in the cabbage when the other vegetables are almost cooked. Serve with rice ■

SIERRA LEONE

Sweet potato leaf stew

Serves 4

'The Mende people in south east Sierra Leone eat rice as their staple food. When it is prepared they spread it on a large round platter. A soup or stew, like this one, is served over the rice and then the people gather round to share the food from the common dish.

'This is a very basic recipe and you can alter it by using beef or chicken instead of fish; or by substituting 1 cup/ 175 g cooked beans (kidney beans, garbanzos/chickpeas or lentils) for the peanut paste.' *Ruth van Mossel, Freetown, Sierra Leone*

I N G R E D I E N T S

4 cups / 500 g green vegetable leaves (sweet potato or spinach), washed and chopped very finely

1/2 pound / 225 g smoked dried fish or 1 pound / 450 g fresh fish *

3 cups / 700 ml water

1 1/2 cups / 360 ml red palm oil +

1 large onion, chopped

1-2 fresh chilis, crushed, or 1-2 teaspoons chili powder

1/2 cup / 110 g groundnut paste / peanut butter

salt and pepper

+ Red palm oil can be found in Indian and Caribbean shops. If you cannot find it, use peanut oil instead.

*NOTE: If using fresh fish, first remove the bones and cut into bite size pieces. Stir-fry it in a little oil with the onion, chili or chili powder and salt. Add 1 cup/240 ml water, cover and simmer for 5 minutes or until the fish is cooked. Then proceed as in step 4 below.

1. First soak the dried fish for 15 minutes and then take the bones out. Wash the fishmeat and place it in a medium-sized saucepan. Pour the red palm oil over and add 1 teaspoon of salt. Heat up gently and then let it simmer for 5 minutes.

2. Now add 1 cup/240 ml of water to the simmering mixture as this cooks and softens the dried fish. Put the lid on.

3. Next put in the onion, chilis or chili powder, some more salt and 1 cup of water. Continue to simmer until the fish is tender, about 15 minutes.

4. When it is cooked, remove the lid from the pot and lay the chopped green leaves on top of the fish mixture. Drizzle a little palm oil on before replacing the lid and then leave it to simmer again.

5. In a bowl, stir about 1 cup/240 ml water into the peanut butter to make a thin, smooth paste, adding more water if necessary, and pour this into the stew. Stir well, adjust the seasoning, and put in more water if the stew is too thick.

6. Serve over cooked rice and accompany the dish with an array of fresh fruits ■

SOMALIA

Seafood stew

Serves 6-8

Somalia is unusual, especially among Islamic countries, In passing a law to allow women to sue for divorce. It is also unusual in having a high literacy rate (around 80 per cent) since the introduction of a script for the previously unwritten Somali language. Hosting the world's fourth largest refugee population is another Somali distinction (mostly ethnic Somalis from Ethiopia). Nomadic livestock rearing is the main way of life, with animals the prime export.

For this stew, you can use a mixture of virtually any seafood; the recipe just gives a few suggestions.

I N G R E D I E N T S

2 pounds / 900 g seafood eg shrimps, prawns, mussels, shelled

1/4 cup / 60 ml peanut oil

2 medium onions, finely chopped

2 cloves garlic, crushed

1 teaspoon curry powder

1 red bell pepper, finely chopped

1 pound / 450 g tomatoes, cut in wedges

2 tablespoons peanut butter

salt

1. To make the stew, first pour the oil into a large pan and lightly brown the onions and garlic for a few minutes. Stir in the curry powder, ginger, red bell pepper and salt.

2. Next, add the tomatoes and peanut butter and simmer gently for 2-3 minutes. At this point, put in the seafood; cook lightly for 10 minutes, stirring from time to time, and then spoon the stew onto hot rice and serve ■

SOUTH AFRICA

Bobotee

Serves 4

'*Bobotee* is an old Cape dish which blends spicy Dutch East Indian empire tastes from Indonesia and Malaysia with local ingredients such as apricots. Many of the Cape slaves came from the East Indies and although they lost their language they retained their Islamic religion and their cookery. You can adapt *bobotee* by using different combinations of fruit and spices. But whatever you include it is best to keep the meat moist, the curry mild and the balance of sweet and sour ingredients that make this so distinctive.' *W. Beinart, Oxford, UK*

I N G R E D I E N T S

1 pound / 450 g ground/ minced lamb or beef

1 slice bread

1½ cups / 360 ml milk

1 tablespoon oil

1 large onion, chopped finely

2 cloves garlic, sliced

½ - 1 teaspoon chili powder or curry powder

seeds from 2 cardamom pods, crushed

1-2 teaspoons ground cilantro / coriander

2 bayleaves

1 clove +

½ cup / 60 g almonds +

1-2 teaspoons turmeric

1 egg

1 teaspoon dry mustard

½ teaspoon finely grated lemon peel

1 small apple, grated

½ cup / 50 g dried apricots, chopped

½ cup / 50 g raisins or sultanas *

2 tablespoons lemon juice (if using lamb) or red wine vinegar (for beef)

2 tablespoons dry white wine or orange juice +

salt

+ optional ingredient

* other dried fruit such as figs can be used or fresh fruit.

Heat oven to 325°F/160°C/Gas 3

1. Put the bread in a bowl and pour over the milk to soak for half an hour.

2. While that is happening heat the oil in a pan and soften the onion and garlic. Then add the chili powder or curry powder, cardamom, cilantro/coriander, bayleaves, clove and almonds. Cook for 5-10 minutes and stir often to prevent sticking. Remove from heat.

3. Now remove the bread from the milk and squeeze it, keeping the milk in the bowl. Add the turmeric and the egg with a little salt to the milk and beat until the mixture is an even light yellow color.

4. Using a large bowl, put in the bread, half of the yellow milk and all the other ingredients including the onion and spices. Mix well with your hand so that the mixture is even and fairly smooth.

5. When this is done, put the meat into a deep greased oven dish and smooth the top. Pour on the rest of the milk, fleck with margarine and then bake in the oven for about 1 hour or until the top is golden brown. Serve with chutney, sliced bananas, shredded coconut and sliced tomatoes ■

SOUTH AFRICA

Bobotee

Serves 4

This version is less spicy and more moist than the previous one. Lamb gives a better flavor than beef, but either can be used.

INGREDIENTS

1 pound / 450 g ground/minced lamb or beef

1 slice bread

1 1/2 cups / 360 ml milk

2 eggs

2 tablespoons / 25 g margarine

1 medium onion, chopped

1-2 teaspoons mild curry powder or to taste

juice of 1 lemon

1/2 cup / 60 g almonds, halved and lightly toasted

1 cup / 100 g dried apricots, chopped

1/2 cup / 50 g raisins or sultanas

2 bayleaves

2 tablespoons chutney +

salt and pepper

+ optional ingredient

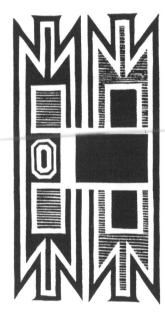

Heat oven to 325°F/160°C/Gas 3

1. First, using a mixing bowl, soak the bread in the milk for 30 minutes. Then take it out and squeeze it well, keeping the milk in a basin. Now beat the eggs into the milk.

2. When this is done, melt the margarine and sauté the onion until it is golden.

3. While that is cooking, mix the meat in a bowl with the bread, curry powder, lemon juice, almonds, apricots, raisins or sultanas, bayleaves, chutney, salt and pepper.

4. Now pour in half of the egg mixture and the onion and mix it well.

5. Spoon the meat into a shallow, greased oven-proof dish and smooth the top. Then pour on the rest of the egg mixture and bake for about 1 hour until the topping sets. Serve with yellow rice (see p.124), or plain rice and a salad ∎

Fish curry with lemon juice

Serves 6-8

Thousands of Indians were brought to South Africa in the last century as indentured laborers for the sugar plantations of Natal. Nowadays many live in the towns, as professionals and industrial workers. Some Indian markets, as in Durban, have stalls piled high with spices, rice and different types of lentils.

INGREDIENTS

2 pounds / 900 g white fish, cut into portions

4-5 tablespoons oil

1/2 teaspoon mustard seeds

1/2 teaspoon cumin seeds

2 large onions, finely sliced

4 cloves garlic, crushed or chopped finely

10 curry leaves or 1 teaspoon curry powder

4-5 teaspoons garam masala

1 teaspoon turmeric

4 tomatoes, chopped

1/2 cup / 120 ml water

juice of 2-3 lemons

handful fresh cilantro/coriander leaves, chopped

salt

1. Toasting the mustard seeds and cumin seeds is the first step. Take a large pan, heat the oil in it and then add the seeds. When they start to jump, put in the sliced onions, garlic and curry leaves or curry powder and cook until the onions are golden brown.

2. Now add the garam masala, turmeric, salt and tomatoes. Let the mixture cook gently over a low heat, stirring often, until it becomes thick like a purée.

3. When this is done, mix some of the water with the

lemon juice and stir this into the sauce to thin it a little; not too much though because it should remain a thick sauce. Then simmer again for a further 10-15 minutes.

4. Put in the fish now and continue cooking, adding more water or lemon juice if necessary, until the fish is ready, about 15-20 minutes. Decorate with cilantro/coriander and serve on a bed of rice ■

Meat curry with cilantro/coriander

Serves 4-6

Here is a basic curry which can use whatever meat you prefer (such as lamb/mutton, beef or chicken), or that may be left over. The word 'curry' just means sauce and there are endless combinations of spices to give different flavors. This one uses cinnamon and ginger in addition to the curry leaves and turmeric.

I N G R E D I E N T S

2 pounds / 900 g meat, cut into 1 inch / 2.5 cm cubes	1/2 inch / 1 cm fresh ginger root, peeled and chopped or 1 teaspoon ground ginger
1 medium onion, chopped	
1 stick cinnamon or 1 teaspoon ground cinnamon	2 cloves garlic, sliced finely or crushed
2 tablespoons oil (use less if meat is fatty)	1 large tomato, sliced
2 teaspoons curry powder	2 teaspoons garam masala
1 teaspoon turmeric	handful fresh cilantro/ coriander leaves, chopped
salt	

1. Cook the onion together with the cinnamon in the heated oil. When the onion is lightly browned, add the curry powder, turmeric, ginger, garlic and tomato. Let this cook slowly, stirring now and again, until it thickens.

2. Now add the meat, mix it in well and then cover the pan and cook until tender – the time will depend on what meat you are using. Beef and lamb will take up to 2 hours, chicken 30-40 minutes. If you are using cooked meat then it only needs to cook for about 15 minutes to heat through. If the mixture looks too dry or too thick, add a little water and stir to prevent sticking.

3. When the meat is cooked add the garam masala and salt. Simmer for another 10 minutes before removing from the heat and garnish with the cilantro/coriander leaves. Serve with rice or chapatis ■

Sosaties (Lamb kebabs)

Makes 12

These kebabs show the Southeast Asian influence in South African cooking – 'sosaties' is a variation of 'saté', the tasty little kebabs cooked over charcoal on food stalls in Malaysia, Indonesia and Singapore. Allow at least one hour for the marinating of the meat.

I N G R E D I E N T S

1 pound / 450 g ground/ minced lamb (or use cubed meat, cut in 1 inch / 2.5 cm pieces)	1/2 teaspoon ground cilantro / coriander
	1/2 teaspoon turmeric
6 dried apricots +	dash of dry white wine +
1-2 tablespoons lemon juice	1 tablespoon sugar +
1 medium onion, finely chopped	1/2 teaspoon black pepper
	salt
+ optional ingredient	

1. The apricots should be cut up into small pieces if you are using ground/minced meat, so do this first. Leave them whole if you are using meat chunks.

2. Prepare a marinade of the lemon juice, onion, apricots, cilantro/coriander, turmeric, wine, salt and pepper in a bowl. Add the meat and mix well. Leave for at least 1 hour, preferably longer.

3. If using ground/minced meat, take a small handful of the mixture and roll with your hands into a cylindrical shape. Then insert the skewer through it lengthwise. If using chunks, simply put them onto the skewers and insert the apricots between. Repeat until the meat is used up. Keep any remaining marinade and heat it up gently to accompany the dish.

4. Broil/grill the sosaties under a high heat or over hot charcoal. Serve with rice or pita bread and salad ■

STAPLE FOODS: BANANAS

Most bananas are grown and eaten locally in tropical regions from the Caribbean to Africa, India and Southeast Asia. Only about 15 per cent enter world trade — mainly the yellow-skinned dessert ones sent to rich countries. In the West those are the ones we're most familiar with, but in Southeast Asia there are varieties of small tasty red-skinned ones. In West and East Africa and the Caribbean, a starchy green banana — also called *ndizi, pisang, plantain* and many other names is a staple food for millions of people while a variety called *ensete* has long been grown in the Ethiopian highlands where it is a major food crop.

Edible bananas probably evolved in the Malay peninsular several thousand years ago. From that region, Indonesian migrants brought the fruit to Madagascar from where it crossed to Africa's east coast before the Portuguese arrived in the late fifteenth century.

About the same time as bananas came to Africa, during the first thousand years AD, they were also borne eastward across the Pacific. In the Philippines and Borneo one species, *musa textilis*, gave the Manila hemp that was for a long time the source of cords and ropes used in shipping. The fruit may have travelled to the New World from West Africa on the slave ships, or possibly they went directly from the Malay/Indonesian region to the Caribbean. At all events, the crop was well established throughout the tropics by the end of the seventeenth century.

Export trade for dessert bananas expanded with plantation production and today Ecuador is the largest exporter. Production is based mainly on one type, the *Gros Michel,* which is adapted to large-scale cultivation and slow sea travel in refrigerated ships.

But dependence on one variety has its perils. The market collapses when crops are ravaged. *Gros Michel* is susceptible to two major diseases — leaf spot and Panama disease (banana wilt). Losses from crop failure are reckoned to cost the West Indies about $4.8 million (£3 million) each year.

Aside from the yellow-skinned plantation-produced dessert bananas, there are red-skinned ones and green plantains. These cooking bananas are more diversified because they are not plantation crops; people still grow a wide variety.

All bananas are picked before they are ripe, and the different stages of maturity alter the taste and texture. When eaten early the plantain is yam-like and starchy, changing to a more soft and fruity flavor as it ripens. Some varieties are good for steaming, others for roasting, and some for making beer.

Wherever these cooking bananas grow they are turned into chips, (fried and flavored with salt, paprika or turmeric). In places where they are a staple food they are mashed into *fufu* or dipped into peanut stews. They are used for *koftas,* Indian spicy dumplings, and Venezuelan fritters. And eating is not all the plant is used for. The leaves give welcome shade in the tropics, and thatch for houses, as well as making excellent platters for a meal of curry and rice.

Main producers (not in order) Ecuador, Honduras, Uganda, Tanzania, Ghana, Nigeria, India, Malaysia, Indonesia, Philippines.

World production (1985) 42.5 million tons.

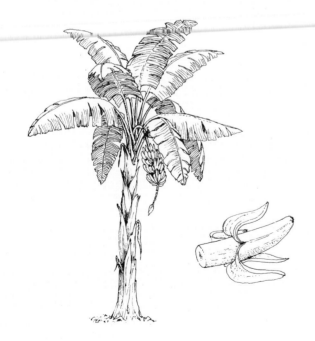

Illustration: Steve Weston

UGANDA

Matoke (Steamed plantain with chicken)

Serves 4-6

Plantains – savory bananas – are used extensively in African cooking. In Uganda, where they are one of the main food crops, plantains grow in the humid areas around Lake Victoria. *Matoke*, often served with a peanut sauce where the food budget does not run to chicken, is a staple meal. This recipe should be served as soon as it is ready because the plantains tend to harden quickly.

I N G R E D I E N T S

6 green plantains

3 pound / 1.5 kg chicken,
skinned and cut into joints

2¹/₂ tablespoons / 30 g ghee
or margarine

1 cup / 125 g flour

1 medium onion, sliced

1 teaspoon curry powder

2 medium tomatoes, sliced

1 cup / 240 ml stock

a little milk and margarine

salt and pepper

1. Melt 2 tablespoons/25 g of the ghee or margarine in a pan. Sprinkle the flour on a plate and roll the chicken joints in it, and then cook them in the fat until they turn golden brown. Remove from the pan and set to one side.

2. Now soften the onion in the pan for 5 minutes and then add the curry powder and, after about 1 minute, the tomatoes. Let them cook for a few minutes and then put the chicken pieces back in.

3. Next, pour on the stock, add the salt and pepper and simmer, covered, for approximately 30 minutes until the chicken is tender.

4. While that is happening, boil some water in a saucepan and cook the plantains in their skins for 20-25 minutes until they are soft. Then take them out of the pan and let them cool a while. When you can handle them, peel off the skins and mash the plantains in a bowl, adding a little milk and margarine, salt and pepper.

5. Put the plantain mash into the bottom of a serving bowl. Place the cooked chicken pieces on top and pour over the sauce. Serve at once with spinach or zucchini/courgettes ■

> **IN ALL RECIPES**
> ● **PEPPER AND SALT ARE TO TASTE**
> ● **CHILI AND SUGAR ARE GIVEN AS GUIDE QUANTITIES ONLY.**
> **VARY TO TASTE**
> ● **MEASURES FOR BEANS AND GRAINS REFER TO DRY**
> **INGREDIENTS.**

WEST AFRICA

Peanut stew with minced beef

Serves 4

Peanuts – or groundnuts as they are commonly known in Africa – are a major source of protein for many people in tropical parts of the world. As well as being eaten as a snack or in stews like this one, peanuts are made into cookies or sweets and also pressed into cooking oil.

For the stew you can used fresh, shelled peanuts, crushed or coarsely chopped. Roasting them a little first enhances the flavor (see step 1 below). Or you can simply use peanut butter – the crunchy type is better for the stew. Any left-over stew is good heated up and spooned over fresh lettuce, cucumber and cooked carrot slices as an adaptation of the Southeast Asian dish, *Gado-Gado* (see p.42)

I N G R E D I E N T S

1 pound / 450 g lean minced/ground beef

3/4 cup / 100 g raw peanuts or 1/4 cup / 60 g peanut butter

1 tablespoon oil

1 onion, chopped finely

1 tablespoon tomato paste

1/2 teaspoon chili powder or cayenne pepper

1/2 inch / 1 cm fresh root ginger, peeled and sliced finely or 1/2 teaspoon ground ginger

1/2 teaspoon mixed spice +

1 medium can tomatoes, mashed or chopped

1/2 cup / 120 ml water

juice of half a lemon

salt and pepper

+ optional ingredient

1. If using raw peanuts, first toast them under the broiler/grill, shaking the tray frequently so they toast evenly. Leave nuts to cool before handling them. If you prefer to remove the skins, rub the nuts gently between your fingers, and then chop or blend them coarsely.

2. Now heat the oil in a large saucepan and soften the onion in it. Then increase the heat and put in the beef, turning it frequently until it browns all over.

3. Now add the tomato paste, chili or cayenne, ginger, mixed spice, salt and pepper. Then stir in the peanuts or peanut butter. Put a lid on the pan and cook gently for about 3 minutes.

4. After this add the canned tomatoes, cover, and simmer for 20 minutes. Stir frequently to prevent sticking, and add water as required. Pour on the lemon juice and mix it in.

5. Before serving, check the seasonings and add more lemon juice, chili or salt according to taste. Serve with rice or cassava or yam fufu (see pps.121 and 137) ■

ZAIRE

Chicken à la Moambe (Chicken with peanut sauce)

Serves 6

Once self-sufficient in foodstuffs, Zaire now is a large importer. Subsistence farming provides a livelihood for 70 per cent of the population but suffers from a lack of resources which are channeled instead into copper and diamond mining, and the shadow economy.

I N G R E D I E N T S

3 pound / 1.5 kg chicken, skinned and cut into joints

4 tablespoons oil

4 tablespoons tomato paste

1 medium can tomatoes, chopped

1 tablespoon lemon juice

1/4 cup / 60 ml water

2 tablespoons peanut butter

salt and pepper

Heat oven to 325°F/160°C/Gas 3

1. Brown the chicken pieces first by cooking them on each side in the hot oil. Leaving the chicken in the pan, carefully pour off any excess oil into a cup.

2. Now mix the tomato paste in a bowl with the chopped tomatoes, lemon juice and the water and pour this over the chicken pieces. Stir gently and then simmer, covered, for 30-40 minutes or until the chicken is cooked. Add more water if it seems too dry.

3. After this, take out the chicken pieces, put them in a serving dish and place it in the oven to keep warm. Pour off the sauce into a bowl, add the peanut butter, salt and pepper and mix well. Now spoon this over the chicken, stir gently so that all the pieces are coated and return the dish to the oven for a further 10 minutes before you serve ■

ZAMBIA

Polenta pie

Serves 4

'Polenta' is an Italian term for a type of corn meal used in northern Italy, and pizza base was originally made with it. The maize/corn flour was cooked into a thick porridge and then poured onto a wooden slab and topped with tomato sauce to become a bulwark for hungry peasants.

Varieties of polenta pie are found in several countries. It is a good way to use up cooked meat, but you can also make it with cooked red lentils.

I N G R E D I E N T S

1 cup / 150 g corn meal/polenta

1½ cups / 350 ml stock

2 tablespoons / 50 g margarine

1 small onion, sliced

1 clove garlic, crushed

½ pound / 225 g cooked chicken, cut in small pieces, ground / minced beef or cooked lentils, or a mixture of meat and vegetables

1 tablespoon flour

handful fresh cilantro/ coriander leaves, chopped

½ teaspoon basil

½ - 1 tablespoon lemon juice

salt and pepper

Heat oven to 400°F/200°C/Gas 6

1. Bring 1 cup/240 ml of the stock to the boil in a heavy pan. Mix a little of the remainder (keeping some to make a gravy below) in a bowl with the cornmeal/polenta. When the stock has boiled, pour it slowly into the polenta, stirring all the time to prevent lumps.

2. Return the mixture to the pan and cook it slowly, stirring constantly until it becomes smooth and thick like a porridge. Add half the margarine and stir it in.

3. In another pan, heat up the remaining margarine and cook the onion and garlic until they soften. Put in the cooked filling, sprinkle on the flour and cook for 1 minute. Then add enough stock to make a little gravy.

4. Now take two-thirds of the polenta mixture and spoon it into a greased 7 inch/17.5 cm pie dish, pressing it into place with the back of a metal spoon. Bake this case for 10 minutes. Then remove from the oven and reduce the heat to 350°F/180°C/Gas 4.

5. Put the cooked meat or lentil mixture into the pie dish and spread the rest of the dough over the top, distributing it with a spoon and smoothing with a fork.

6. Put the pie in the oven and cook for 20-30 minutes ■

79

ASIA

Chicken with cashewnuts

Serves 4

Cashewnuts, native to tropical Central and South America, were transplanted in suitable parts of Asia and Africa by Portuguese and Spanish travellers. The nuts grow on trees, and make a curious sight as they hang from the bottom of the cashew 'apple'. India's Kerala state is a leading producer as are Mozambique and Tanzania.

The chicken should marinate for about 20 minutes.

I N G R E D I E N T S

1 pound / 450 g chicken breasts, skinned

2-3 tablespoons oyster sauce *

1/2 teaspoon sugar

1/2 teaspoon cayenne pepper or chili powder

1/2 pound / 225 g egg noodles

2-3 tablespoons peanut or other oil

2 cloves garlic, finely sliced

1 inch / 2.5 cm fresh root ginger, peeled and chopped finely

1 teaspoon turmeric

3/4 cup / 100 g cashewnuts, unsalted

2 carrots, very finely sliced

handful fresh cilantro/ coriander leaves, chopped

salt and pepper

* obtainable in supermarkets or oriental food stores

1. First of all, cut the chicken breasts into thin slices and put them into a bowl with 2 tablespoons of the oyster sauce, the sugar and the cayenne pepper or chili powder. Mix well so that the chicken is well coated and then leave to marinate for 20 minutes.

2. Now cook the egg noodles as directed on the packet. When they are ready, drain them and set aside.

3. Pour the oil into a wok and when it is hot put in the garlic, chopped ginger, turmeric and cashew nuts, stirring them round. Next, add the chicken and stir for 3-4 minutes before putting in the carrot slices. These should cook for 2 minutes before you put in the egg noodles and the rest of the oyster sauce. Season to taste.

4. When everything is cooked, and the noodles have been re-heated, sprinkle the cilantro/coriander leaves on top and serve at once ■

BURMA/ MYANMAR

Shrimp rice with lemon grass

Serves 4

Elephants are used as draught animals in Myanmar (formerly Burma), especially for the work of heaving unwieldy trunks of felled trees in the forests – the country contains three-quarters of the world's teak-wood resources. About 70 per cent of Burmese people work on the land, growing enough rice both to meet local needs and also to provide the main export.

'Lemon grass, in the recipe, is usually available in Asian markets and health food stores as *daun sereh*. Both fresh and dried types should be soaked before adding to the recipe. Use thinly sliced lemon peel as a substitute if necessary.' *Peter Stockton, Oxford, UK*

I N G R E D I E N T S

1 pound / 450 g brown rice

3 cups / 700 ml water

4 inch / 10 cm stalk lemon grass, or thinly pared peel from half a lemon

4 shallots or 1 medium onion, grated

3 cloves garlic, crushed

1 1/2 teaspoons turmeric or 1/4 teaspoon saffron

1 chili, sliced finely, or 1 teaspoon chili powder

1/4 pound / 100 g shelled shrimps

3 tablespoons oil

1 1/2 tablespoons fish sauce or 2 teaspoons anchovy essence

1 tablespoon lemon or lime juice

handful fresh cilantro/ coriander or parsley, chopped

salt

1. To begin, heat the water in a saucepan and when it is boiling throw in the rice. Put in the lemon grass or lemon peel, cover, and cook until the liquid has been absorbed.

2. Using a pestle and mortar or a blender, grind the shallots or onion, garlic, turmeric or saffron, chili and shrimps, adding the oil, fish sauce or anchovy essence and lemon or lime juice to make a paste.

3. Stir this into the rice, add salt to taste and cook gently, stirring often, for another 5 minutes.

4. Remove from heat and allow to stand, covered, for a few minutes before serving. Decorate with pieces of red chili and cilantro/coriander or parsley ∎

CHINA

Chicken with ginger

Serves 4-6

Women tend to outnumber men in a country's population, partly because they live longer. But in some countries, including China, India and several of the Gulf states, women form a smaller proportion of the overall population. The reasons are hard to pinpoint but may be associated with a woman's status, as unwanted girl babies who may be neglected and die or as lowly underfed adult child-bearers and chattels who succumb to disease and die untimely.

For this recipe, it is best to use a fairly deep pan so that the chicken and other ingredients can to be covered by the liquid while they cook.

I N G R E D I E N T S

1¹/₂ pounds / 675 g chicken, skinned, boned and cut into small pieces

3 tablespoons oil

1 large onion, finely chopped

2-3 cloves garlic, crushed

1¹/₄ cups / 300 ml rice wine or dry sherry

3 tablespoons soy sauce

1 inch / 2.5 cm fresh ginger root, peeled and chopped finely or 1 teaspoon ground ginger

1 teaspoon sugar

salt

1. Taking a deep pan or wok, heat up the oil and cook the onion and garlic until they are soft. Then add the chicken and the other ingredients, making sure that the liquid covers the meat.

2. Cover the pan and bring to the boil, then turn down the heat and simmer for 30-40 minutes or until the chicken is tender. Serve with rice or noodles and green vegetables ∎

Fish in sherry sauce

Serves 2-4

Soybeans have long been prized by the Chinese for their nutritional value, and also as a medicinal ingredient. Today soybeans are also made into milk and tofu or bean-curd as well as into soy sauce. The US is the biggest producer of soybeans, with China next.

I N G R E D I E N T S

2 pounds / 900 g fish fillets (cod, bream, halibut, haddock)

2 tablespoons oil

3 tablespoons soy sauce

¹/₂ inch / 1 cm fresh ginger root, peeled and chopped finely or ¹/₂ teaspoon ground ginger

2 scallions / spring onions, chopped finely

2 tablespoons sherry

2 teaspoons sugar

salt and pepper

1. Wash and dry the fish and then rub it with a little salt. Heat the oil and cook the fish gently for 5 minutes before adding the soy sauce, sprinkling this evenly over the fish.

2. Next, add the ginger, scallions/spring onions and salt and pepper. Continue to cook for a few minutes to let the seasonings penetrate the fish.

3. When this is done, add a little water and bring to the boil. Then pour in the sherry and sugar and leave to simmer on a reduced heat for 15 minutes before serving ∎

CHINA

Prawn fu-yung

Serves 4-6

Most Chinese people work on the land, growing wheat and maize/corn in the North and rice and soybeans in the South. Wheat, rice and soybeans are three of China's 'five sacred crops', cultivated since earliest times and venerated as mainstays of the diet – the others being millet and barley.

Prawn fu-yung is quite simple and quick to do; serve it on its own as a starter or with rice and vegetables for a main course dish.

INGREDIENTS

1/2 pound / 225 g shelled prawns, washed

6 eggs

1/2 inch / 1 cm fresh ginger root, peeled and chopped finely

1 tablespoon sherry

1 teaspoon soy sauce

2 tablespoons oil

salt and pepper

1. In a mixing bowl, beat the eggs and then fold in the prawns. Add the ginger, sherry, soy sauce, salt and pepper.

2. Next, heat the oil in a pan and when it is very hot pour in the prawn mixture, stirring and tossing it for 3-4 minutes until cooked. Serve immediately ■

(Opposite) Breakfast time in Shaoxing, China.
Photo: Wang Gang Feng/Panos Pictures

Fried rice

Serves 6

There are of course many variations on the theme of fried rice; so if you like, use this recipe as a launch-pad for some experimentation of your own.

INGREDIENTS

1 1/2 cups / 300 g rice, cooked and kept warm

3 tablespoons oil

1/2 pound / 225 g pork, cut into thin strips*

1 1/2 inch / 3 cm fresh ginger root, peeled and chopped finely or 2 teaspoons ground ginger

1/2 pound / 225 g shelled prawns or shrimps, cooked for 5-10 minutes in a little margarine

1 egg, beaten

1-2 tablespoons soy sauce

6-8 scallions / spring onions, finely chopped

salt and pepper

* Pork is normally used, but you could also use ham and/or bacon, or chicken.

1. Heat the oil in a heavy pan or wok and then add the pork, ginger, cooked rice and salt and pepper. Cook gently for 10 minutes, stirring constantly.

2. Next put in the prawns or shrimps and mix well.

3. Now make a well in the mixture and pour the egg into it. Let it cook a while in the heat of the rice until it is set. Then break it up with a fork and mix it into the rice.

4. Pour on the soy sauce and stir round to distribute. Pile the fried rice onto a serving plate, sprinkle on the scallions/spring onions and serve at once ■

> **IN ALL RECIPES**
> ● PEPPER AND SALT ARE TO TASTE
> ● CHILI AND SUGAR ARE GIVEN AS GUIDE QUANTITIES ONLY. VARY TO TASTE
> ● MEASURES FOR BEANS AND GRAINS REFER TO DRY INGREDIENTS.

CHINA

Lamb with bean sprouts

Serves 4

Although pork is the most common meat in Chinese cooking, lamb is favored in the South around Canton. For this recipe, shoulder or leg of lamb can be used, cut into very fine slivers so that it cooks rapidly.

I N G R E D I E N T S

1 pound / 450 g lean lamb, cut into thin slices

1 tablespoon cornstarch/ cornflour

³/₄ cup / 200 ml water

2-3 tablespoons oil

1 clove garlic, crushed

salt

4 tablespoons soy sauce

¹/₄ teaspoon ground ginger or ¹/₄ inch / 0.5 cm fresh ginger root, peeled and grated or chopped finely

1 teaspoon sugar

4 scallions / spring onions, chopped finely

2 cups / 100 g bean sprouts

1. First, take a small bowl or cup and mix the cornstarch/cornflour with the cold water, adding the water a little at a time to create a smooth paste.

2. Then heat the oil in a pan or wok until hot. When it is ready, put in the slivers of meat and the crushed garlic, salt, soy sauce, ginger and sugar. Mix well, reduce the heat if necessary and cook gently for 3 minutes, stirring all the time.

3. Now turn up the heat and add the scallions/spring onions and bean sprouts. Cook them briskly for 1 minute, moving them around continuously so they cook but remain crunchy.

4. When this is done, quickly pour in the cornstarch/cornflour paste, mix it in and bring to the boil, stirring until it thickens slightly. Serve at once with plain boiled rice ■

Shredded pork chow mein

Serves 4

Ovens for baking are not much used in China, since they require more wood or other fuel which is scarce there. Most cooking is done in a wok, an iron pan with a curved base that has been used by the Chinese for 5,000 years. 'The shape of the wok allows the food to cook quickly. This saves fuel and keeps the vegetables crunchy.' *J. Eng, Hong Kong*

I N G R E D I E N T S

³/₄ pound / 330 g lean pork

2 cups / 300 g egg noodles

¹/₂ tablespoon sugar

2 tablespoons soy sauce

1¹/₂ tablespoons cornstarch / cornflour

3-4 mushrooms, sliced finely or Chinese dried mushrooms

3 cups / 150 g bean sprouts

1 onion, sliced finely

2 cloves garlic, crushed or sliced finely

¹/₂ cup / 75 g green bell pepper or string / green beans, sliced thinly, or snow peas / mangetout

¹/₂ cup / 75 g carrots, sliced very thinly

2-4 scallions/spring onions, sliced very thinly

2 tablespoons oil

¹/₂ teaspoon chili powder, or ¹/₂ fresh red chili, sliced

¹/₂ tablespoon sesame oil *

handful fresh cilantro/ coriander or parsley, chopped

¹/₂ tablespoon dry sherry

salt and pepper

* Sesame oil is best if you can get it; otherwise use sunflower oil.

1. To begin, cut the pork into small pieces the size and shape of matchsticks. Sprinkle and rub the pieces with a little salt, half of the sugar and soy sauce and ¹/₂ tablespoon of the cornstarch/cornflour. Leave to marinate for 30 minutes.

2. If you are using Chinese dried mushrooms, soak them in warm water for half an hour and then drain and slice them thinly.

3. When all the vegetables are prepared, cook the noodles as directed on the packet – this usually takes about 7 minutes. Then drain them, keeping about ¹/₂ cup/120 ml of the water they were cooked in for later use.

4. In a wok or heavy pan, heat the oil (not the sesame oil) and cook the garlic, onion, chili or chili powder, carrots and mushrooms gently for 1-2 minutes, stirring constantly. Now increase the heat, add the pork and stir-fry for 2 minutes until the meat is cooked and browned all over.

5. Now put in the scallions/spring onions, the bean sprouts and the bell peppers or string/green beans or peas. Sprinkle them with a little salt, the remaining sugar and half of the noodle water. Continue cooking and stirring for a further 2-3 minutes.

6. When this is done, spoon the noodles into the wok or pan and mix them well with the vegetables. Pour in the sherry.

7. In a small bowl, blend the remaining cornstarch/corn-flour with the rest of the noodle water and pour over the mixture. Stir round to mix it in. Sprinkle on the sesame oil and cilantro/coriander or parsley and serve immediately ∎

Shrimps with rice and peas

Serves 4

In Chinese and eastern cooking, it is the preparation of food which takes the most time, chopping up a range of ingredients and mixing spices so that everything is ready the instant you need to cook it. The cooking time is comparatively short which means that vegetables keep their fresh taste – and their goodness.

Instead of the peas in this recipe you can use fresh snow peas/*mangetout*, or add other thinly sliced vegetables such as carrots.

INGREDIENTS

1 cup / 200 g rice, cooked	1 cup / 100 g onion, grated
1 cup / 175 g shelled shrimps or prawns	¹/₂ cup / 80 g peas, frozen or fresh, cooked
3 tablespoons oil	salt
1 egg, beaten	

1. With all the ingredients prepared, heat 1 tablespoon of the oil in a pan. Add the cooked rice and salt and stir-fry briskly for 2 minutes.

2. Then pour in the beaten egg and stir until cooked. Remove the pan from the heat.

3. Now, in another pan, heat up the rest of the oil and cook the onion until it is soft. Add the shrimps and peas and/or other vegetables.

4. When they are cooked, put in the rice and egg mixture and mix everything well. Turn up the heat, stirring frequently, until all the ingredients are piping hot and serve at once ∎

INDIA

Badami murghi (Chicken with almonds)

Serves 2

Almonds probably originated in the Near East but are now mainly grown in southern Europe and western Asia as well as in South Africa and California. Of all the nuts, almonds have the largest share of world trade. A bitter variety is used to make almond oil for flavorings and cosmetics.

I N G R E D I E N T S

2 chicken breasts, skinned and cut into small pieces

2 tablespoons oil

1-2 cloves garlic, crushed

1/2 inch / 1 cm fresh root ginger, peeled and chopped finely

1/2 cup / 60 g almonds

1/2 teaspoon allspice

1 tablespoon lemon juice

2 tablespoons orange juice

1 tablespoon fresh cilantro / coriander leaves, chopped

salt and pepper

1. Start by browning the chicken on all sides in hot oil.

2. When this is done, add all the other ingredients except the lemon juice, orange juice and cilantro/coriander leaves. Mix everything thoroughly so that the meat and almonds are well coated with spices. Cook, uncovered, over a fairly high heat for about 10 minutes until the chicken is cooked.

3. Just before serving, pour in the lemon juice and orange juice, stirring well. Serve hot, garnished with the cilantro/coriander leaves ∎

Chicken curry with coconut

Serves 4-6

This is a quick curry to make since it uses ground spices. One of these, turmeric, is rarely bought in any other form since it is difficult to grind at home. It comes from the root-like stem (rhizome) of a plant of the ginger family and is used for its color and slightly musty flavor.

I N G R E D I E N T S

3 pound / 1.5 kg chicken, skinned and cut into portions

4 tablespoons / 50 g margarine or ghee

1 large onion, finely chopped

2 cloves garlic, crushed

1 tablespoon ground cilantro / coriander

1 tablespoon desiccated coconut

1 teaspoon turmeric

1/2 teaspoon ground cumin

1/2 teaspoon chili powder

2 teaspoons ground almonds

juice of 1 lemon

1 1/4 cups / 300 ml plain yogurt

salt and pepper

1. Melt the margarine or ghee in a pan and cook the onion and garlic until they are golden. Now put in the chicken pieces and brown them on each side.

2. After this, add the cilantro/coriander, coconut, turmeric, cumin, chili powder, ground almonds, lemon juice, salt and pepper. Cook for 2-3 minutes, stirring a little. Then cover the pan and simmer gently for 30-40 minutes or until the chicken is cooked.

3. When it is ready, remove the pan from the heat and stir in the yogurt. Serve at once with rice ∎

Chicken palak (Spicy chicken with spinach)

Serves 4

The tropical monsoon climate with its extremes of droughts and floods dominates India's farming and the life and death of people as well. The caste system, although officially discouraged, and religion also shape people's lives: 80 per cent are Hindu and the rest Muslim, with some Christians, Sikhs, Parsis, Jains, Buddhist and animist. Each

Hindu was born into a caste, with the Brahmin priests at the top and the 'untouchable' out-caste at the other. Gandhi renamed the untouchables the *Harijans* – children of God.

I N G R E D I E N T S

4 chicken pieces, skinned

2 tablespoons margarine or ghee

1 large onion, finely chopped

2 cloves garlic, crushed

¹/₂ inch / 1 cm fresh root ginger, peeled and chopped finely

1 green chili, finely chopped or 1 teaspoon chili powder

2 teaspoons ground cumin

2 teaspoons ground coriander

2 teaspoons turmeric

1 cup / 225 g fresh or frozen spinach, chopped

1 medium can tomatoes, chopped

salt and pepper

1. Melt the margarine or ghee in a pan and then cook the chicken pieces until they are golden on all sides. When that is done, remove the chicken and put in the onion, cooking until it is soft.

2. Now add the garlic, ginger, chili, cumin, coriander and turmeric and cook for 2-3 minutes.

3. Next stir in the spinach and tomatoes. Season, and then put the chicken pieces back in.

4. Cover the pan and cook on a low heat for 30 minutes or until the chicken is done. Add water if the mixture becomes too dry. Serve hot with rice or chapatis and dhal ■

Chicken with sesame seeds

Serves 2-4

Allspice, one of the flavorings used here, is a dark red-brown berry so named because its aroma and flavor resembles several spices: cinnamon, cloves and nutmeg. The plant, which belongs to the myrtle family, is native to the tropical Americas. Most allspice is now produced in Jamaica.

The chicken needs to marinate for at least 1 hour.

I N G R E D I E N T S

2 pound / 1 kg chicken, skinned and cut into pieces

juice of 1 lemon

¹/₂ inch / 1 cm fresh root ginger, peeled and finely chopped

1 clove garlic, crushed

1 tablespoon oil (sesame oil if possible)

¹/₂ teaspoon chili powder

¹/₂ teaspoon allspice

3-4 tablespoons sesame seeds

salt

Heat oven to 350°F/180°C/Gas 4 after step 1 below.

1. First, make deep cuts in the chicken pieces to allow the marinade to soak in. Then mix all the ingredients, except the sesame seeds, in a bowl. Add the chicken and leave it to marinate for at least 1 hour. Turn the pieces from time to time to cover them evenly.

2. After this, take out the meat, keeping the marinade.

3. Sprinkle the sesame seeds on a flat dish and coat the chicken pieces with them on all sides.

4. Now place the chicken on a baking tray or shallow ovenproof dish and put it in the oven for 30-40 minutes until it is tender.

5. While that is cooking, pour the marinade into a saucepan and bring it to the boil. Then reduce the heat, simmer gently for 5 minutes and serve as an accompanying sauce for the meat, together with rice or chapatis ■

STAPLE FOODS: RICE

Bustling, teeming Hangzhou (Hangchow) city was an eye-opener to the traveller Marco Polo when he visited China in the thirteenth century. The citizens were discerning if voracious rice consumers — eating up to two pounds a day each was common and plenty was fermented into the 54 recorded varieties of rice wine.

The 'life-giving seed', as rice is called in Sanskrit texts, is one of the world's oldest and most important foods. Archaeological digs in China unearthed sealed jars of the grain that had been harvested almost 7,000 years ago.

Growing rice was then a very hit-or-miss affair. The grain came from wild grass that grew in swampy areas from north India across to south China. Harvesting it was hazardous, requiring a foray into the watery domain of snakes and leeches. Such a task usually fell to the lowliest people in a household: slaves or women.

It was in China, about 5,000 years ago, that haphazard cultivation was replaced by the controlled flooding of land in small plots to give the familiar paddy fields of China and Southeast Asia. By 2800 BC rice was being named one of China's Five Sacred Crops.

From China, rice spread to Japan. From India, it was probably taken by traders to the Middle East and Europe and thence to the Americas. Rice was first planted in the US during the seventeenth century. Africa has its own variety, 'red' rice (because the bran layer is reddish), which grows in the swampy reaches of the upper Niger River. Many countries were self-sufficient in rice until colonialists' desire for cash crops took away the paddy fields; in Indonesia in the nineteenth century about one-third of the land that had been used for food-growing nurtured sugar and tobacco instead.

Today, over 7,000 varieties of rice are grown around the world. Asia produces most of it — and eats it too. Unlike many cereals, rice is not usually fed first to animals which are in turn fed to humans. So it is the staple that directly feeds most people.

All rice is brown to start with. But frequently the grains are stripped of the bran layer and then polished shiny white — losing their nutritional fibre in the process. Rice is mainly carbohydrate, with a lower protein content than most cereals. People relying on a diet of polished white rice can get 'beri-beri' a disease due to lack of vitamin B1 — one of the vitamins lost when the bran is removed.

Rice is the basis of many famous meals. In southern China it is often eaten as *congee*, mildly-flavored gruel; as *nasi goreng*, Indonesian fried rice or *biryani* in India. *Pullao or pilaff* with the Middle East; European dishes include Italian *risotto* and Spanish *paella*; the Dutch enjoy *rijsttafel* — rice-table — brought back from their colonies in the East Indies (Indonesia), while generations of British children have spooned their way through bowls of rice pudding — short-grain rice baked in sweetened milk.

Main producers (in descending order) China, India, Indonesia, Bangladesh, Thailand, Vietnam, Japan, Burma, Brazil, Philippines.

World production (1985) 474 million tons.

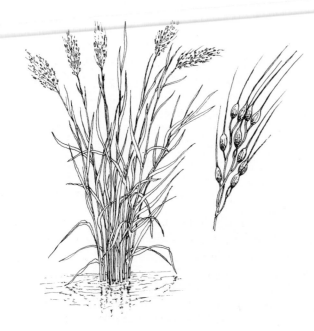

Illustration: Steve Weston

88

INDIA

Coconut curry

Serves 4-6

Cumin, or *jeera*, the dried fruit of a parsley-related plant, is a common spice in Indian cookery. It looks like caraway but has a very different taste (caraway seeds are not really used in Indian cooking). Aside from flavoring curries, cumin is also used in India as an aid to digestion.

INGREDIENTS

3 pound / 1.5 kg chicken, skinned and cut into portions

4 tablespoons / 50 g margarine or ghee

2 medium onions, sliced

2 cloves garlic, crushed

1/2 cup / 50 g creamed coconut, dissolved in 1/2 cup / 120 ml of the hot stock (see below)

1 teaspoon ground cumin

1/2 teaspoon chili powder

2 whole cardamom pods

1 teaspoon ground cilantro / coriander

1 tablespoon curry powder

1 1/4 cups / 300 ml chicken stock

salt and pepper

1. Heat half the margarine or ghee in a pan and cook the chicken portions until they are brown on all sides.

2. Meanwhile, in another pan put the rest of the margarine or ghee and add the onions and garlic. Cook them for a few minutes until they are soft and then put in the coconut milk, cumin, chili powder, cardamom seeds, cilantro/coriander, curry powder, salt and pepper and stir well. Cook this for 2-3 minutes over a medium heat.

3. Now spoon the mixture onto the chicken, pour in the remaining stock, cover, and bring to boil. Reduce the heat and simmer for 40 minutes or until the chicken is cooked. Serve with rice or chapatis ∎

Fish with tomatoes and spices

Serves 2-4

Jesus made a few fishes feed the five thousand; we have succeeded in doing the opposite. Huge quantities of fish are caught but very little is eaten directly by people. Most of the catch is processed and fed to animals which we then kill for food.

In the rice fields of Asia, fish are often reared with the paddy, ensuring a fresh supply of protein to eat with the rice. Such fish farming makes up about a quarter of all inland fresh-fish production in Indonesia.

INGREDIENTS

1 pound / 450 g fresh white fish fillets

1/2 teaspoon garam masala

1 inch / 2.5 cm fresh root ginger, peeled and chopped or 1 teaspoon ground ginger

2 cloves garlic, crushed

1/2 cup / 60 g flour

4-6 tablespoons oil

1 large onion, chopped finely

1/4 teaspoon chili powder

1/2 cup / 120 ml water

6 large tomatoes, chopped

handful fresh cilantro/ coriander leaves, chopped

salt

1. First wash the fish thoroughly and then pat it dry with paper towels.

2. Next, mix the garam masala, ginger, garlic, salt and flour in a bowl. Shake this over a large plate and then coat the fish in it.

3. When that is done heat up 2 tablespoons of oil in a pan and cook the fish for a few minutes on each side. Remove and set aside.

4. Using the rest of the oil if necessary, cook the onion over a low heat. When soft, add the chili powder, water and tomatoes and allow to simmer gently for 5-10 minutes.

5. Put the fish back in the pan with the other ingredients and cook slowly for 15 minutes or so until the fish is ready.

6. Scatter the cilantro/coriander leaves over and serve with rice and salad ∎

INDIA

South Indian biryani

Serves 6-8

This *biryani* uses cardamoms which are native to the hills of South India and Sri Lanka. Cardamom is related to the ginger family and is now sometimes grown between rows of tea bushes or rubber trees on the plantations. First mentioned in European literature in the 12th century, cardamom has long been an important spice, the seeds from its dried pods lending delicate fragrance to curries and desserts.

The meat should be marinated for 30 minutes.

I N G R E D I E N T S

2 pounds / 900 g beef, chicken or lamb, cut into small chunks*

1 green chili, crushed or 1 teaspoon chili powder

1 large tomato, cut finely

handful of fresh parsley or mint, chopped or 2 teaspoons dried

1 teaspoon turmeric

$1/2$ cup / 120 ml yogurt

1 inch / 2.5 cm ginger root, peeled and grated or 1 teaspoon ground ginger

2 cloves garlic, chopped finely or crushed

4 cups / 940 ml water

2 cups / 400 g rice

3 tablespoons oil

3 tablespoons / 40 g margarine

2 sticks cinnamon or 2 teaspoons ground cinnamon

seeds from 2 cardamom pods, crushed

5-10 curry leaves

3 large onions sliced in rings

2 teaspoons garam masala

$1/2$ cup / 110 g black or other lentils, cooked until just tender but not too soft

* With lamb, you can use a half or whole shoulder and cook it as one piece, cutting the meat as you serve.

Heat oven to 325 F/160 C/Gas 3

1. Put the meat in a bowl and add the chili, tomato, mint or parsley, turmeric, yogurt, salt, ginger and garlic. Leave it to marinate for 1 hour.

2. Now, in a heavy pan, heat the oil and margarine together and cook the cinnamon, crushed cardamom, curry leaves and onions until they are golden brown. Keep some of the onion rings to use later to decorate the dish with.

3. When this is ready, add the meat and its marinade and cook on a low heat until the meat is nearly tender – this will take about 30 minutes for chicken and up to 2 hours for lamb or beef, depending whether you are using a whole joint or pieces. It does not need to be completely cooked at this stage since it will cook some more in the oven (see below).

4. Meanwhile bring the water to the boil in a large pan, adding a little salt, and cook the rice for 5 minutes if using white rice, 10 minutes if using brown. It is important that the grains are not completely cooked at this stage as they cook more later (see below) and the biryani should not be too wet. When the rice is ready, set aside.

5. Now put the garam masala and cooked lentils into the pan containing the meat and simmer for a further 10 minutes.

6. At the end of this time, transfer the mixture to an oven-proof dish and add the rice, stirring gently to combine the ingredients.

7. Garnish with the onion rings and place the dish in the oven for 30 minutes or so. This lets the flavors mingle and finishes the cooking of the meat, rice and lentils. It should end up fairly dry, but add more water if you wish. You can serve the biryani with side dishes such as cucumber raita, chutney, slices of banana, hard-boiled egg, chopped apples, sultanas and desiccated coconut ■

INDONESIA

Petjel Ajam (Coconut chicken)

Serves 4-6

After China, India, the USSR and the US, Indonesia's 175 million people make it the world's most populous country. It has the largest Muslim population in the world although the island of Bali is mainly Hindu. Oil, natural gas and wood are the leading exports and Indonesia is now self-sufficient in rice, the staple food.

Throughout Southeast Asia, people often eat at the street stalls where food is prepared, cooked and served up in a flash as you wait and pass the time of day with the stallholder.

INGREDIENTS

3 pound / 1.5 kg chicken, skinned and cut into joints

1¹/₂ tablespoons oil

2 onions, chopped

4 cloves garlic, crushed

1 dried red chili, chopped finely or 1 teaspoon chili powder

1 cup / 125 g roasted peanuts

1 tablespoon lemon juice

1 tablespoon sugar

1 teaspoon ground ginger

¹/₄ cup / 50 g creamed coconut melted in ¹/₂ cup/ 120 ml hot water

salt and pepper

1. Heat the oil in large pan and brown the chicken joints. When golden, take them out of the pan and set aside.

2. Now cook the onions, garlic and chilis. When they are soft, put the chicken pieces back into the pan and add the peanuts, lemon juice, sugar, ginger, salt and pepper. Pour in the coconut milk, cover the pan and simmer for 30-40 minutes or until the chicken is cooked. Serve with boiled rice, chutney and sultanas ∎

Rempah (Spicy hamburger)

Serves 4-6

Most of Indonesia's people are of Malay origin but there are also some 300 minority groups in the country. About 80 per cent live in the countryside growing rice, cassava/manioc, corn/maize, sugar, bananas and other fruits and vegetables.

Rempah make a change from regular hamburgers. The spices are distinctively Asian, but you may like to experiment with other seasonings.

INGREDIENTS

1 pound / 450 g ground/ minced beef or lamb

1¹/₄ cups / 100 g desiccated coconut

1 clove garlic, crushed

¹/₂ teaspoon ground cilantro/ coriander

¹/₄ teaspoon ground cumin

1 egg, beaten

a little flour

1 tablespoon oil

salt and pepper

1. First put the coconut into a small bowl and pour over enough boiling water to cover it. Leave for 15 minutes and then squeeze out the excess liquid.

2. Now mix the meat with the coconut, garlic, spices and beaten egg so that they combine well. Divide the mixture into 12 burgers.

3. Sprinkle the flour onto a plate and dust the patties on both sides. Then either fry or broil/grill them for 5 minutes on each side. Serve with rice, or inside pitas, together with salad ∎

IN ALL RECIPES
● PEPPER AND SALT ARE TO TASTE
● CHILI AND SUGAR ARE GIVEN AS GUIDE QUANTITIES ONLY. VARY TO TASTE
● MEASURES FOR BEANS AND GRAINS REFER TO DRY INGREDIENTS.

INDONESIA

Saté ayam (Chicken kebab)

Serves 2-4

Saté – grilled meat on skewers with peanut sauce – is found in most parts of Southeast Asia. The street hawkers can be seen fanning their charcoal stoves with a coconut palm leaf, and then the little wooden skewers of meat are laid on top and soon a delicious snack is ready. You can use lamb, beef or pork as well, and turn this into a main meal by serving with rice and salad. Marinate the meat for at least 30 minutes before you cook it.

I N G R E D I E N T S

3 chicken breasts, skinned or 1 pound / 450 g beef, pork or lamb, cut into 1 inch / 2.5 cm cubes

2 cloves of garlic, crushed

2 tablespoons soy sauce

2 tablespoons water

SAUCE

1 small onion, chopped

5 macadamia nuts +

1 red chili, finely sliced or 1 teaspoon chili powder

1 tablespoon sugar

3/4 cup / 100 g peanuts, roasted or 1/2 cup / 110 g coarse peanut butter

1 tablespoon peanut oil

1/2 cup / 50 g creamed coconut melted in 1/2 cup/ 120 ml warm water

1 tablespoon lime or lemon juice

1 1/2 tablespoons dark soy sauce

salt

+ optional ingredient

1. Start by combining the garlic, 2 tablespoons of soy sauce and 2 tablespoons of water in a bowl and put the meat in to marinate for at least 30 minutes.

2. Now, using a blender or mortar, grind the onion, macadamia nuts, chili, half the sugar and the peanuts or peanut butter until they form a smooth paste, adding some of the oil if necessary.

3. Next heat up the remaining oil and cook the peanut mixture for 1-2 minutes, stirring all the time. Add the coconut milk and mix well. Keep the sauce warm.

4. When this is done, put the meat on the skewers and cook over a charcoal grill/barbecue or under the broiler/grill for a few minutes, turning as required, until they are cooked.

5. Meanwhile stir the lime or lemon juice, soy sauce and remaining sugar into the peanut mixture and season. You can either pour the sauce over the skewers before serving or hand it round separately ■

MALAYSIA

Chicken and vegetable curry

Serves 4-6

'I was in the UK studying for a year. I'd not done much cooking before I came although I used to make a fish curry which was just about all right for me … But the bland English pie-and-beans diet soon made me reach for the spices and now I have more confidence to cook. And yes, I have carried on back at home, cooking for the family.' *Joe Paul, Kuala Lumpur, Malaysia.*

I N G R E D I E N T S

3 pound / 1.5 kg chicken, skinned and cut into joints

3 tablespoons oil

1 onion, thinly sliced

5 cardamom pods

2 cinnamon sticks or 2 teaspoons ground cinnamon

5 cloves

3 teaspoons curry powder, mixed to a paste with a little water

2 medium potatoes, chopped

1 carrot, sliced

1/2 cup / 50 g creamed coconut melted in 1/2 cup/ 120 ml warm water

2 tomatoes, sliced

salt

Daging goreng (Marinated beef strips)

Serves 4

The trading centres of Singapore, Malacca and Penang, the tin mines and rubber plantations meant that thousands of foreign laborers came to Malaysia, especially Indians and Chinese. One of the earliest groups, the 'Straits' Chinese have lived in Malaysia for more than 100 years.

This is an easy meal to prepare and very quick to cook – and it tastes even better if you can cook the strips over a charcoal grill or barbecue. You can also try the recipe with lamb or chicken, but note that the meat should marinate for 1 hour.

I N G R E D I E N T S

1 pound / 450 g lean beef, sliced as in (1) below

1 teaspoon ground cilantro/coriander

1½ teaspoons turmeric

1 small onion, chopped very finely

1 clove garlic, crushed

1 teaspoon sugar or to taste

handful fresh cilantro/coriander leaves, chopped +

salt and pepper

+ optional ingredient

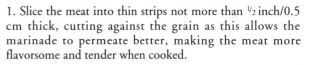

1. Using a large saucepan, heat the oil and cook the onion for a few minutes until it softens. Then add the cardamoms, cinnamon, cloves and salt together with the curry paste and cook for a few more minutes, pouring in a little water to prevent sticking.

2. Now put in the chicken pieces and let them brown a little. Mix all the ingredients well. The potatoes and carrot go in next, with enough water added to cover them.

3. Cover the saucepan, bring to the boil, and then reduce the heat and simmer gently for 30-40 minutes until the chicken is cooked.

4. Add the tomatoes and the creamed coconut. Cook for 2-3 minutes more and then serve with rice, chapatis and cucumber raita (see p.39) ∎

1. Slice the meat into thin strips not more than ½ inch/0.5 cm thick, cutting against the grain as this allows the marinade to permeate better, making the meat more flavorsome and tender when cooked.

2. Combine the ground cilantro/coriander, turmeric, onion, garlic, sugar, salt, pepper and fresh cilantro/coriander and sprinkle over the meat. Leave it to stand for at least 1 hour, turning occasionally to coat all pieces.

3. After this, put the meat on a charcoal grill, or under a broiler/grill, and cook quickly for 3-5 minutes on each side, according to how well done you like the meat. Serve with salad and rice or bread ∎

MAURITIUS

Boef Rougaille

Serves 4-6

'This is a typical Creole dish. Lamb, chicken, goat or fish can also be used, but whatever meat you use it should be left after seasoning for 15 minutes. *Rougaille* is thought to come from French "roux" meaning sauce and "ail" – garlic. We are an Anglo-Mauritian family and this is a firm favorite with us.' *Stella Bruce, Asha and Shona Brewer, Ilkley, UK*

INGREDIENTS

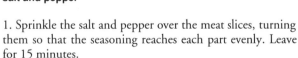

1¹/₂ pounds / 675 g lean beef, cut against the grain into very thin slices

2 tablespoons oil

3 onions, sliced

¹/₂ inch / 1 cm fresh ginger root, peeled and chopped finely

1 teaspoon fresh thyme

3 cloves garlic, crushed

4-6 chilis, split lengthwise

1 tablespoon fresh parsley, chopped

1 pound / 450 g tomatoes, chopped

6 scallions / spring onions, sliced

1 tablespoon fresh cilantro/coriander, chopped

salt and pepper

1. Sprinkle the salt and pepper over the meat slices, turning them so that the seasoning reaches each part evenly. Leave for 15 minutes.

2. After this time, heat the oil in a heavy pan and cook the meat for 1 minute, stirring frequently.

3. Take out the meat and put in the onions, ginger, thyme, garlic, chilis and parsley and cook for 3 minutes. Next add the chopped tomatoes and cook for a further 2 minutes.

4. Now return the meat to the pan and simmer for 15 minutes or longer if required, until it is tender.

5. When the meat is cooked, add the chopped scallions/spring onions, half the cilantro/coriander leaves and more seasoning if required and continue to cook for a further 2 minutes.

6. Before serving, garnish with the remaining cilantro/coriander and then serve with rice or other accompaniment such as potatoes ∎

MONGOLIA

Marinated beef strips

Serves 4

In Mongolia, domestic animals outnumber people 11 to one. The 22 million head of sheep, horses, goats, camels and yaks provide the wool, milk, meat and skins that are the country's main source of wealth. Wrestling, archery and horse-racing are the national sports, involving men, women and children, calling for the same qualities of rugged fitness as life around the herds.

The meat should marinate for 1 hour to allow the flavors to penetrate well. If you cannot get yak meat, you will have to make do with beef.

INGREDIENTS

1 pound / 450 g lean beef, sliced as in (1) below

1/2 cup / 120 ml soy sauce

1 teaspoon sugar +

1 clove garlic, crushed

1/4 teaspoon pepper

1 scallion / spring onion, finely chopped

1 tablespoon dry red or white wine +

salt

+ optional ingredient

1. Slice the beef into 1/4 inch/0.5 cm thick strips, cut across the grain so that the flavors can enter easily, the meat cook and become tender quickly.

2. Now mix together the soy sauce, sugar, garlic, pepper and chopped scallion/spring onion and pour over the beef pieces. Leave to marinate for at least 1 hour, turning occasionally.

3. After this, set the broiler/grill to a high heat and cook the beef for 3-5 minutes each side, according to how well done you want it to be.

4. Using a small pan, heat up the remaining marinade with meat juices (add the wine if desired) and pour it over meat.

5. Serve the meat with rice, barley or cracked wheat and salad, or on its own as an appetizer ∎

VIETNAM

Shrimp and chicken salad

Serves 4

Firecrackers explode, homes are decked with peach blossom and sweet rice cakes are eaten: that's how the Vietnamese celebrate *Tet* – Lunar New Year. It was during *Tet* in 1968 that the Vietnamese launched the offensive that was a turning point in the war against the Americans. Still recovering from those years, Vietnam now grows just about enough food for its people (rice, cassava/manioc, pulses, peanuts, fruit and vegetables), and fish is an important source of protein.

INGREDIENTS

1/2 pound / 225 g shelled shrimps, cooked

1/2 pound / 225 g cooked lean chicken meat, cut into small cubes

4 cups / 200 g bean sprouts

2 tablespoons lemon juice

1-2 teaspoons sugar

2 tablespoons fish sauce *

1 carrot, grated

6 inch / 15 cm cucumber, sliced

handful fresh cilantro/ coriander leaves, chopped

1/2 cup / 60 g peanuts, crushed or coarsely chopped

salt and pepper

* Fish sauce, called *nuoc nam* is obtainable from Chinese food shops; or you could use 1 tablespoon anchovy essence instead.

1. Pour in just enough water to cover the bottom of the saucepan. Heat it up and when it is boiling throw in the bean sprouts, for a few seconds only. Drain them and allow to cool.

2. In a bowl, mix the lemon juice with the sugar, fish sauce, salt and pepper.

3. Now arrange the bean sprouts, carrot and cucumber on a serving dish and pour the dressing over.

4. Place the chicken and shrimps on top of the salad and garnish with the cilantro/coriander leaves and crushed peanuts ∎

BOLIVIA

Meat and vegetable soup with quinoa

Serves 4

'Quinoa is cultivated in Bolivia as a staple grain; it is an ancient food for our country, very nutritious and rich in protein. With the flour we make bread and biscuits; fermented quinoa becomes the drink *chicha*. For soup we buy bones and boil them early in the morning; then add the quinoa and boil some more; then throw in the vegetables and cook again…and by lunchtime it is ready. But of course you don't have to cook it for so long.' *Alonzo Urquizu, Potosi, Bolivia*

INGREDIENTS

1 pound / 450 g bones with meat

1/2 cup / 110 g quinoa *

3 cups / 700 ml water

2 onions, sliced

1/2 pound / 225 g potatoes, cubed

1 carrot, sliced, or other vegetables

1/2 teaspoon ground cumin

1/2 -1 teaspoon chili powder

salt and pepper

* available at health food stores

1. Start the soup by heating up the bones and water to make the stock. Allow up to 2 hours for this. Then add the quinoa and let it cook for about 10 minutes.

2. Next, put in the potatoes, carrot and any other vegetables you are using. Sprinkle in the cumin and chili powder to taste, and season with salt and pepper.

3. Let the soup simmer for a further 20-30 minutes, adding more stock if a thinner soup is desired ■

Stuffed avocados

Serves 6

The US and Argentina are the main exporters of food to Bolivia whose rice, maize/corn, potatoes and wheat production falls short of local needs. Although still a major tin producer, Bolivia's output has declined in response to falling tin prices, while coca leaf cultivation has increased.

INGREDIENTS

6 ripe avocados

6 lettuce leaves, chopped finely

1/4 pound / 100 g chicken, fish or prawns, cooked

2-3 tablespoons mayonnaise

1 hard-boiled egg, sliced

salt and pepper

1. Cut the avocados in half lengthwise and remove the stone. Then take a bowl and mix the chopped lettuce with the diced meat or fish and mayonnaise; add seasoning.

2. Pile the mixture into the avocados and garnish with the egg slices ■

BRAZIL

Feijoada (Black beans with meats)

Serves 6

Regarded as Brazil's national dish, *feijoada* is international in its ingredients: beans and hot peppers originally came from Mexico, cassava/manioc from pre-Portuguese Brazil, meats and sausage from Europe and cooking skills from Africa.

I N G R E D I E N T S

1 pound / 450 g black beans, soaked and cooked

¼ pound / 100 g tongue, sliced and cut into small pieces *

½ pound / 225 g pork, cut into 1 inch / 2.5 cm cubes *

1/2 pound / 225 g smoked sausage, sliced *

2 onions, sliced

2-4 cloves garlic, crushed

2 handfuls fresh parsley, chopped

2 tablespoons oil

1 cup / 240 ml stock or water

2 bayleaves

salt and pepper

* other meats may be used, eg Polish or Spanish sausage, ham hock.

1. To begin, sauté the onions, garlic and half the parsley in the oil for a few minutes. Now put in the cubed pork and let it brown on all sides before adding the other meats. Cook them together for 10 minutes.

2. Now put the cooked beans into a large pan. Spoon in the meat and onions, together with the stock and bayleaves. When this is done, cover the pan and cook gently for 30-40 minutes until the meat is tender.

3. Near the end of the cooking time, add the salt and pepper. Just before serving, remove ½ cup of beans; mash them well and return them to the pot to thicken the liquid.

4. Scatter the remaining parsley on top before serving with rice, mashed potatoes or cassava/manioc. Fresh orange slices are excellent too, both to complement the *feijoada's* richness and as a colorful garnish ■

Moqueca (Fish stew)

Serves 4-6

'In Latin America and the Caribbean, domestic service is almost entirely done by women and up to 80 per cent of all women who earn wages work as servants.

'Fish is an important source of protein in Brazil with cod, crab, lobster and shrimp among the catch eaten locally. In this recipe, the dish needs to stand for 1 hour, after an initial cooking.' *Vanessa Baird, Oxford, UK*

I N G R E D I E N T S

2 pounds / 900 g white fish fillets

1 lemon

2 tablespoons oil, preferably coconut oil

2 medium onions, sliced

3 tomatoes, sliced

1 chili, cut finely

1 cup / 150 g shelled shrimps or prawns

fresh parsley, chopped

salt and pepper

1. Cut the lemon in half and rub the fish with it. Then squeeze the lemon and keep the juice.

2. Now heat the oil in a shallow pan and cook the onions and chili until they are soft. Add the tomatoes, fish, shrimps or prawns, lemon juice to taste and salt and pepper. Cook the mixture over a high heat for one minute, then turn off the heat, cover the pan and leave it to stand for one hour.

3. After this time, warm up the pan again and allow the contents to simmer for a few minutes until the fish is soft. Garnish with parsley and serve with rice ■

CARIBBEAN

Boljaw (Salt fish salad)

Serves 2-4

'This dish – also spelled *buljol, bull chow* and *booljow* – is probably an original piece of West Indian slave cuisine. To maximize the use of land, slaves were not allowed to keep their own livestock and were fed imported food, like salt fish or salt beef, rice and maize/corn. They supplemented this with vegetables they grew themselves in small gardens. The salted cod from the fishing grounds off Newfoundland was, and still is, a mainstay of the diet. It can be found in Caribbean or Asian food stores.

'Boljaw can be served either to start the meal or as a side dish. In Trinidad it is often eaten for breakfast.' *John Haigh, Kumasi, Ghana*

I N G R E D I E N T S

1/2 pound / 225 g salted cod

1/2 pound / 225 g white cabbage, chopped finely

1 avocado

1 onion, finely chopped

2 tomatoes, sliced

1/2 red chili, finely chopped, or 1/2 teaspoon chili powder

1 green bell pepper, chopped

4 tablespoons oil, preferably coconut

1 tablespoon lime or lemon juice

pepper

1. The first step is to remove the salt from the fish. To do this, put the fish into a pan with plenty of water, bring to the boil and simmer for 10-15 minutes. Then drain it two or more times with cold water. At this stage, the skin and bones can easily be removed and the fish divided into small pieces.

2. Now boil up some water and cook the cabbage in it lightly for 2 minutes and then drain.

3. Next, slice the avocado in half lengthwise and remove the stone. Peel, and cut the flesh into chunks or slices.

4. In a salad bowl, mix together the lightly-cooked cabbage, onion, tomatoes, chili, bell pepper, avocado and fish. Pour over the oil, lime or lemon juice and pepper and stir it round before serving ∎

Pelau (Savory rice)

Serves 4-6

'*Pelau*, or pilau, is a basic Muslim dish of savory rice which may have reached the Caribbean with the Asian indentured laborers who were taken there in the 19th century. But this pilau, or *pillow* (just one of many alternative spellings) served in homes and bars of St Vincent is very different from its Indian original. The Caribbean version will often use the cheap off-cuts of chicken refused by US consumers – wings, back or neck – which are exported frozen to the islands.

'The meat is seasoned and left to marinate, ideally overnight, and the rice is sweetened and flavored with caramelized sugar. It is quite a taste.' *John Haigh, Kumasi, Ghana*

I N G R E D I E N T S

3 pound / 1.5 kg chicken, skinned and cut into portions

juice of 1 lemon or lime

2 tomatoes, sliced

1 onion, finely sliced

1-2 cloves garlic, finely sliced

1/2 teaspoon curry powder

1 teaspoon thyme

1 tablespoon soy sauce

4 tablespoons oil, preferably coconut

2 tablespoons sugar

1 pound / 450 g rice

salt and pepper

1. Begin by putting the chicken portions into a bowl. Squeeze the lemon or lime juice over them and then add the tomatoes, onion, garlic, curry powder, thyme, soy sauce, salt and pepper. Mix well. Cover and place in the fridge overnight if possible, or for at least 4 hours.

2. Taking a pan with a cover, pour in 2 tablespoons of oil and when it is hot put in the portions of chicken, keeping

the marinade. Brown the chicken on all sides and then add the marinade. Cook for 2-3 minutes.

3. After that, cover the pan, reduce the heat and allow it to simmer for 30-40 minutes or until the chicken is cooked. Check from time to time that it is not catching; add a little water if necessary but not too much as the chicken produces some liquid as it cooks.

4. While that is happening, take another saucepan and heat the remaining 2 tablespoons of oil together with the sugar, stirring constantly until the sugar begins to caramelize and turn dark. Remove from the heat and let it cool a little, about 1 minute, stirring all the time.

5. Then very, very carefully, add a little water and stir as the sugar mixture sizzles. As you stir, the water should be incorporated into the sugar mixture.

6. After this put in the rice and mix it round. Then pour in more water as necessary to cover the rice by 2 inches/5 cms. Bring it to the boil and cook for 20 minutes or so until the rice is almost ready (see 8 below).

7. When the chicken is done, lift it out of the pan and remove the meat from the bones. Put the meat back into the onion and tomato sauce and continue to cook slowly. (The bones are not needed for this recipe but you can keep them to make stock).

8. Five minutes before the rice is cooked, mix in the chicken pieces and sauce. When everything is ready, turn the mixture out into a warmed dish or serve it from the cooking pot, with a salad ■

CHILE

Empanadas (Meat turnovers)

Serves 4-6

Transport is all-important in Chile, a ribbon of land hemmed in by mountains and sea. A strike by truck drivers can bring the economy to a halt, as happened in the events leading to the assassination of President Allende in 1973. Wheat and potatoes are the country's major staples, with beans, lentils and fruits. This recipe uses meat, but empanadas are delicious with a cheese or lentil filling (see p. 46); you can serve a variety.

I N G R E D I E N T S

1 packet / 200 g frozen flaky pastry, thawed

FILLING

$1/2$ pound / 225 g ground/ minced beef

2 onions, chopped

1 clove garlic, chopped or crushed

$1/2$ teaspoon chili powder

2 tablespoons oil

8 green olives, sliced +

$1/2$ cup / 50 g raisins or sultanas

$1/4$ cup / 30 g almonds, toasted and chopped

$1/4$ teaspoon paprika

$1/4$ teaspoon marjoram

2 tablespoons tomato paste

1 small can tomatoes, drained

salt and pepper

Heat oven to 400°F/200°C/Gas 6

1. In a bowl, mix the meat with the onions, garlic and chili powder.

2. Next heat the oil in a pan and cook the filling until the meat is brown. Add the tomatoes and tomato paste and mix well, cooking for a further 3 minutes.

3. Let the mixture cool a little and then add the olives (if using), raisins or sultanas, almonds, paprika, marjoram and seasoning.

4. Roll out the pastry on a floured board and cut it into circles approximately $3^{1}/_{2}$ inches/10 cms across, using a saucer or small bowl to press out the shape with.

5. Cover one half of each circle with some of the filling, leaving an edge of about $1/4$ inch/0.5 cm. Brush the edges with a little water, and then fold the empanada together, using a fork to press the sides closed.

6. Place the empanadas on a greased baking tray and cook them in the oven for 25-35 minutes until golden. Serve hot with salad ■

STAPLE FOODS: CORN OR MAIZE

In the sixteenth century in Mexico, when Hernan Cortes' mounted troops tried to ride their horses across the Aztec fields of corn (maize), they had a problem. For the plants grew so high, and so thickly that they were *'inpenetrable as a stone wall.'* The corn grew tall, almost like a forest, in the fertile Mexico basin. Indeed the *conquistadores* thought they they must have found Paradise, so abundant was the food in this country. And so easy to grow, only requiring a few months' work a year. This in turn released labor for other projects such as the making of magnificent cities and temples, elaborate handicrafts and class societies. Maize, as the centrepiece of this bounty, was soon despatched to Europe with the returning adventurers.

Maize or corn is the only major cereal crop of American origin. Cultivated for over 6,000 years, its development is woven into the history of the continent's indians. There are four main types; popcorn and flint which both have smooth and rounded or pointed kernels; and dent and sweetcorn which do not. Dent has a dented appearance, and sweetcorn is very wrinkled. The grains come in many colors — yellow, blue, red and black. Sometimes a corn cob bears more than one color of grain.

The Andes mountains are home to the greatest variety of corns. Inca indians developed the crop and extended their farming techniques by building elaborate terracing and irrigation systems.

Guatemalan and North Andean flint type corns may have been spread by the Chibchan culture. The Aztecs of what is now central Mexico cultivated a conical corn which was suited to their high land. In lowland Central America the Maya indians grew dent corn, the one that was cross-bred by North American farmers in the eighteenth century to produce today's major crop variety, the Corn Belt Dent.

In the sixteenth century the Portuguese carried maize to the west coast of Africa. Here it was planted to grow the food which would provision the ships bearing slaves to the Americas. Its rich harvests led to a population boom which ensured a steady supply of men and women to be transported into slavery.

Corn is now the mainstay food in many parts of Africa. Called *mealie* in South Africa, it is usually made into a mush (boiled and partly mashed kernels) served with stews while the flour makes porridge and cornmeal cakes.

Today, corn is the world's second largest cereal crop after wheat — but less than a quarter of the production is eaten by humans. In the US for instance where it takes up nearly 25 per cent of all cropland, corn is mostly fed to pigs.

Maize or corn is low in protein and dependence on it as a complete food can lead to pellagra, a disease caused by lack of nicotinic acid. Processing the grain with ash or soaking it in slaked lime, as the indians do, enhances its protein content.

The Hopi indians in Arizona cultivate blue corn, a hardy variety which can cling to life on cold windswept hills with thin soils. It is often prepared with the ash of local sagebrush plants. Hopis say *'Corn is like our mother. The blue variety is like our compass — wherever it grows we can go. Blue corn directed our migrations. It survives where others die.'*

Main producers (in descending order) US, China, Brazil, Romania, Soviet Union, Mexico, France, Argentina, Yugoslavia and South Africa.

World production (1985) 490 million tons.

CHILE

Pastel de choclo (Corn/maize pie with chicken)

Serves 4-6

Variations of this pie are found in Bolivia and other Latin American countries. Corn or maize is the only major cereal grain native to the Americas (**see Staple Food opposite**). In North America, it was introduced to the colonists by the Iroquois indians. Among the many varieties is the distinctively-flavored blue corn, grown in Arizona and New Mexico by the Hopi indians.

For this recipe you can also use left-over cooked chicken, and miss out the first two steps in the method.

I N G R E D I E N T S

3 pound / 1.5 kg chicken, skinned and cut into portions

2 tablespoons oil

2 onions, chopped

1 teaspoon ground cumin

1 teaspoon dried marjoram

1 tablespoon flour

1 ¼ cups / 300 ml stock or water

½ cup / 50 g raisins or sultanas

½ cup / 75 g olives, cut in halves

2 hard-boiled eggs, sliced +

2 eggs, beaten

¾ cup / 180 ml milk

1 medium can corn kernels

1 teaspoon sugar +

salt and pepper

+ optional ingredient

Heat oven to 350°F/180°C/Gas 4

1. First place the chicken portions into a large pan and pour in just enough water to cover them. Put a lid on the pan and bring it to the boil. Then lower the heat and simmer for 30-40 minutes or until the chicken is cooked.

2. Lift out the chicken pieces, keeping the stock, and allow them to cool. Then remove the meat from the bones.

3. Now heat the oil in a pan and sauté the onions for a few minutes before adding the cumin and marjoram. Cook for 2 minutes before sieving in the flour, a little at a time.

4. After that, slowly add the stock or water, stirring constantly so that you get a smooth sauce. Bring this to the boil and then put in the chicken pieces, seasoning with salt and pepper.

5. Next, spoon the chicken mixture into an oven-proof dish and scatter the raisins or sultanas, sliced olives and hard-boiled eggs on top.

6. Then whisk the beaten eggs and milk together in a bowl, adding the corn. Pour this over the chicken and sprinkle the sugar on top. Bake in the oven for 45 minutes or until the topping is set. Serve with baked potatoes and salad ∎

IN ALL RECIPES
● PEPPER AND SALT ARE TO TASTE
● CHILI AND SUGAR ARE GIVEN AS GUIDE QUANTITIES ONLY. VARY TO TASTE
● MEASURES FOR BEANS AND GRAINS REFER TO DRY INGREDIENTS.

COLOMBIA

Beef and fruit stew

Serves 6

Spain was a Moorish (Arab) colony from the 12th to the 14th century, and when the Spaniards came to South America the Moorish influence came with them – manifest here in the use of dried fruit with the meat. Instead of using exactly the fruit listed below, you can substitute the same weight from a packet of mixed dried fruit. Whichever you use, soak it for 1 hour first.

I N G R E D I E N T S

3 pounds / 1.5 kg lean beef, cut into 1 inch / 2.5 cm cubes

1/2 cup / 50 g dried apricots

1/2 cup / 50 g raisins or sultanas

1/2 cup / 50 g dried apples or pears

1/2 cup / 50 g dried prunes

3 tablespoons oil

2 onions, finely chopped

2-4 cloves garlic, crushed

2 carrots, sliced

1 teaspoon ground cilantro/coriander

1 1/4 cups / 300 ml dry red wine

salt and pepper

Note: The liquid should cover the beef while it is cooking, so use a saucepan which is deep enough to allow this, and which has a tight-fitting lid.

1. After soaking the fruit for 1 hour in a little water, drain it and the keep the liquid.

2. Using a heavy pan, heat the oil and sauté the onions and garlic for 2-3 minutes. Then add the beef and carrots and continue to cook for a few more minutes, turning the ingredients often. Add the salt, pepper and cilantro/coriander.

3. Now pour in the wine and liquid from the dried fruit and bring to the boil. Reduce the heat, cover the pan and simmer for about 2 hours or until the beef is nearly tender.

4. Put in the fruit, cutting it into smaller pieces if you prefer. Cover the pan and simmer again for another 30 minutes. Check the sauce, adding more wine if it is too thick. Serve with rice ∎

HAITI

Soupe au Giraumon (Vegetable Soup)

Serves 8

Haiti's agriculture suffers from drought and poor resources; food imports are needed to top up subsistence farming of maize/corn, rice, sorghum, beans, fruit and vegetables. Coffee, mangoes and sugar are among the goods exported. Many of the richest Haitians reside outside the country and take their wealth with them.

For this thick soup/stew, the meat should first marinate in the orange juice for 1 hour. When serving, you may prefer to take out the meat and vegetables at the end and have them as a separate course after the soup.

I N G R E D I E N T S

1 pound / 450 g chicken pieces, skinned

1 pound / 450 g ham hock, unsalted if possible

1 cup / 240 ml orange juice

1/2 cup / 100 g rice

2 carrots, sliced

2 cups / 300 g summer squash, zucchini/courgette or vegetable marrow, cubed

1/2 pound / 225 g white cabbage, shredded

1 stalk celery, sliced

1 onion, sliced

oil

3 cloves

1 tablespoon cider vinegar

salt and pepper

1. To start, marinate the chicken and ham in the orange juice for 1 hour. Then take them out and keep the juice.

2. Rub the meats with salt (if using salted ham hock, reduce or omit the salt here). Place them in a large pan and cover with water nearly to the brim. Bring to the boil,

cover, and then simmer for $2^1/_2$ - 3 hours. Skim the top of the liquid from time to time to remove any froth.

3. After this time, add the rice and carrots and continue to boil for 10 minutes. Now put in the squash, cabbage and celery, adding more water if needed.

4. Next, sauté the onion in a little oil and put it into the pot containing the meat, together with the cloves and vinegar. Boil for 1-2 minutes and season with pepper and salt. Add the retained orange juice just before serving.

5. If you are serving this as a soup course first, remove the meat and vegetables and put them in a dish to keep hot for serving after the soup ■

MEXICO

Chiles en nogada (Bell peppers in walnut sauce)

Serves 4-6

Walnut trees are grown both for their edible seeds – the nuts – and also for their attractive wood. The most widely-grown type is found from Mediterranean Europe through to China. Introduced into Britain in the 15th century, the species was taken to California 300 years later. A native American variety produces a more strongly-flavored black nut than its European counterpart, and either will do for this recipe.

I N G R E D I E N T S

6 green bell peppers

2 eggs, separated

flour

4 tablespoons oil

FOR THE FILLING – Picadillo

1 pound / 450 g ground/ minced beef

2 tablespoons oil

1 onion, finely chopped

1 clove garlic, crushed

1 teaspoon chili powder

1 medium can tomatoes, drained

$^1/_2$ cup / 50 g raisins or sultanas

$^1/_2$ cup / 60 g almonds, slivered or chopped

1 cooking apple, peeled and diced

salt and pepper

FOR THE SAUCE

1 cup / 125 g walnuts, finely ground

$1^1/_4$ cups / 300 ml cream or milk

1 cup / 225 g cream cheese

$^1/_4$ teaspoon ground cinnamon

1 tablespoon sugar

Heat oven to 350°F/180°C/Gas 4

1. Using a sharp knife cut round the top of the peppers carefully and draw out the core and seeds. Wash and dry the shells.

2. Then prepare the picadillo by first heating the oil and cooking the onions and garlic for a few minutes until they soften. Stir in the chili powder and then add the meat and other ingredients. Cover the pan and cook gently for 10 minutes, stirring now and again.

3. After that, whisk the egg whites until they are stiff. Beat the yolks lightly and fold them into the whites.

4. Now sprinkle some flour on a board or plate and roll the empty peppers in it, and then dip each one into the egg mixture to coat the outside.

5. In a large pan, heat the oil and gently cook the peppers all over until the egg coating turns golden. Drain them and pat lightly with paper towel. Now stand them in an oven-proof dish.

6. After this, fill the peppers with the picadillo mixture, putting any that remains in the bottom of the dish. Cover the container with a lid or foil and put it into the oven for 20 minutes or until the peppers are tender.

7. For the sauce, combine the ground walnuts, cream cheese and half the cream or milk, adding the cinnamon and sugar as desired. Use a blender for this, or beat well with a spoon. Pour in more cream or milk to produce a smooth but thick sauce and pour it over the peppers. If you want the sauce to be warmed, heat it gently in a pan taking care that it does not boil. The dish can be eaten warm or cold ■

MEXICO

Enchiladas (Filled pancakes)

Serves 6

Cortez, the Spanish conqueror, soon realized that a grain called *amaranth* was central to Aztec culture in Mexico. It was believed to give mystical power and was offered as tribute to the ruler Montezuma. So Cortez outlawed the grain and killed anyone caught growing it – an effective way to demoralize his enemy.

The earliest *enchiladas* could well have been made with *amaranth* flour; today corn/maize or wheat flour would more likely be used.

INGREDIENTS

4 eggs

2¼ cups / 280 g flour

2 cups / 470 ml milk

oil for cooking

½ teaspoon chili powder

½ teaspoon paprika

1 onion, sliced finely

1 clove garlic, chopped finely or crushed

½ pound / 225 g cooked ham, cut into small pieces

6 tomatoes, chopped

handful fresh parsley, chopped

1 tablespoon tomato paste

½ teaspoon fresh or dried marjoram or thyme

1 cup / 110 g cheddar cheese, grated

salt and pepper

1. Start by making a pancake batter. Crack three of the eggs into a bowl and whisk them. Then sieve the flour into a separate basin and make a well in it. Add the beaten eggs and gradually pour in two-thirds of the milk and a pinch of salt, stirring all the time to make a smooth mixture.

2. Using a shallow pan, put in just enough oil to coat the base. Heat it gently and then test to see if it is hot enough for cooking the pancakes by dropping a little bit of the mixture into the oil – if it sizzles then you can go ahead.

3. Pour in a little batter and tilt the pan to spread the mixture evenly over the base. Let it cook for a while over a medium heat and shake the pan gently to free the pancake. Now toss or turn it over to cook the other side. Do not cook the pancake for too long since it is to be browned later (see below). Remove it, put in a little more oil and cook the next one. Repeat until all the batter is used up.

4. Combine the remaining milk, egg, chili, paprika, salt and pepper in a bowl and pour this into a shallow dish. Dip each pancake in this mixture and then brown them in the hot oil. When this is done, put the pancakes aside to keep warm.

5. Now cook the onion and garlic in a little oil for 3 minutes to soften before adding the ham, tomatoes and parsley. Add the tomato paste, the marjoram and seasoning.

6. Fill each pancake with the mixture and fold it over. Place the pancakes on a heat-proof dish, scatter the grated cheese on top and broil/grill for a few minutes until the cheese melts ■

Picadillo (Savory beef with almonds)

Serves 4-6

Most of Mexico's farming is done by small rural collective units or *ejidos* growing food crops of maize/corn, sorghum, wheat, rice, barley, potatoes and beans. Export crops like tobacco and tomatoes have been given priority over food for local needs.

This is the basic *picadillo* which can be used to stuff peppers or to fill *empanadas* and *tacos* – or for a cross-cultural taste use chapatis (see p. 128) or pita bread.

INGREDIENTS

1 pound / 450 g ground beef or pork

1 onion, finely chopped

1 clove garlic, peeled and thinly sliced

1 tablespoon oil

1 medium can tomatoes, drained (keep the liquid)

1-2 tablespoons tomato paste

½ cup / 50 g raisins

½ cup / 75 g olives

½ cup / 60 g almonds, lightly toasted *

salt and pepper

* To toast the almonds, first halve or chop them. Heat a shallow pan and cook the nuts, preferably without any oil, for a few minutes until they turn slightly brown. They can also be broiled/grilled or roasted.

1. Using a heavy pan, cook the onion and garlic in the oil until soft. Now add the meat and brown it all over.

2. After this put in all the other ingredients except the almonds and reserved tomato juice. Cover the pan with a lid and cook gently for 20 minutes or so.

3. Stir occasionally, and if the mixture looks too dry pour in some of the drained tomato juice, or a little water.

4. Put the mixture into a dish, scatter the almonds on top and use as a filling (see above) or on its own with rice and a green salad ■

PERU

Ceviche (Marinated fish)

Serves 4-6

In the 1430s the Incas, the last of the indigenous conquerors, began to create their empire in Peru. The Spanish took over in 1532, but kept the Incas' exploitative structures; with the added twist of outlawing local culture and deeming indians as inferior.

With its extensive coastline, Peru has a long connection with the sea and fishing. It was the leading fishmeal exporter in the 1970s but the depletion of anchoveta led to today's emphasis on increasing pilchard and mackerel catches for local consumption.

The *ceviche* is not cooked, but it needs to marinate for 20-40 minutes before serving. If you like, keep the marinade (see 4 below) to mix with *pisco* (white grape brandy) or vodka. Serve in small cups to accompany the meal.

I N G R E D I E N T S

2 pounds / 900 g white fish fillets (sea bass or hake are best)

juice of 4-6 limes or lemons

1 large onion, sliced finely

$^1/_2$-1 chili, chopped finely or $^1/_2$-1 teaspoon chili powder

$^1/_2$ cup / 75 g sweet potato, sliced and cooked +

1 cup / 150 g cassava/ manioc, sliced and cooked

3 tomatoes

$^1/_2$ cup / 75 g olives

salt and pepper

+ optional ingredient

1. To begin, cut the fish fillets into small pieces. Then place them in a bowl or dish and pour on enough lime/lemon juice to cover them.

2. Now add the other ingredients and mix them in gently. Squeeze on more lemon or lime juice if necessary to make sure everything is covered. Leave the fish to marinate for 20-40 minutes.

3. After that time, drain off some of the liquid, keeping it, and transfer the fish and other marinated ingredients to a serving bowl. The ceviche is now ready to be eaten.

4. If liked, mix the retained juices with pisco (white grape brandy) or vodka to taste and serve in small cups to drink with the ceviche ■

IN ALL RECIPES
● **PEPPER AND SALT ARE TO TASTE**
● **CHILI AND SUGAR ARE GIVEN AS GUIDE QUANTITIES ONLY. VARY TO TASTE**
● **MEASURES FOR BEANS AND GRAINS REFER TO DRY INGREDIENTS.**

PERU

Roast lamb with mint

Serves 6-8

Rearing animals is a major activity in Peru's southern region: sheep, chickens, turkeys, cattle and cavies which are guinea-pig like rodents that often end up in the cooking pot. Lamb or kid is not so widely eaten as beef in South America. This recipe is a variation of a Peruvian Creole-style dish. 'Creole' originally meant a person born and naturalized in a country (eg the Caribbean or Mauritius) but of European or African descent.

INGREDIENTS

4 pound / 2 kg leg or shoulder of lamb, with most of the fat cut away

3 large potatoes, cut in half lengthwise and parboiled

3 tablespoons oil

6 cloves garlic, crushed

4 tablespoons fresh mint, chopped

$1^1/_4$ cups / 300 ml dry white wine

salt and pepper

Heat oven to 400°F/200°C/Gas 6

1. First place the lamb in a roasting pan and arrange the potato halves around it.

2. After this, mix the oil, garlic, salt, pepper and mint in a bowl. Spread this evenly over the meat and then put the lamb into the oven.

3. Cook at the above heat for 10 minutes to seal the meat and then lower the temperature to 325°F/170°C/Gas 3 and pour in $^1/_2$ cup/120 ml of the wine.

4. Let the lamb cook for 1-1$^1/_2$ hours, basting every 15 minutes or so with the wine, using the rest of this and more if required. It is important to keep the joint moist.

5. When the lamb is cooked, serve with the potatoes and pour the juices over the meat. Serve with sautéed red bell peppers, and a green salad ∎

EGYPT

Samak kamounieh (Baked fish with cumin)

Serves 4

'Egypt is the Nile and the Nile is Egypt': the saying reflects the impact of the longest river in the world on the land and people around it. Egypt's farming has a long history. The Egyptians were probably the first people to grind wheat into flour for making bread; there were bakeries in Egypt as long ago as 2000 BC.

INGREDIENTS

4 fish steaks such as cod, bream, haddock or bass

3 tablespoons oil

1 onion, sliced finely

2 cloves garlic, sliced finely

1 tablespoon ground cumin

2 tablespoons tomato paste

$^1/_2$ cup / 120 ml water

2 tomatoes, sliced

handful fresh parsley, chopped

salt and pepper

Heat oven to 350°F/180°C/Gas 4

1. Heat 2 tablespoons of the oil in a pan and gently cook the onion and garlic together with the cumin for 5 minutes.

2. Then stir in the tomato paste, salt, pepper and water and cook for a further 5 minutes or until most of the water has evaporated and the mixture is quite thick.

3. Place the fish in a greased shallow oven-proof dish and pour over the sauce. Arrange the tomato slices on top and drizzle the remaining oil over.

4. Now cover the dish (foil will do) and put it into the oven for 15 minutes. At this point, check that there is enough liquid; if not, add some more water. Now continue to cook, uncovered, for another 10 minutes or until the fish flakes easily.

5. Then decorate with the parsley and serve with rice and vegetables or salad ∎

IRAN

Lamb with apricots

Serves 4

Persian influence spread to India with the Moghuls, and the legacy is seen not only in Shah Jehan's Taj Mahal, the breathtaking mausoleum for his wife, Mumtaz, but also in the *pullaos, samosas* and other foods, indigenized and still eaten today in India.

If you can, use slightly sharp-tasting dried apricots (rather than very sweet dessert ones) for this recipe since they offset the richness of the meat and the sweetness of the raisins. Whichever you use, this is a delicious stew.

INGREDIENTS

1 1/2 pound / 675 g lamb joint (shoulder will do)

1 tablespoon olive oil

2 tablespoons / 25 g margarine

1 onion, finely chopped

1/2 teaspoon ground cinnamon

2 tablespoons raisins or sultanas

1 cup / 100 g dried apricots, halved

salt and pepper

1. Using a large heavy saucepan with a lid, heat the oil and margarine and cook the onion until it is transparent. Add the meat and turn it over so that each side browns. Season with the cinnamon, pepper and salt.

2. Now put in the raisins or sultanas and the apricots and stir them round while they cook for a few minutes.

3. After this, pour in enough water to come half way up the joint of meat, cover the pot and simmer for up to 2 hours until the meat is tender. If you want to have a thicker sauce, turn up the heat and boil rapidly for a few minutes to reduce the liquid. Serve with baked potatoes or rice ∎

JORDAN

Basal badawi (Onions with meat, nuts and fruit)

Serves 4

This is a traditional dish of the Bedouin, the nomadic 'guardians of the desert'. It is easy to prepare and can be made more festive with the addition of saffron or turmeric in the accompanying rice. Red lentils can be used instead of meat.

INGREDIENTS

4 large onions

1/4 pound / 100 g ground/minced lamb

3/4 cup / 180 ml plain yogurt

2 tablespoons dates, stoned and finely chopped *

2 tablespoons walnuts, chopped

1 tablespoon raisins or sultanas

2 tablespoons breadcrumbs

handful fresh parsley, chopped

salt and pepper

* Fresh dates are best if you can get them. Otherwise use packet dates and rinse them to remove some of the sweetness.

1. Peel the onions and place them in a large pan of boiling water. Reduce the heat and let them simmer for 15-20 minutes until they are fairly tender. When they are ready, take them out and set aside to cool.

2. Now remove the center section of each onion to leave a shell about 3/4 inch/1.5 cm thick. In a bowl mix together the meat, pepper, salt, yogurt, dates, walnuts, raisins or sultanas and breadcrumbs. Fill the onions with this mixture. Keep any that is left over and mix it with the chopped discarded centers of the onions.

3. Now place the onions in an oven-proof dish, spoon any remaining mixture around them and then cook for 1 hour . Garnish with parsley and serve with boiled barley, cracked wheat or rice ■

(Opposite) Plant life – a woman in Borneo picking medicinal leaves.
Photo: Nigel Dickinson/Still Pictures

LEBANON

Daoud Pasha (Meatballs with pine nuts)

Serves 4

This recipe takes its name from an Armenian, Pasha Davoudian, who became first governor of the Lebanon from 1868-73. He was the first Christian to hold such high office in an Ottoman administration. Other names associated with Lebanon are that of a Syrian monk, Maro, from whom the Christian Maronites take their title, and Ismail al-Darazi, founder of the Druze sect.

INGREDIENTS

1 pound / 450 g ground/minced lamb

1/2 teaspoon ground cumin

1/2 teaspoon allspice

1 teaspoon ground cilantro/coriander

2 tablespoons olive oil

1 onion, finely sliced

2 tablespoons pine nuts/pignoles or almonds

2 tablespoons tomato paste mixed with 1 1/4 cups/300 ml water

1/2 tablespoon lemon juice

1/2 teaspoon fresh or dried basil

salt and pepper

1. In large bowl, mix the meat, salt, pepper, cumin, allspice and half the cilantro/coriander. Shape this mixture into balls about the size of a large walnut.

2. Next heat the oil in a pan, add the onion and cook it until it becomes golden and soft.

3. Now put the meatballs in and cook them for about 10 minutes, gently turning them until they are brown all over.

4. Shake in half the nuts, cooking them for 2 minutes before you pour in the thinned tomato paste, lemon juice, basil and remaining cilantro/coriander. Stir well to coat the meatballs.

5. Now turn down the heat and simmer, covered, for about 30 minutes, stirring occasionally. At the end of this time, transfer the meatballs and sauce to a heated serving dish, and sprinkle the remaining nuts on top. Daoud Pasha goes well with a plain boiled cereal such as barley and a crisp green salad ■

LEBANON

Kibbeh (Bulgur with lamb and pino kernels)

Serves 4-6

Pignoles/pine nuts, used here, come from the Mediterranean Stone Pine tree. The nuts are widely used in Middle Eastern cookery and impart a delicate pine flavor. *Kibbeh* is a sort of flan made with meat. It probably originated in Syria although today it is popular throughout the Middle East.

I N G R E D I E N T S

1 cup / 225 g bulgur

1 pound / 450 g ground/minced lamb

1 medium onion, finely sliced or grated

handful fresh mint leaves, chopped

2 teaspoons ground cumin

1 egg, beaten

1 clove garlic, sliced finely

$1/4$ cup / 30 g pine nuts/pignoles

salt and pepper

Heat oven to 350°F/180°C/ Gas 4

1. Soak the bulgur in a bowl of water for 30-45 minutes until it has plumped up.

2. Drain the liquid from the bowl and then squeeze the bulgur with your hand to remove any more liquid. Now transfer it to a mixing basin with the ground/minced lamb, the onion, mint leaves and cumin.

3. After this, pour in the beaten egg, season with salt and pepper and mix well.

4. Now turn out the mixture into a 10 inch/25 cm pie dish and press it down using the back of a spoon or clean fingers.

5. Scatter the slivers of garlic and the pine nuts on top of the meat mixture, pressing them in slightly.

6. Bake the kibbeh for about 45 minutes and then serve it cut in slices like a flan, accompanied by a green salad ■

MIDDLE EAST

Dajaj souryani (Chicken with yogurt)

Serves 4

This dish comes from the region known once as Assyria – now Iraq, Syria and Jordan. About three thousand years ago the Assyrians were the most powerful people in the Middle East with a rich culture that extended into the kitchen.

I N G R E D I E N T S

3 pound / 1.5 kg chicken, skinned and cut into 8 pieces

4 tablespoons / 50 g margarine

4 tablespoons oil

1 onion, finely sliced

1 green bell pepper, sliced

1 teaspoon chili powder

1 teaspoon ground cumin

1 cup / 240 ml chicken stock

2 tablespoons sumak powder *

2 tablespoons ground almonds

$1^1/4$ cups / 300 ml yogurt

salt and pepper

* Sumak powder can be bought in stores selling Middle Eastern groceries. If you cannot find it, use the grated peel and juice from half a lemon.

1. Begin by melting the margarine and oil in a large pan and then cook the chicken pieces so that they brown on each side. Season with salt and pepper, and when they are ready remove them and set aside to keep warm.

2. Now put the onion and bell pepper into the pan and cook them gently until they are soft. Add the chili powder and cook for a further minute or so.

3. After that, pour in the stock and add the sumak powder, or lemon zest and juice, and the chicken pieces. Bring to the boil, then reduce the heat and simmer for about 30-40 minutes or until the chicken is tender.

4. When cooked, take out the chicken and keep warm in a serving dish. Skim off any excess fat from the chicken juices in the pan.

5. In a bowl, add a little water to the ground almonds to form a smooth paste. Add this mixture to the juices in the pan and bring to the boil, stirring constantly until it thickens.

6. Remove the pan from the heat and allow it to cool slightly. Then stir in the yogurt and adjust the seasoning. Pour this sauce over the chicken pieces, sprinkle on a little more chili powder and cumin and serve at once, with bulgur, rice or potatoes ■

Lamb, apricot and raisin stew
Serves 2-4

Lamb is the most common meat in the region and the fat rendered from lambs' tails – *alya* – has been the main cooking medium. Many dishes are cooked very slowly, for several hours, and rare meat is not eaten unless it is in a dish meant to be taken raw.

INGREDIENTS

1 pound / 450 g lean lamb, cut into ¼ inch / 0.5 cm thin strips, or ground/ minced lamb

½ cup / 50 g dried apricots

½ cup / 50 g raisins, sultanas or prunes

1¼ cups / 300 ml water

1-2 tablespoons oil

1 onion, finely chopped

¼ teaspoon ground nutmeg

¼ teaspoon ground cinnamon

juice of ½ lemon

salt and pepper

1. To begin, soak the dried fruit for 1 hour in a bowl with just enough water to cover.

2. When almost ready, heat the oil in a large pan and cook the onion gently until it is golden. Then add the lamb, stirring to prevent sticking, and to brown the pieces on each side. Now put in the nutmeg, cinnamon, salt and pepper.

3. Next, drain the fruit, keeping the liquid. Pour this liquid and the lemon juice into the pan containing the onion and lamb.

4. Cover the pan and simmer for about 1 hour or until the lamb is tender. When it is ready, add the apricots and other fruit, and a little more water if required.

5. Put the lid back on and simmer for a further 10-15 minutes and then serve with rice or cracked wheat ■

MIDDLE EAST

Margog (Lamb and zucchini/courgette stew)

Serves 4-6

Bedouin dishes like this one are tasty, filling and usually quite simple to make. *Margog* can be served on rice or bulgur and accompanied by apples, oranges and bananas cut into pieces.

I N G R E D I E N T S

1/2 pound / 225 g packet frozen puff pastry, thawed

1 1/2 pounds / 675 g lamb shoulder, cut into 1 inch/ 2.5 cm pieces

3 tablespoons oil

1 onion, finely sliced

1/2 teaspoon chili powder

seeds from 6 cardamom pods, crushed

2 cups / 000 g zucchini/ courgettes, cut into 1/2 inch/ 1 cm slices

3 tomatoes, chopped

2 teaspoons cornstarch/ cornflour

1 cup / 240 ml stock or water

salt and pepper

Heat oven to 375°F/190°C/Gas 5

1. To start, heat the oil in a large pan and cook the onion until soft. Add the meat pieces and brown them all over.

2. Next, add the chili powder, cardamom, salt and pepper and mix well. Continue cooking gently for 10 minutes and then remove from the heat.

3. Stir in the stock or water and then put in the sliced zucchini/courgettes and tomatoes and bring slowly to the boil, stirring from time to time.

4. Now reduce the heat to low and continue to cook, covered, for about 2 hours or until the meat is almost ready.

5. While that is happening, roll out the pastry on a floured surface to a thickness of 1/4 inch/0.5 cm and cut into 1 inch/2.5 cm squares.

6. When the meat is nearly cooked, drain off any fat from the stew and thicken the sauce if necessary with the cornstarch/cornflour mixed to a smooth paste with a little water. Return the pan to the heat and stir in the cornstarch mixture gradually. The sauce should be thick enough to support the pastry squares (see 7 below).

7. Put the Margog into an oven-proof dish and allow it to cool slightly. Now, carefully arrange the squares of pastry over the surface, overlapping them to form a pie-crust. They should rest on the meat and vegetables and not be submerged in the liquid, otherwise they will not crisp up properly. Remove excess liquid if necessary.

8. Place the dish in the oven and cook for 15 minutes or until the crust is golden ■

Prawns with rice and pineapple

Serves 4-6

Variations of prawns with rice are found all along the Gulf coast. In Kuwait, egg, soy sauce and pineapple are included while Bahrainis often add curry powder – all ingredients coming from the ancient trade between the Arabs and the East.

I N G R E D I E N T S

1 pound / 450 g shelled prawns or shrimps, fresh, canned or frozen

2 tablespoons almonds, flaked

3 tablespoons oil

1 stalk celery, sliced

3/4 cup / 120 g French beans, cut into 2 inch / 5 cm pieces

4 scallions / spring onions, sliced

2 tablespoons soy sauce

1 cup / 100 g pineapple, fresh or canned, cubed

2 eggs

2 cups / 400 g rice, cooked and kept warm

salt and pepper

1. First toast the almonds by placing them on a flat baking sheet and placing them under the broiler/grill for a few minutes, turning from time to time. Leave to one side.

2. In a pan, heat the oil and cook the celery, French beans and half of the scallions/spring onions for 3 minutes, stirring frequently.

3. Now add the soy sauce, the prawns or shrimps and pineapple pieces and continue to cook gently.

4. Meanwhile, break the eggs into a bowl and beat them lightly before pouring them into the pan. Turn down the heat now and stir the mixture until the eggs are cooked.

5. To serve, arrange the rice on a large flat dish and spoon on the egg and shrimp mixture. Garnish with the toasted almonds and remaining scallions/spring onions ■

MOROCCO

Chicken salad with bulgur

Serves 4

Morocco's romantic image in the West – fostered by tales of Beau Geste, the French foreign legion and the film *Casablanca* – belies the iron rule of king Hassan, reinforced by Islam (the word means 'submission' in Arabic). Although Morocco is rich in phosphates (for fertilizers) and agricultural produce, most rural people are poor. The war against nationalist Polisario guerillas in phosphate-rich Western Sahara, annexed by Morocco in 1975, continues.

INGREDIENTS

1 cup / 225 g bulgur	handful fresh mint, chopped
2 tomatoes, finely chopped	
1/2 pound / 225 g chicken, skinned, cooked and cut into small pieces	2-3 tablespoons olive oil
	2 tablespoons wine vinegar or lemon juice
handful fresh basil, chopped	salt and pepper
2 cloves garlic, crushed	

1. First of all, cook the bulgur in plenty of boiling salted water for about 15 minutes, or according to the instructions on the packet. Then drain it and allow to cool.

2. In a salad bowl, combine the cooled bulgur, tomatoes, chicken, basil, garlic and mint (keep a little back for decoration).

3. Beat the oil with the vinegar or lemon juice, season and then pour the dressing over the salad and stir lightly to distribute it evenly. Scatter the remaining mint on top and serve ■

Lamb with ginger and honey

Serves 6

Wheat, barley and corn/maize are Morocco's main food crops along with beans and pulses, potatoes, olives and citrus fruit such as oranges. Orange blossoms are distilled into orange-blossom water, used in this recipe, and added to many Middle Eastern drinks, almond pastries and desserts such as *muhallabia* (see p 165).

INGREDIENTS

2 pounds / 900 g lean lamb, cut into 1 inch / 2.5 cm cubes	1-2 tablespoons honey
	1 teaspoon orange-blossom water *
2 tablespoons oil	
1/2 teaspoon ground ginger	1 tablespoon toasted sesame seeds +
1 teaspoon ground cilantro/coriander	salt and pepper
2 teaspoons ground cinnamon	* Available from shops selling Middle Eastern foods: if you cannot find it, use a little grated orange peel instead.
2 onions, sliced finely	
2 cups / 200 g dried prunes or dried apples, or a mixture, soaked for 1 hour	

1. First of all put the meat pieces into a large pan and pour in just enough water to cover them. Then add the oil, ginger, salt and pepper, coriander, cinnamon and onions.

2. Bring the pan to the boil and then cover and simmer slowly for about 2 hours, until the lamb is tender and the liquid quite thick. Add more water during this time if it appears to be becoming too dry.

3. Next, add the prunes or other dried fruit and simmer for 20 minutes before stirring in the honey. Cook gently for a further 10 minutes and then sprinkle on the orange-blossom water and sesame seeds just before serving with rice ■

SYRIA

Fasouliyeh (French bean and lamb stew)

Serves 4-6

The area known today as Syria forms part of the pre-historic 'fertile crescent' where it is thought people first cultivated wheat, barley and pulses. The earliest known grains of domesticated wheats have been found in the region and date back to around 7500-6500 BC.

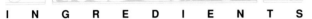

I N G R E D I E N T S

1½ pounds / 675 g lamb shoulder, cut into 1 inch/ 2.5 cm cubes	1 teaspoon allspice or use 3-4 whole cloves or ½ teaspoon ground cloves
2 tablespoons / 25 g margarine	2½ cups / 590 ml water
1 large onion, chopped	1½ pounds / 675 g French beans, prepared but left whole
2 cloves garlic, crushed	4 tomatoes, chopped
2 tablespoons tomato paste	1-2 tablespoons lemon juice
½ teaspoon chili powder	salt and pepper

1. To begin the fasouliyeh, heat the margarine in a large pan and cook the onion and garlic until they are golden. Then add the meat and let it brown, turning frequently.

2. Now put in the tomato paste, salt, pepper, chili powder and allspice and cook for 5 minutes, stirring often.

3. When this is done pour in the water, cover the pan and bring to the boil. Reduce the heat now and let the dish simmer for about 1½ hours or until the meat is tender, stirring from time to time.

4. A few minutes from the end, put in the French beans and tomatoes together with the lemon juice and cook gently for a further 30 minutes, until the beans are soft. Serve with pita bread or potatoes ∎

(Opposite) Gold mine worker in Brazil eating local dish *Feijoada*.
Photo: Julio Etchart/Reportage

Kabab halabi (Lamb kebab with yogurt)

Serves 4-6

Syria was carved out of the Turkish Ottoman Empire in 1920, but the area has long been a fruit garden of the Arab world with apples, pomegranates, plums, figs, pears, cherries and many varieties of apricot. Fruit and vegetables are exported along with cotton, tobacco and the main income-earner, petroleum.

For this kebab, the lamb should be marinated for 2 hours if possible.

I N G R E D I E N T S

2 pounds / 900 g lean lamb, cut into 1 inch / 2.5 cm cubes	
1 onion, chopped finely	
3 teaspoons paprika	
3 tablespoons oil	
3 large tomatoes, chopped	
3 pitas	
2 tablespoons / 25 g margarine, melted	handful fresh parsley or mint, chopped
1 cup / 240 ml yogurt	salt and pepper

1. Put the lamb into a basin with the onion, paprika, salt, pepper and 2 tablespoons of the oil and leave it to marinate for 2 hours.

2. Now, keeping the marinade, take the meat out and thread it onto skewers. Broil/grill for 10-15 minutes, turning often, until cooked.

3. Meanwhile, heat the remaining oil in a pan and gently cook the tomatoes for 5 minutes. Then add the marinade mixture and let it heat through gently.

4. Heat the pitas and cut into ½ inch/1 cm strips. Lay them on the serving plate and pour the melted margarine on top.

5. When the kebabs are ready, pour the tomato mixture onto the bread strips and slide the kebabs from the skewers onto this.

6. Pour the yogurt over the meat and serve at once, garnished with parsley or mint ∎

115

Samak bi tahina (Fish with tahina sauce)

Serves 6

This is a popular dish in Syria and Lebanon. The fish can be served hot or cold and the cooking time will vary according to whether you are using a large whole fish, small whole fish or fillets. Red mullet would be used in the Middle East, but any fish will do. Leaving the fish to soak in the lemon juice and herbs for 1 hour enriches the flavor.

I N G R E D I E N T S

3 pound / 1.5 kg fish, or equivalent in small fish / fillets	2 large onions, sliced
	4 tablespoons tahina
4 tablespoons oil	2 cloves garlic, crushed
juice of 2 lemons	12 tablespoons water
handful fresh basil leaves, chopped or 1 teaspoon dried basil *	fresh parsley to garnish
	salt and pepper

* Other herbs can be used: tarragon, marjoram, oregano or parsley.

Heat oven to 325°F/160°C/Gas 3 (But allow for marinating time of 1 hour, see step 2)

1. If using whole fish, clean them thoroughly and rub with salt inside and out. Make slits in the skin to prevent curling while cooking and to allow the heat and flavors to penetrate.

2. Now mix together 2 tablespoons oil and 1 of lemon juice; add the basil or other herbs and pour over the fish. Leave to marinate for 1 hour.

3. After this, heat the remaining oil in a pan and cook the onions until they are golden and soft. Place half of them in a shallow oven-proof dish and lay the fish on top, keeping the marinade. Arrange the remaining onions on top.

4. Put the marinade into a bowl, add the tahina and crushed garlic. Stirring with a spoon, pour in the remaining lemon juice and enough water to make a smooth sauce.

5. Now pour the sauce over the fish and bake for 30-45 minutes until the flesh flakes easily. Decorate with a bit of parsley or other herbs and serve with pita bread and salad ■

TUNISIA

Chicken with honey and almonds

Serves 4-6

Fleeing the Assyrians, in 814 BC Phoenician princess Dido founded Carthage ('new capital') in what is now Tunisia. Six hundred years later, Carthage's most famous son, Hannibal, rocked the Roman empire with his daring elephant raid over the Alps. Today Tunisia is Western-oriented –to the irritation of Muslim fundamentalists – and tourism is a major income-earner.

The chicken is stuffed with an almond mixture and so will take a bit longer to cook than usual.

I N G R E D I E N T S

3 pound / 1.5 kg chicken	lemon juice
1/2 cup / 50 g breadcrumbs	3 tablespoons honey
1/2 cup / 60 g almonds, chopped finely	2-3 tablespoons olive oil
1/2 cup / 100 g ground almonds	1/2 cup / 120 ml water
1 egg, beaten	2 tablespoons / 25 g margarine
2 tablespoons fresh basil, chopped	salt and pepper

Heat oven to 350°F/180°C/Gas 4

1. Combine the breadcrumbs and chopped almonds with the ground almonds and beaten egg in a bowl. Season with 1 tablespoon of the basil, lemon juice, salt and pepper and then stuff the chicken with the mixture.

2. Now take the honey and oil and blend them together in a bowl. Prick the chicken skin with a fork and rub in the mixture. Dot the margarine over the chicken and scatter the remaining basil over.

3. Place the chicken in a casserole, cover, and roast in the oven for about 1 1/2 hours, basting frequently with the honey juices. Remove the lid for the last 30 minutes ■

Side

DISHES,

SALADS,

VEGETABLES

STAPLE FOODS: CASSAVA

Arrows and blowpipe darts used by indians in the South American rainforests may well have been tipped with cassava juice, for until it is cooked this liquid is poisonous. Also known as manioc and tapioca the swollen roots of this shrub are one of the most important food crops in tropical regions which have good rainfall. The cylindrical roots have wrinkled coarse brown skin with white flesh inside.

Cassava is very starchy and low in protein. Yet it is increasingly widely grown because it is easy to cultivate, requiring little attention from the farmer. For instance, after reaching maturity the crop can be left in the ground for another two years, unattended, and will not spoil. Tolerating both drought and locust attack, cassava is a bulwark against famine. It is mostly grown by peasants as a subsistence food, but some enters the world market as animal feed, (Thailand is a major exporter), industrial starches and tapioca used in soups and milk puddings.

It is a plant native to America. Precursors of cassava were thought to have been among the plants used as food when people were migrating from North into Central and South America. Cassava flour appears to have been an important trading item in north-western South America several thousand years ago.

It reached West Africa and the river Congo area at the end of the sixteenth century as the Europeans travelled to seek slaves; round to the East Coast of Africa via Madagascar and Zanzibar by the end of the eighteenth century and on to India a little later.

Cassava's importance as a famine-reserve crop was recognized by the Europeans — local people had probably realised this already — in the mid-nineteenth century. As a consequence the plant was developed further as a food crop. But there is a snag, aside from cassava's poor nutritive qualities: it contains enzymes that produce prussic acid. The tuber should always be cooked before eating.

Fresh cassava root, washed, peeled, steamed and pounded becomes *fufu* in Africa, a starchy accompaniment to soups and stews. The tubers can also be grated to produce meal — *farinha* — in Brazil, *gari* in Nigeria which can be cooked into small cakes handy for traveling. Juice of bitter varieties is boiled and made into a spiced liquid called *casareep*, which is an essential ingredient of a popular Caribbean dish, Pepperpot.

Main producers (in descending order) Brazil, Thailand, Zaire, Indonesia, Nigeria, Tanzania, India, China, Mozambique, Vietnam.

World production (1985) 92 million tons.

Illustration: Steve Weston

118

AFRICA

Cassava/manioc scones

Serves 4

Cassava/manioc is a vital food in Africa, where it was brought from South America originally by the Portuguese. However it contains substances that give rise to prussic acid. The Amerindians may well have tipped their arrows and blowpipes with its juice. But don't worry, the noxious substance is readily removed by cooking. Cassava is usually peeled, boiled and then mashed into *fufu* (see p.121) – or made into scones as in this recipe – to accompany stews and soups.

INGREDIENTS

1 cup / 150 g cassava/manioc, boiled and mashed

1 cup / 125 g flour

1 teaspoon baking powder

2 tablespoons / 25 g margarine, melted

2 tablespoons oil

salt

1. To begin with, put all the ingredients except the oil into a basin and knead until you have a ball of dough.

2. Now sprinkle some flour onto a flat surface or board and roll out the dough to a thickness of ¹/₂ inch/1 cm. Then cut it into scone-size rounds using a cutter or glass.

3. When this is done, heat up the oil in a shallow pan and cook the scones on each side until they are light brown. Serve right away, with main dishes ∎

Sweet potato bread

Serves 6

This recipe calls for corn/maize flour which is finer than corn or 'mealie' meal yet retains the distinctive flavor. You can use white or yellow cornmeal instead, available in supermarkets or health stores.

INGREDIENTS

¹/₂ pound / 225 g sweet potatoes, cooked and mashed

1 cup / 125 g corn / maize flour

1 cup / 125 g wheat flour

2 teaspoons baking powder

a little milk

salt

Heat oven to 400°F/200°C/Gas 6

1. Put the mashed sweet potato into a bowl and sieve in the flours, baking powder and salt. Mix everything together, adding enough milk to make a stiff mixture.

2. Now spoon the bread into a greased tin and cook for about 30 minutes. When it is ready, let it cool for a while and then serve it warm or cold ∎

CHAD

Zucchini/courgettes with peanuts

Serves 4-6

Like Caesar's Gaul, Chad divides into three parts: the Sahara in the North; the drought-ridden and war-torn Sahel region; and the South-West where most people live. Peanuts are an important source of protein in this country, the third poorest in the world.

INGREDIENTS

1¹/₂ pounds / 675 g zucchini / courgettes, sliced

1-2 cloves garlic, crushed

1 tablespoon lemon juice

2 tablespoons / 25 g margarine

1¹/₂ cups / 185 g peanuts, toasted and coarsely chopped

salt and pepper

1. To begin, simmer the zucchini/courgettes in very little boiling water for 5-10 minutes until they are tender. Drain well and put them into a bowl.

2. Now add the garlic, lemon juice, margarine, salt and pepper and mash all the ingredients with a fork. Add more lemon juice if required. Spoon the mash into a bowl and scatter the toasted hot peanuts on top before serving with millet or rice ∎

119

ETHIOPIA

Yataklete kilkil (Potatoes with nutmeg)

Serves 6

Many years ago an Ethiopian goatherd watched one of the flock tugging at a small bush and eating its berries. A few moments later, the goat began to race and frolic as if charged with energy. Taking a tip from the animal, the goatherd collected some berries and tried them. They tasted better roasted, but the effects were the same – the caffeine packed its punch and coffee has been a popular drink ever since.

I N G R E D I E N T S

1 pound / 450 g new potatoes, diced

2-3 heads of broccoli

3 large carrots, sliced

6-8 cauliflower florets, chopped

2-3 tablespoons / 25-40 g margarine or ghee

1 onion, finely chopped

2 cloves garlic

1 teaspoon turmeric

1-2 teaspoons ground nutmeg

1 teaspoon ground cinnamon

$\frac{1}{2}$ inch / 1 cm fresh root ginger, peeled and finely chopped

1 clove

salt and pepper

1. First, steam or boil the potatoes, chopped broccoli stalks and the carrots for 10 minutes or so until nearly ready.

2. Then add the broccoli heads and cauliflower pieces and steam or boil together for another 4 minutes until all the vegetables are done. Drain.

3. Next heat the margarine or ghee and sauté the onion and garlic before adding the turmeric, nutmeg, cinnamon, ginger and clove. Then mix in the vegetables, season with pepper and salt and cook for 6-8 minutes, stirring frequently. Serve with millet or rice ∎

THE GAMBIA

Koocha 'Fatty Kunda' (Spinach and peanut butter)

Serves 4

'This is *koocha* – hibiscus leaves – as cooked at the Fatty family home in Saruja village in The Gambia. As fresh hibiscus leaves are hard to come by, you can substitute fresh, canned or frozen spinach and add lemon juice to produce a slightly sour flavor – the perfect counterbalance to the rich peanut butter … delicious.' *Rosemarie "Mariyama Fatty" Daly, London, UK*

I N G R E D I E N T S

1 pound / 450 g spinach, fresh or frozen, chopped

1 tablespoon peanut or other vegetable oil

2 medium onions, chopped finely

2 cloves garlic, crushed

12 black peppercorns, crushed

juice of 1 lemon

1 cup / 240 ml chicken stock

a few dashes of Tabasco sauce, or $\frac{1}{4}$ teaspoon chili powder

1-2 tablespoons crunchy peanut butter

salt and pepper

1. Using a large pan, heat the oil and soften the onions in it. Add the garlic and peppercorns and cook for 3 minutes.

2. After this, put in the spinach, lemon juice, half the stock, chili powder or Tabasco sauce, salt and pepper and simmer gently for 8-10 minutes.

3. Stir the remaining stock into the peanut butter in a bowl and then add this to the cooking pot and mix it in well. Continue cooking for a further 10 minutes and then serve ∎

GHANA

Fufu (Cassava/manioc mash)

Serves 4

The first sub-Saharan colony to become independent (in 1957), Ghana set the pace for post-colonial Africa. Economic depression soon slowed the momentum and has been made worse by a decline in the key export crop, cocoa.

Cassava/manioc originated in South America (**see Staple Food p.118**) and after being sun-dried, it is exported by countries such as Thailand to the West for animal feed. In this recipe, the cassava/manioc is made into dumplings to put in stews.

I N G R E D I E N T S

1 pound / 450 g cassava/ manioc, cut into chunks *

* Sweet potatoes can be used instead and will need less cooking time.

1. Bring a large pan of water to the boil and put in the chunks of cassava. Let them cook for 40-50 minutes until they are soft.

2. Now drain the cassava/manioc and leave it to cool a little. Then put it in a bowl and mash it, or you can use a food-processor.

3. When it is a dough-like consistency, wet your hands and shape it into small balls. Drop these into a spicy soup or stew and let them cook for 5-10 minutes to heat through ∎

KENYA

Rice and spinach

Serves 4-6

Spinach has a high vitamin A content and is richer in protein than other leaf vegetables. This makes it a valuable addition to the diet in developing countries. A spinach-like plant, *amaranth*, is used as spinach in parts of Africa, while another type of *amaranth* is grown for its seeds (used as grain) in Central and Andean South America.

I N G R E D I E N T S

1 pound / 450 g spinach, fresh or frozen, chopped

3 tablespoons olive oil

1 onion, sliced

1 pound / 450 g rice

2$^1/_2$ cups / 590 ml chicken stock

4 medium tomatoes, chopped

1 tablespoon fresh fennel, chopped or 1 teaspoon dried

1 medium tomato, sliced

1 hard-boiled egg, sliced

salt and pepper

1. Heat the oil in a large saucepan and cook the onion until it is soft and golden. Add the rice and fry for 1 minute.

2. Next put the chopped spinach in the pan and then the chicken stock.

3. After this, cover the pan and bring to the boil. Reduce the heat and cook gently until most of the liquid is absorbed, about 20 minutes.

4. Now add the 4 chopped tomatoes and fennel and carefully mix this in. Cover and cook again until all the moisture is absorbed and the rice is ready.

5. Season, and then decorate with the sliced tomato and egg slices ∎

KENYA

Sweet potatoes with tomatoes

Serves 4

Sweet potatoes have been grown since prehistoric times in Peru. Today however it is the Pacific islanders who are the main consumers of this tuber. It is a versatile vegetable which can be made into desserts and sweets as well as savory dishes.

INGREDIENTS

1 pound / 450 g sweet potatoes, peeled

2-4 tablespoons / 25-50 g margarine

1/2 teaspoon sugar

1 teaspoon chili powder

3 medium tomatoes, sliced

salt and pepper

1. Boil the sweet potatoes, whole, in water until they are soft, about 30 minutes depending on the size of the vegetable. Drain and allow them to cool and then cut into 1/4 inch/0.5 cm slices.

2. In a pan, melt the margarine and sauté the potato slices for about 5 minutes until golden brown. Add the chili powder, salt, pepper and sugar and mix well. Now put in the sliced tomatoes and cook for a further 5 minutes. Serve hot with grated cheese or cooked sliced sausage on top if desired ■

MALAWI

Masamba (Green vegetables with nuts)

Serves 4

Small-holders in Malawi produce most of the country's food crops such as maize/corn, and also a little tobacco, while estate farmers grow sugar, tea and tobacco for export. As in many African countries, peanuts provide an important source of protein.

In this recipe, the peanuts are boiled which gives them a flavor more like chestnuts or beans.

INGREDIENTS

1 pound / 450 g greens such as spinach, finely chopped

4 medium tomatoes, sliced into circles

2 small onions, sliced in rings

1 cup / 125 g peanuts

salt

1. Heat up a little water in a saucepan and when it boils, add salt and put in the greens.

2. Let them cook for 4-5 minutes and then lay the tomato slices, onion rings and peanuts on top but do not stir.

3. Now lower the heat and simmer for 20 minutes before serving. If you prefer not to cook the greens for so long, boil the peanuts first for 20 minutes before combining them with the greens, tomatoes and onions ■

SOUTH AFRICA

Putu (Porridge with maize flour)

Serves 4-6

Porridge is a standard accompaniment to many African meals. It can be made of maize, cassava/manioc, sorghum, plantains or other local staples. It is called *ugali* in Kenya, *bidia* in Zaire and *nsima* in Malawi and Zambia. One way to eat it is to tear off a small piece, make a dent in it with your thumb and use it as a scoop for sauces and stews.

I N G R E D I E N T S

1¼ cups / 190 g white cornmeal

1 cup / 240 ml water

1 cup / 240 ml milk

1. First, bring the water to the boil in a medium saucepan.

2. While this is heating up, gradually mix half the cornmeal with the milk in a bowl, stirring briskly to make a smooth paste.

3. Add this slowly to the boiling water, stirring continuously.

4. Cook for 4-5 minutes, sieving in the remaining cornmeal and mixing the porridge with a spoon all the time.

5. When the mixture begins to pull away from the sides of the pan, remove it from the heat.

6. Now place the putu into a basin and, with damp hands, shape it into a ball, flipping it so the rounded sides of the bowl help to make it smooth. Serve right away ■

Umbido (Greens and peanuts)

Serves 6

After soybeans, peanuts pack the most food value of non-meat items. They have no vitamin A or C but contain more vitamin B5 than any known foodstuff apart from yeast, and are very rich in protein (up to 30 per cent). For a different flavor, try boiling them instead of toasting or using them raw.

I N G R E D I E N T S

2 pounds / 900 g spinach or pumpkin leaves, fresh or frozen

1 cup / 125 g peanuts

2 tablespoons / 25 g margarine

salt and pepper

1. (See also 3 below) To make with boiled peanuts, first put them into a pan containing enough boiling water to cover them and cook for 20-25 minutes. About 5 minutes before the end, toss in the spinach or pumpkin leaves and let them cook for 4-5 minutes. Flavor with salt and pepper.

2. When everything is cooked, drain and put into a dish. Add the margarine and mix it in well before serving.

3. To make with toasted peanuts, put them in the oven or under the broiler/grill, or fry them in a little oil. In all cases, shake or turn them frequently so that they do not burn. Then cook the spinach or pumpkin leaves in a very little water for 4-5 minutes; drain well and toss in the toasted peanuts. Season with pepper and salt and mix in the margarine before you serve ■

> **IN ALL RECIPES**
> ● PEPPER AND SALT ARE TO TASTE
> ● CHILI AND SUGAR ARE GIVEN AS GUIDE QUANTITIES ONLY. VARY TO TASTE
> ● MEASURES FOR BEANS AND GRAINS REFER TO DRY INGREDIENTS.

SOUTH AFRICA

Yellow rice

Serves 6

The usual accompaniment to *bobotee* (see pps. 73 & 74), this rice is also good with other curry dishes where its slight sweetness complements the savory tastes.

INGREDIENTS

1 pound / 450 g rice

3 cups / 700 ml water

2 teaspoons sugar

1 tablespoon margarine

1^1/$_2$ teaspoons turmeric

^{1}/$_2$ cup / 50 g raisins or sultanas

salt

1. First bring the salted water to boil in a saucepan and then add the rice and all the other ingredients.

2. Reduce the heat and simmer, covered, for about 25 minutes, or until the rice is tender and most of the liquid has been taken up. Drain if necessary before serving ■

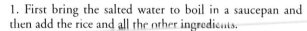

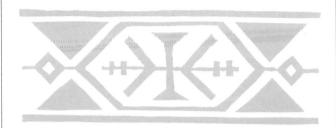

TANZANIA

Curried cabbage

Serves 6-8

About 1,500 years ago, along the coast of East Africa, the Swahili culture emerged, a blend of African and Arab history. Based on trade, the *dhows* (ships) would ply between Mombasa, Kilwa, Zanzibar, the Arab peninsular and then on to India and China. Zanzibar, now part of Tanzania, was last century a center for the slave trade with the African interior.

INGREDIENTS

1 large onion, finely chopped

6 tablespoons oil

1 large tomato, sliced

^{1}/$_2$ teaspoon curry powder or 2 teaspoons ground cumin and ^{1}/$_2$ teaspoon turmeric

2 carrots, sliced in rounds

1 medium cabbage, finely sliced

1 green bell pepper, chopped

^{1}/$_2$ cup / 120 ml water

salt and pepper

1. In a large shallow pan with a lid, sauté the onion in the oil over a moderate heat until it is lightly browned. Now add the tomato, salt and curry powder or spices and continue to cook for 2-3 minutes, stirring frequently.

2. Next put in the carrots and cook for 5 minutes. Then add the cabbage and bell pepper and mix well.

3. Pour in the water, cover the pan and simmer until the liquid is absorbed and the vegetables are cooked ■

Futari (Coconut milk pumpkin)

Serves 6-8

Coconuts, grown in tropical regions, have many uses: copra, the dried 'meat' of the nut; edible oil which is extracted from copra and used in soap and for cooking; and the fibrous husk for *coir* matting. The biggest copra-producing country is the Philippines, followed by Indonesia.

INGREDIENTS

2 cups / 300 g pumpkin, peeled and cut into 1 inch/ 2.5 cm chunks

1 pound / 450 g sweet potatoes, peeled and diced

1 onion, finely chopped

1 tablespoon oil

juice of $^{1}/_{2}$ lemon

2 cloves

$^{1}/_{2}$ cup / 50 g creamed coconut melted in 1 cup/ 240 ml hot water

1 teaspoon ground cinnamon

salt and pepper

1. In a heavy pan, cook the onion in the oil until it is golden. Then combine it with the pumpkin and sweet potato pieces.

2. Now add the lemon juice, cloves, salt and the coconut milk. Cover and simmer slowly for 10-15 minutes.

3. After this, add the cinnamon and seasoning. Cook, uncovered, for another 15-20 minutes until the vegetables are tender, stirring frequently to prevent sticking. Add more coconut milk or plain milk if the mixture becomes too dry ∎

Mint chutney

Serves 4

Tanzania's pattern of agriculture has been affected by the disease *trypanosomiasis* which can kill both cattle and humans. Carried by the tsetse fly, the disease thrives in humid parts of Africa and has no known cure. Burdened by this, and by the poor soil in other parts of the country, Tanzanian agriculture remains very poor. Most people grow food and raise livestock, with export crops including cashew nuts, used in this recipe, sisal, coffee and cotton.

INGREDIENTS

$^{1}/_{2}$ cup / 30 g fresh mint leaves

$^{1}/_{2}$ cup / 30 g fresh cilantro/ coriander leaves

handful cashewnuts

1 bell pepper

juice of 2 limes or lemons

1 tablespoon sugar

3-4 cloves garlic

1-3 teaspoons cilantro/ coriander seeds

$^{1}/_{4}$ teaspoon chili powder

water

1. Combine all the ingredients except the water in a blender, or chop them very finely and mix together. Add water as required and serve with meat dishes ∎

125

ASIA

Coconut milk

This is widely used in Southeast Asia to flavor curries and other dishes. There it is usually made with fresh coconuts, but you can substitute coconut cream or desiccated coconut. You can buy coconut cream from health or wholefood shops. It usually comes in a small block and you simply add hot water or follow the instructions on the packet. For shredded or desiccated coconut, see below.

INGREDIENTS

2 cups / 150 g desiccated coconut

2¹/₂ cups / 590 ml boiling water

1. Soak the coconut in the boiling water and let it cool.

2. Then mash or liquidize the mixture until it is smooth. It can be used like this, or sieved or squeezed through a piece of muslin cloth to remove the coconut pulp.

3. Always add the coconut milk towards the end of cooking time so its flavor is retained. Store in the refrigerator ∎

Miso potatoes

Serves 2

'Miso is a fermented soybean paste made with barley. It has a long history in China, being rich in protein and considered good for the digestion. It is quite salty and can be used in soups, sauces and other vegetarian dishes. You can buy *miso* in powder form in health food stores. By the way, this dish makes a good alternative to chips and fries.'
Valerie Sherriff, British Columbia, Canada

INGREDIENTS

4 medium potatoes, cut into chip / French fry shape

1 tablespoon miso

1 tablespoon oil

2 tablespoons / 25 g melted margarine

Note: To reduce the cooking time, parboil the potatoes first for 5 minutes.

Heat oven to 350°F/180°C/Gas 4

1. Mix the miso with the melted margarine in a bowl.

2. Then spoon the oil into an oven-proof dish which has a tight-fitting lid and add the sliced potatoes.

3. Pour the miso-margarine mixture over the potatoes and stir round gently to distribute the sauce.

4. Cover and bake for about 20 minutes or until the potatoes are tender ∎

BURMA/ MYANMAR

Chutney rice

Serves 4

The British ruled Burma as a province of India from the 1850s. They used the country as a rice bowl to feed other colonies in the region, notably Malaya and Ceylon where the colonialists required people to grow rubber and tea instead of rice. Until the Second World War Burma was the world's leading exporter of rice.

To turn this dish into a main meal add cooked chicken or prawns; vegetarians could substitute cooked garbanzos/chickpeas or other beans.

I N G R E D I E N T S

1½ cups / 300 g rice

2-4 tablespoons sugar

4 tablespoons wine vinegar

3 cloves or ¼ teaspoon ground cloves

2 large cooking apples, chopped

4 tablespoons raisins or sultanas

2 tablespoons oil

3 cups / 700 ml water

½ cup / 60 g unsalted cashewnuts

salt and pepper

1. Taking first the sugar, vinegar and salt, gently stir them together in a pan. Now add the cloves, apple and raisins or sultanas.

2. Next heat the mixture slowly, stirring frequently, and cook it for about 30 minutes or until it thickens. Allow to cool a little.

3. Meanwhile, gently heat the oil in a large saucepan. Add the rice and stir for about 1 minute, seasoning with salt and pepper. Then pour in the water, put the lid on, and bring to the boil. Now turn down the heat and simmer the rice for 20 minutes or until it is cooked as you like it.

4. When this is done, turn the rice into a dish and spoon the chutney over it, scattering the cashewnuts on top before serving ∎

CAMBODIA

Cucumber and sesame seed salad

Serves 4-6

Most of the people in Cambodia are Khmer, a group probably descended from early Chinese immigrants. Before the turmoil of the 1970s Cambodians lived in a similar manner to their Thai and Lao neighbors, in small, self-sufficient villages. Wet rice cultivation was the main means of livelihood.

Toasting the sesame seeds first for this recipe gives them a nuttier flavor.

I N G R E D I E N T S

1 large cucumber

½ cup / 120 ml white wine or cider vinegar

1 tablespoon sesame seeds

1 tablespoon sesame oil

1 onion, sliced finely

2 cloves garlic, sliced finely

1 teaspoon turmeric

1-2 teaspoons sugar

salt

1. First peel the cucumber and cut into 2 inch/5 cm pieces. Cut these again into lengthwise sticks. Now put them into a pan with the vinegar and salt; add a little water to cover, heat and simmer for a few minutes until the cucumber is slightly tender and transparent. Drain, keeping the liquid, and let the cucumber cool. Set aside.

2. Now toast the sesame seeds in a pan with a little oil until they begin to jump and turn golden. Then let them cool.

3. After this, heat 1 tablespoon of the oil in a pan and cook the onion and garlic without burning until they are golden brown. Remove them from the pan and set aside.

4. Now pour in the remaining oil, turmeric, sugar and half the drained vinegar liquid. Stir this over a gentle heat until the sugar is dissolved. Add the onion and garlic and heat them through.

5. Arrange the cucumber pieces in a salad bowl and pour over the dressing. Mix well and then scatter the sesame seeds on top. Serve warm or cold ∎

FIJI

Tomato salad with buttermilk

Serves 4

Fijian clans or *matagali* have historically held most of the island's land, growing food crops such as rice, sorghum and pulses. Today much land is used for export commodities such as sugar, bananas, cocoa and ginger. Livestock rearing and dairying are also part of life. Buttermilk, used in this recipe, is the slightly sour liquid left after the butter has been separated from the milk in butter-making.

INGREDIENTS

6 large tomatoes, sliced

1 medium onion, chopped finely

4 tablespoons fresh cilantro/coriander leaves or parsley

1 fresh green chili, chopped finely or 1 teaspoon chili powder

$^1/_4$ teaspoon mustard powder

$^1/_4$ teaspoon ground cumin

$^3/_4$ cup / 180 ml buttermilk

1. In a salad bowl, mix everything together except the buttermilk.

2. When the ingredients are well mixed, pour on the buttermilk and stir round. Serve cold ■

INDIA

Chapatis

Makes 12

Chapatis and other breads such as *nan* are the main accompaniment to meals in the wheat-growing (northern) areas of India. In the South, rice is the staple.

INGREDIENTS

2 cups / 250 g flour $^1/_2$ cup / 120 ml water

1. First, sieve the flour into a bowl and then gradually pour in the water to form a stiff dough. Add more flour or water as required to make the mixture easy to handle.

2. Then make a ball of the dough and place it on a board or surface and knead it for 5 minutes until it is smooth and elastic. Cover it with a damp cloth and let it rest for 30 minutes.

3. After that, roll the dough into a cylinder shape with your hands and divide it into 12 pieces. Sprinkle some flour on the board and shape each piece into a ball. Then flatten and using a rolling pin form into a circle about 5 inches/13 cms across.

4. Now place a heavy pan on the cooker and heat it slowly, using no oil if possible. Cook the first chapati for 1 minute until bubbles appear on top; then turn it over and cook the other side for 1 minute also. Cook all the chapatis like this and put them in a hot cloth to keep warm; serve as soon as possible ■

Curried potato fries/chips

Serves 2

Potatoes have a place as a prime staple food in many countries, and provide a good source of vitamins and protein (**see Staple Food p.14**). Their development through selective breeding has until recently been geared mainly to Western needs and temperate climates; increasingly now research and breeding is being adapted to requirements of countries like Kenya and India.

I N G R E D I E N T S

4 medium potatoes

oil

1/2 teaspoon turmeric

1-2 cloves garlic, crushed

1 tablespoon sesame seeds, toasted

salt

1. Start by cutting the potatoes into French fry/chip shapes. Soak them in water for 30 minutes and then drain and dry.

2. After this, heat some oil in a heavy-based pan and add the potatoes and salt. Cook for 15 minutes, stirring round.

3. Now sprinkle on the turmeric and mix it well to spread the color evenly.

4. When the potatoes are nearly done, put in the crushed garlic and sesame seeds. Stir well and then serve with dhal (see p. 39) ■

INDONESIA

Peppery potatoes with egg-plant/aubergine

Serves 2

In the 17th century the Spice Islands, now Indonesia, came under the control of four Dutch trading companies who joined to form the United East India Company. Competition was fierce and the Company sometimes resorted to drastic measures to gain control of the European markets, even burning spice trees to keep prices high.

I N G R E D I E N T S

2 tablespoons oil

1 small onion, sliced

1/2 teaspoon chili powder

1/2 teaspoon mustard powder

1/2 teaspoon turmeric

1/2 inch / 1 cm fresh ginger root, peeled and grated

2 medium potatoes, diced and parboiled

1 medium egg-plant/ aubergine, sliced thinly

salt

1. The first step is to heat the oil in a pan and cook the onion until it is clear and soft.

2. After that put in the chili, salt, mustard, turmeric and ginger. Then add the partly-cooked potatoes and egg-plant/aubergine and lightly brown them all over, turning constantly to prevent them catching.

3. Add just enough water to come half-way up the vegetables, cover the pan and cook gently until the vegetables are tender and the liquid is absorbed ■

129

LAOS

Njum (Bamboo shoot salad)

Serves 2

Laos is the only land-locked country in Indochina and has always been prey both to foreign powers seeking dreamed-of mineral wealth, like gold, and also to more populous neighbors in quest of better lines of communication. The French and American wars in the region catapulted Laos and its sleepy capital, Vientiane, into the jet-age, leaving the largely rural population devastated and impoverished.

I N G R E D I E N T S

1 medium can bamboo shoots, drained

1-2 fresh red chilis, cut very finely or minced

1 clove garlic, crushed

1 tablespoon lime or lemon juice

3 teaspoons sugar

1 tablespoon fish sauce or 1 teaspoon anchovy essence*

$^1/_2$ cup / 50 g creamed coconut melted in $^1/_2$ cup/ 120 ml warm water

3 scallions / spring onions, finely chopped

1 tablespoon fresh basil, chopped

1 tablespoon fresh mint, chopped

a few sprigs fresh fennel or dill

salt and pepper

* Fish sauce, called *nuoc nam* in Laos, can be obtained in some Asian stores.

1. To begin, boil the bamboo shoots for 2-3 minutes in slightly salted water. Drain and rinse them in cold water. When cool, cut them into very thin slices and place in a salad bowl.

2. Now prepare the dressing by mixing the chilis, garlic, lime or lemon juice, sugar, fish sauce or anchovy essence and coconut milk. Pour this over the bamboo shoots. Add salt and pepper.

3. Scatter the chopped scallions/spring onions, basil and mint on top and toss the salad. Garnish with sprigs of fennel or dill ∎

KOREA

Carrot and radish salad

Serves 2

The white radish, *mooli* or *daikon*, is commonly eaten with *sashimi* (raw fish) in Korea and Japan. Radishes have been cultivated widely throughout the world and there are many varieties. In China the white radish is prized for its digestive and diuretic qualities; in India it is used to help people with respiratory disorders.

If possible, leave this salad to stand for 1 hour before it is to be served.

I N G R E D I E N T S

1 medium carrot, thinly sliced in rounds

$1^1/_2$ cups / 250 g white radish, thinly sliced in rounds *

1 tablespoon sesame or other oil

1 tablespoon rice or white wine vinegar

$^1/_4$ teaspoon soy sauce

$^1/_4$ teaspoon sugar

pinch cayenne pepper

salt

* White radish (mooli) can be found in larger supermarkets, Indian and oriental stores. If you cannot find it, use another kind of radish.

1. Put the carrot and radish slices into a salad bowl.

2. Then mix together all the other ingredients in a small basin and pour the sauce over the sliced vegetables, stirring well to distribute evenly. Leave the salad to soak for up to one hour before serving ∎

Tamari (Dipping sauce)

Soy sauce – made from fermented soybeans – is a basic part of many Asian sauces and flavorings. It comes in different strengths and sweetnesses, but basically there is light and dark, the latter colored with caramel and sometimes containing molasses. Use whichever you prefer, though the light varieties may be better for more fragrant dishes.

I N G R E D I E N T S

3 tablespoons soy sauce

3 tablespoons sesame oil

1 tablespoon sesame seeds

$^1/_2$ tablespoon sugar

1. Heat a drop or two of oil in a heavy pan over a gentle heat. Now put in the sesame seeds and wait for them to start popping, shaking the pan to prevent burning. When they turn golden, turn off the heat and let them cool.

2. Meanwhile combine the soy sauce, oil and sugar in a bowl. Whisk them together and pour over the seeds. Serve in a shallow bowl ■

Honsik bab (Rice with barley)

Serves 4-6

Barley can grow in high, cold and windswept parts of the world, making it one of the toughest grains. This ability to survive was one reason why barley was fed to Roman soldiers, to make them strong in battle. Nowadays in the West barley is mainly used as cattle feed while in countries like China and Libya it still grown to feed people (**see Staple Food p. 160**). In this recipe, the rice and barley should soak first for half an hour (see 1 below).

I N G R E D I E N T S

$^1/_2$ pound / 225 g rice

$^1/_2$ cup / 100 g barley

4 cups / 950 ml stock or water

salt and pepper

1. First rinse the rice and barley and put them together in a bowl. Pour over enough stock or water to cover and leave them to soak for 30 minutes.

2. Then transfer them, with the stock, into a large pan. Cover and bring to the boil. When steaming, turn down the heat and allow to simmer very gently for 20-30 minutes, or until the grains are cooked.

3. After this take the pan from the heat but leave the rice and barley inside for a few more minutes before serving with vegetables or another main dish ■

Rice with millet

Serves 4-6

In the West, millet is mostly thought of, if at all, as birdseed or other animal fodder. Yet it is a major cereal for many people in the Third World (**see Staple Food p. 50**). And with reason: it is nutritious as well as having a pleasant, delicate flavor which you can bring out by first toasting the grains in a pan for about 5 minutes until they turn golden brown and begin to pop.

In this recipe, the rice and millet should soak for 30 minutes.

I N G R E D I E N T S

$^1/_2$ cup / 110 g hulled millet

1 pound / 450 g rice

4 cups / 950 ml stock

a little fresh cilantro/ coriander or parsley, chopped

salt and pepper

1. To begin, toast the millet (see above). Then put it into a bowl with the rice and add enough stock to cover. Leave to soak for at least 30 minutes.

2. After this, put the grains and their liquid together with any remaining stock into a large pan with a lid. Bring this to the boil, then reduce the heat to simmer gently for 20-30 minutes or until cooked.

3. Before serving, leave the rice and millet to sit for a few minutes in the pot. Garnish with cilantro/coriander or parsley, and serve with vegetables, salad or as an accompaniment to a meat dish ■

131

KOREA

Yang bai chuna mool (Marinated cabbage salad)

Serves 4

Fruit and vegetables are grown in both North and South Korea; in the North on state farms and in the South on small-holdings. The main crops tend to be the same, however, whether in North or South: rice, maize/corn and potatoes, sweet potatoes, millet and barley.

This salad is easy to make, but it needs to stand for up to 5 hours to get the full benefit of the marinade. If you cannot obtain oriental or Chinese cabbage (*bok choy*), you could use white cabbage or Chinese lettuce (*sui choy*).

I N G R E D I E N T S

1/2 pound / 225 g Chinese cabbage or equivalent, chopped finely

1 tablespoon sesame seeds

6 inch / 15 cm cucumber

1 1/2 tablespoons sesame oil

1 inch / 2.5 cm fresh ginger root, peeled and grated

1/2 tablespoon sugar

2 scallions / spring onions, chopped very finely

1 1/2 tablespoons white wine vinegar

2 tablespoons light soy sauce

1/2 -1 fresh green chili, or chili powder to taste

1. To start, toast the sesame seeds in a pan with a minimum of oil until they are golden and beginning to jump. Remove and allow to cool.

2. After this, cut the cucumber in half and then slice it into thin lengthwise strips. Now put the cucumber pieces, together with the Chinese cabbage, into a salad bowl.

3. Using a small bowl or cup, mix together the oil, ginger, sugar, scallions/spring onions, vinegar, sesame seeds, soy sauce and chili. Pour this over the salad and stir well. Then leave it to marinate for 5 hours if possible before serving ∎

SRI LANKA

Coconut rotis (Coconut bread)

Makes 12

'Serendib' was Sri Lanka's Arab name, giving the English word *'serendipity – the faculty of making happy, unexpected discoveries'*. It's a notion that might seem remote at times for Sri Lanka's people facing daily realities of survival against a backdrop of unrest in the 1980s. Many work the state-owned plantations producing tea, rubber and coconuts for export. Local food, including rice and soybeans, cashews and spices, is grown on small-holdings.

I N G R E D I E N T S

2 cups / 250 g flour

1 1/2 cups / 150 g desiccated coconut

a little ghee or margarine

salt

1. To begin, gently warm the flour in a pan over a low heat.

2. Then mix it with the coconut in a basin and add a little boiling water to make a thick paste.

3. Shape this mixture into balls the size of an egg and then flatten them to the size of a saucer.

4. Put a little ghee or margarine in a pan and cook the first roti on one side for about 1 minute, then turn it over and cook for a further minute. When it is done, remove it and keep warm while you repeat the process with the remaining rotis. Serve as soon as possible after cooking ∎

Pepina saladeh (Cucumber salad)

Serves 6

'Family recipes from Sri Lanka like *pepina saladeh* were given to us when we were living for a time in the village of Konkatuwa, working as Canadian World Youth Service volunteers. The recipe calls for *ambala kada*, Maldive fish paste, but you can use fish powder or anchovy essence. The cucumber should soak in salted water for 30 minutes.' *Christian Delaquis, Manitoba, Canada*

I N G R E D I E N T S

3 cups / 300 g cucumber, sliced

2-4 teaspoons salt

1/2 cup / 120 ml water

2 teaspoons pepper

1-2 green chilis, sliced thinly

3 small red onions, sliced

2 teaspoons ambala kada (see above) or a few drops anchovy essence

juice of 1 orange

1. Start by putting the cucumber slices into a bowl. Then stir the salt into the water and pour this over the cucumber, mixing well and pressing the cucumber slices a little as you do it. Leave to soak for 30 minutes.

2. After this time, squeeze the water from the cucumber slices and add the other ingredients. Mix well, and chill before serving ■

Roti (Bread)

Serves 6

'Friends of mine – Dorothy, Ramini, Brigitte and Shuba – and I took down a few recipes from our respective 'families' (hosts during our stay in Sri Lanka) who prepared them. My *amma* ('mother') and *akka* ('elder sister') never measured the ingredients, so it is all down to the taste … These *rotis* are great for breakfast with spicy *seeni sambol* (sauce) – or jam.' *Christian Delaquis, Manitoba, Canada*

I N G R E D I E N T S

3¼ cups / 400 g wheat or rice flour

4 cups / 300 g coconut, grated or desiccated

2 small red onions, sliced very finely or grated +

1 teaspoon salt

2 teaspoons sugar +

+ optional ingredient

1. First, sieve the flour into a bowl and then mix it with all the other ingredients, adding just enough water to make a stiff dough.

2. After this divide the mixture into balls of about 2 inches/5 cms diameter. Flatten each on a slightly greased surface, using the back of a cooking pan or greased hands.

3. Cook the rotis, one at a time, in a heavy ungreased pan over a medium to high heat, or under the broiler/grill. They take about 5-8 minutes each side, depending on how moist the dough is. Serve right away ■

> **IN ALL RECIPES**
> ● **PEPPER AND SALT ARE TO TASTE**
> ● **CHILI AND SUGAR ARE GIVEN AS GUIDE QUANTITIES ONLY. VARY TO TASTE**
> ● **MEASURES FOR BEANS AND GRAINS REFER TO DRY INGREDIENTS.**

VIETNAM

Goi nam phuong (Radish and celery salad)
Serves 6

The fertile deltas of the Red River in the North of Vietnam and the Mekong in the South are sometimes likened to two rice baskets, linked by the 'carrying pole' of the Annam mountains. Vietnam's agriculture was badly hit by the war with the US and the country still needs to import rice, the main staple, (**see Staple Food p. 88**) and other foods.

INGREDIENTS

4 inch / 10 cm white radish, grated *

1 tablespoon oil

12 lettuce leaves, shredded

3 stalks celery, sliced thinly

1 medium red onion, sliced finely in rings

2-3 cloves garlic, sliced thinly

1-2 red or green chilis +

6 scallions / spring onions, finely chopped

2 tablespoons peanuts, roasted and coarsely chopped

handful fresh cilantro/ coriander leaves or parsley, chopped

handful fresh mint leaves, chopped

SAUCE

3 tablespoons white wine vinegar or lemon juice

1 tablespoon sugar or to taste

1¹/₂ tablespoons soy sauce

1 clove garlic, crushed

small piece carrot, finely grated

1. For the salad, boil the white radish quickly for 2 minutes in a little water with the oil added. Drain and cool.

2. Then arrange the lettuce on a flat serving dish, putting the celery and onion rings on top.

3. Now mix together the garlic, chilis, scallions/spring onions, chopped peanuts and radish. Scatter these over the celery and onion rings.

4. To make the sauce, mix together the white wine vinegar or lemon juice with the sugar, soy sauce, garlic and finely grated carrot. Pour this over the salad and toss. Before serving, decorate with the cilantro/coriander and mint leaves ∎

* White radish, mooli or daikon can be bought in most large supermarkets. Substitute red radish if you cannot find it.

+ optional ingredient

(Opposite) On the road – Vietnamese woman with flowers and hens.
Photo: Mark Harris/Tony Stone Worldwide

135

STAPLE FOODS: YAMS

Yams are the underground tubers of vine-like plants originating in West Africa and Asia. The Yellow or Guinea yam and the White yam are the West African types while the Asiatic yam is found in Vietnam, Cambodia and Laos. There is also an American variety, the 'cush-cush' yam. 'Yam' is sometimes used for almost any tropical root plant, even sweet potatoes.

Nigeria grows half the world's total harvest. Yams are an important staple also in the Caribbean, parts of Latin America, Southeast Asia and Oceania, especially Melanesia. Although starchy, yams contain enough protein to make them a valuable part of the diet.

People began to domesticate them more than 5,000 years ago within aboriginal cultures in Africa, Asia and tropical America. The tubers were conveyed across the Pacific in the Polynesian migrations and are associated with the early pre-metallic culture in Melanesia. They were taken to Madagascar and thence to East Africa by Malaysian migrations.

Africa's most important yam is the Common or White yam. This has a gray-brown skin and white sticky flesh. The other major variety here is the Yellow or Guinea yam with its reddish-brown skin and sticky yellow flesh. Both these yams are found in the Caribbean, and they are exported to West Indian communities including those in Britain and North America.

The Greater (Water) or Asiatic yam comes in many shapes and sizes and is found around the world. The tubers can be enormous, an average-sized one in the market might well weigh 10 kg (22 pounds).

In South America, indians were growing yams before Christopher Columbus arrived, but the crop was never as popular as cassava/manioc, perhaps because that plant is easier to grow.

With over 600 species yams provide not only food but also a source of medicines. Traditional healers have used them for centuries and in the years since the second world war, the pharmaceutical companies have also shown interest in them especially for a steroid used in the contraceptive pill. This ingredient comes from wild yams found in Mexico and South Africa. But then, as demand for the steroid grew, the plants were on the way to extinction and means of conserving and regenerating stocks had to be found.

Yams lend themselves to being boiled, roasted and fried. A popular way to eat them is to boil and mash them as an accompaniment to main dish stews (*fufu* in African cookery) and in China yams can be wrapped in lotus leaves and steamed.

No serious selective breeding has been done with yams to improve their food value or to make them easier to cultivate. In some tropical regions as a result, nutritionally-inferior cassava is taking over as the staple because it requires only minimal labor.

Main producers (not ranked) Nigeria, Vietnam, Cambodia, Laos, Ivory Coast, Ghana, Cameroon, Brazil, Oceania and the Caribbean.

World production figures not available.

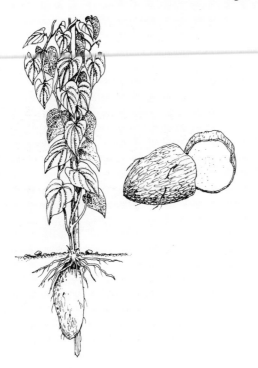

Illustration: Steve Weston

136

CARIBBEAN

Foofoo (Boiled yams)

Serves 4-6

Cassava/manioc, yams and plantains are all used to make *foofoo* or *fufu*, the classic West African mash that accompanies most main dishes. And uprooted Africans, slaves, re-created the tastes of home in their new surroundings in the Caribbean. This is an easy way of cooking yams (**see Staple Food opposite**) and it goes well with spicy dishes.

INGREDIENTS

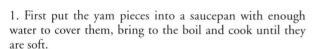

2 pounds / 900 g fresh yams, peeled and cut into chunks

1 tablespoon fresh mint, chopped

2 tablespoons / 25 g margarine

salt and pepper

1. First put the yam pieces into a saucepan with enough water to cover them, bring to the boil and cook until they are soft.

2. Now drain off the water and mash the yams, adding the mint, margarine, salt and pepper. Serve at once ■

Okra and egg-plant/aubergine

Serves 4-6

Okra is used widely around the world, and is known by many different names – *gumbo, bhindi or lady's fingers* are a few of these. One of the cotton family of plants, it is probably indigenous to West Africa and was taken to America on the slave ships. The word 'okra' may have evolved from the Ghanain Twi language *nkuruman* and 'gumbo' from the Angolan *ngombo*.

To make this side dish into a main course, try adding tuna and/or top with grated cheese and serve with rice or boiled yams (see previous recipe).

INGREDIENTS

1 medium egg-plant/aubergine

24 okra

2-3 tablespoons / 25-40 g margarine

1 onion, chopped finely

2 tomatoes, sliced

1 tablespoon fresh parsley, chopped

salt and pepper

1. First chop the egg-plant/aubergine and okra into similar-sized pieces.

2. When this is done, melt the margarine in a pan and add the onion, okra and egg-plant/aubergine. Cook gently for 5 minutes, stirring occasionally.

3. After this, put in the tomatoes and season with salt and pepper. Now cover the pot and stew for about half an hour over a very low heat, stirring frequently, until everything is tender. Add a little water to prevent sticking if necessary. Sprinkle on the parsley before serving ■

137

CARIBBEAN

Pumpkin and cashewnut salad

Serves 2

The hundreds of islands in the Caribbean stretch out in a curve from Florida to Venezuela, and the range of food reflects both the tropical climate and the islands' varied histories. St Lucia, for instance, changed hands between France and Britain 14 times before finally gaining its independence.

You can serve this dish in half of the pumpkin. To do this, cut the vegetable around the middle and put the salad in the scooped-out bottom section.

I N G R E D I E N T S

2 cups / 300 g pumpkin, cubed and boiled or steamed for 10 minutes

¼ cup / 30 g cashewnuts, lightly toasted

4 tablespoons oil-and-vinegar dressing/vinaigrette

slices of watermelon and green bell pepper for garnish or use tomato and parsley

salt and pepper

1. When the cooked pumpkin has cooled a little, mix the cubes carefully with the vinaigrette so that all the pieces are coated. Keep a few of the toasted cashews back for garnish and combine the rest into the pumpkin salad and season.

2. Now pile the salad back into the pumpkin shell or serving bowl and decorate with the watermelon and bell pepper slices or tomato and parsley before serving ■

DOMINICAN REPUBLIC

Ensalada de coliflor (Cauliflower salad)

Serves 4

The Dominican Republic has been a colonial kickabout: Christopher Columbus' son Diego was the first governor for the Spanish; it was then ceded to France in 1795; regained by Spain in 1808; independent in 1821; ruled by Haiti between 1822-44 and thereafter independent.

Today the main export is sugar; and about 10 per cent of food requirements are imported.

Cauliflower originated in the Mediterranean area and was probably cultivated widely in Europe from an early time, although no specific reference occurs until 1576. The Spanish or Portuguese most likely took it to the Americas where it combines happily with the local hero, the avocado pear, as in this recipe.

I N G R E D I E N T S

1 cauliflower, cooked whole and cooled

1 large ripe avocado

1 tablespoon white wine vinegar or lemon juice

2-3 tablespoons oil

¼ cup / 50 g ground almonds

a little milk

salt and pepper

1. To start with, place the whole cauliflower into a serving dish. If preferred you can carefully cut off the florets and arrange these on their own in the dish.

2. Now slice open the avocado, remove the stone and scoop the flesh into a mixing bowl. Mash the avocado, adding the vinegar or lemon juice, oil, milk, ground almonds and seasoning, until you have a smooth coating sauce.

3. Spoon this over the cauliflower and serve immediately ■

HAITI

Avocado pear and pineapple salad

Serves 2-4

The years of 'Papa Doc' and 'Baby Doc' Duvalier's regimes have left Haiti as one of the 30 poorest countries in the world, with a life expectancy of 55 years (compared with 75 years in the US). Most of the population is black, but nearly half a million Haitians live in the Dominican Republic where they went or were sent to cut sugar. Clearly not all Haitians are poor however – the country has a higher percentage of millionaires per capita than the US.

I N G R E D I E N T S

1 large ripe avocado

4 slices fresh pineapple, or a medium can, drained

2 tablespoons olive oil

$1/2$ -1 tablespoon lemon juice

a few lettuce leaves

a little chopped parsley

salt and pepper

NOTE: Add tuna, nuts or cottage cheese to make a more substantial meal.

1. Start by slicing round the avocado to open it and taking out the stone. Then peel off the skin and cut the flesh into small pieces.

2. Remove the skin from the fresh pineapple and cut the fruit into chunks. If using tuna, cottage cheese or nuts, place these in a bowl with the avocado.

3. In a separate container whisk the olive oil, lemon juice, salt and pepper with a fork to make the dressing.

4. Pour this over the salad and stir gently. Place the lettuce leaves on a flat dish and cover them with the avocado and pineapple mixture, garnishing with parsley. Serve with hot bread, potatoes or cracked wheat ∎

MEXICO

Tortillas

Makes 12

Tortillas are the daily bread of Mexico and other parts of Latin America, made from a special corn/maize flour. This recipe uses a mixture of cornmeal and wheat flours.

I N G R E D I E N T S

1 cup / 150 g fine cornmeal

1 cup / 125 g wheat flour

$1^1/2$ cups / 360 ml warm water

a little oil

1. Put the cornmeal and flour in a bowl and add enough water to make a dough. Knead this well until it is smooth and elastic, and then divide it into 12 pieces.

2. Cut 2 pieces of aluminium foil or waxed/greaseproof paper into 8 inch/20 cm squares and grease these lightly.

3. Put a ball of the dough between the paper/foil and roll it with a rolling pin into a 6 inch/15 cm circle.

4. Next, heat a lightly-greased heavy, shallow pan. Remove one of the layers of paper/foil and place the tortilla in the pan, with its remaining paper/foil side uppermost. Cook for about 1 minute.

5. Remove the paper/foil and turn the tortilla over to cook the other side. Both sides should be dry with brown patches.

6. Stack the tortillas, cover to keep warm and serve as soon as possible ∎

NICARAGUA

Egg-plant/aubergine casserole

Serves 4-6

Nicaragua's economy depends on a few agricultural exports (coffee, cotton, sugar and bananas), making it highly vulnerable to world price fluctuations for these. In addition the country was undermined by the US-supported war and trade sanctions.

The egg-plant or aubergine has a string of other names – *apple of love, Jew's apple, widow's comforter* and *brown jolly* being some of the more intriguing. The name of a famous Turkish egg-plant dish, *Imam bayeldi*, means 'the *Imam* (priest) fainted' although whether at delight with the dish his wife served up or with horror at the cost of the ingredients is not known.

INGREDIENTS

1 pound / 450 g egg-plant/
aubergine, cut into $^1/_2$ inch/
1 cm slices

1 tablespoon oil

1 medium onion, finely
chopped

1-2 cloves garlic, crushed	5 tablespoons tomato paste
1 red or green bell pepper, chopped finely	$^3/_4$ cup / 180 ml water
1 green chili or $^1/_2$ teaspoon chili powder	2 cups / 225 g cheddar cheese, grated
$^1/_2$ teaspoon ground cumin	salt and pepper

Heat oven to 400°F/200°C/Gas 6

1. First of all, place the egg-plant/aubergine slices in a single layer on a greased baking sheet and bake uncovered in the oven for 10-20 minutes until soft.

2. Now heat the oil in a pan and sauté the onion, garlic and bell pepper for 5 minutes. Then add the chili, cumin, tomato paste and continue to cook for 3 minutes before pouring in the water.

3. Bring to the boil, stirring from time to time and then lower the heat and simmer, uncovered, for 10 minutes. Add salt and pepper to taste.

4. In a shallow greased oven-proof dish, put a layer of the egg-plant/aubergine slices and spoon on half the sauce. Sprinkle half of the cheese on top. Repeat with the remaining ingredients.

5. Bake, uncovered, for 15-20 minutes. Serve with baked sweet potatoes ∎

Pererreque/Cosa de Horno (Corn/maize cake)

Serves 6

'Pererreque is a traditional Nicaraguan cake which is sold in markets. It is made with corn/maize meal and cheese, sweetened with sugar and lightly aerated with bicarbonate of soda. It is delicious, tasting sweet rather than savory. The cheese makes it nutritious and very filling.' *Tony James, Wantage, UK*

INGREDIENTS

1 pound / 450 g fine white corn / maize meal	2 tablespoons / 25 g margarine
1 pound / 450 g crumbly cheese, grated finely (try monterey jack or wensleydale)	$^1/_2$ teaspoon bicarbonate of soda
1 cup / 200 g sugar	$2^1/_2$ cups / 590 ml milk

Heat oven to 350°F/180°C/Gas 4

1. First mix the corn/maize meal together with the cheese and sugar in a bowl. Then rub in the margarine.

2. Now mix the bicarbonate of soda into a little of the milk and pour this into the other ingredients. Then add more milk to make a mixture which is soft enough to find its own level when spooned into a cake tin. Mix well.

3. Place the cake mixture into a baking tray or cake tin. The mixture should be about 1 inch/2.5 cm thick.

4. Bake for 30-40 minutes until the cake is golden brown. After this time, remove it from the oven, allow to cool and then cut into small pieces or squares before serving cold ∎

EGYPT

Salata baladi

Serves 4

Fragmented land tenure, price controls and increased soil salinity from years of irrigation are just some of the reasons why Egypt's food production has not kept up with demand. Another is that emphasis on cash crops such as cotton, potatoes and tomatoes has meant less land for growing the food people eat locally such as rice and beans.

This salad is a good accompaniment to *Ful Medames* – an Egyptian bean dish (see p. 48), as the fresh mint and cucumber offset the dryish texture of the beans.

INGREDIENTS

1 medium lettuce, shredded	1 tablespoon fresh mint, chopped
6 tomatoes, chopped	
2 cups / 200 g cucumber, diced	3 tablespoons olive oil
	1 tablespoon vinegar
1 medium onion, sliced	salt and pepper

1. In a salad bowl, toss together the lettuce, tomatoes, cucumber, onion and mint.

2. Then make the dressing by mixing the oil with the vinegar, salt and pepper. Pour this over the salad and serve immediately ∎

Tomatoes stuffed with bulgur or cracked wheat

Serves 4-6

'Peruvian apple' was one of the names for the tomato when it first came to Europe from South America in the 16th century. But fears of its possible toxicity (it is related to the nightshade family) persisted in some parts of the world until the 20th century. Nowadays prized for their high vitamin C content, color and flavor, tomatoes are widely grown – they rank second only to potatoes among the US's vegetable crops – and are cultivated in Egypt's Nile valley along with cucumbers, okra, beans and peas.

INGREDIENTS

1/2 cup / 110 g cracked wheat or bulgur, cooked	handful of chives, parsley and fresh mint, chopped
6 big tomatoes	6 scallions / spring onions or 1 medium onion, sliced finely
3 tablespoons olive oil	
1-2 tablespoons lemon juice	a few lettuce leaves
4 small tomatoes	salt and pepper

1. To start, cut the tops off the big tomatoes and scoop out the seeds and pulp (keep these). Make the dressing by mixing the oil, lemon juice, salt and pepper in a bowl.

2. Next, take the skins off the small tomatoes by putting them in a bowl and pouring boiling water over them. The skins will split and can easily be removed. Cut these tomatoes into small cubes and add to the chopped pulp from the large tomatoes.

3. Now mix the tomatoes, wheat, chopped herbs and scallions/spring onions with the dressing. Fill the big tomatoes with this mixture and arrange them on a bed of lettuce leaves ∎

> **IN ALL RECIPES**
> ● PEPPER AND SALT ARE TO TASTE
> ● CHILI AND SUGAR ARE GIVEN AS GUIDE QUANTITIES ONLY. VARY TO TASTE
> ● MEASURES FOR BEANS AND GRAINS REFER TO DRY INGREDIENTS.

141

STAPLE FOODS: WHEAT

Wheat is the staple food for 35 per cent of the world's people, and is the primary cereal in the rich world. But increasingly it is being grown in developing countries and in some, such as Libya and Morocco it has overtaken barley as the main cereal.

The earliest grains, found in northern Syria, date back to the eighth millenium BC. Wheat transformed the way people live, since hunter-gatherer communities discovered that if they planted wheat seeds and stayed nearby to tend them, those grains would flourish and give them a reliable source of food. And so they could settle there, build homes and from that stable base go on to domesticate animals to give milk and materials for clothing. Those original wheat plants have given rise to today's 30,000 varieties. Early forms, einkorn and emmer wheat, spread around the Near East and then to Europe and India.

In 1529 the Spanish took the forerunner of today's bread wheat type to Mexico and it was carried to Australia in 1788. This 'hard' type of common wheat is high in protein. 'Soft' common wheat is grown for cakes and pastry use. The other main type is durum wheat, a hard grain from which we get semolina and pasta.

As with most food crops, people have selected and grown the types best suited to their needs. They wanted increased yields, larger seeds, better quality flour and greater adaptability. After years of selective breeding, wheat lost its brittle spike — which had eased its self-burial for germination in the soil — but which pricked the harvester's fingers. So the grain became as dependent on people for survival as they are on it.

During the last two decades the total amount of wheat grown has doubled, partly through more land being sown with it but mainly due to the increased use of fertilizers. Wheat's high nutritive value, coupled with the fact that it is easy to transport, store and process, puts it ahead of rice as the world's major cereal. Unlike rice, however, which people eat directly themselves, wheat and other grains are commonly fed first to animals which are in turn fed to humans. And since it can take 16 pounds of grain to produce one pound of beef this is an expensive way to feed people.

The spread of wheat was boosted in the 1960s 'Green Revolution' with the development of high-yielding varieties. But the cereal is not always welcome. When the Chinese went into Tibet they insisted people grow wheat instead of the local staple, barley. Such change is hard not just because of taste and familiarity but also because staple foods carry meaning into other parts of people's lives; into the eating and drinking habits which underpin a community.

Main producers (in descending order) China, Soviet Union, US, India, France, Canada, Turkey, UK and Pakistan.

World production (1985) 505 million tons.

IRAN

Chello rice

Serves 4-6

'I learned this dish from my Iranian brother-in-law who cooks it beautifully at family gatherings, the rice and potato mixture reflecting the meeting of East and West. It takes experience to produce a perfect chello but it is a very forgiving recipe. You can add nuts and cooked vegetables if you like, and the first stage (see step 1 below) can be done the day before you want to eat the meal.' *Jacqueline Bright, Luton, UK*

INGREDIENTS

1 pound / 450 g rice

4 cups / 950 ml stock or water, or a mixture

1/2 teaspoon saffron or turmeric +

4 tablespoons / 50 g oil or margarine

1 pound / 450 g potatoes, cut into 1/2 inch / 1 cm slices and parboiled

1/2 cup / 75 g chopped walnuts or pistachios +

1/2 cup / 75 g vegetables, cooked +

salt and pepper

+ optional ingredient

1. Using a large pan, bring the water or stock to the boil and then put in the rice, saffron and seasoning. Return the liquid to the boil and then turn down the heat, cover, and let the rice simmer until it is half cooked (this will be 5-10 minutes for white rice and 10-15 minutes for brown). Drain and rinse with cold water.

2. Now, taking a heavy pan (ideally one you can serve from), heat the oil or margarine and when it is hot put in the potato slices, turning them from time to time so that both sides are coated. Arrange them in a layer or layers to cover the bottom of the pan.

3. Add any nuts or cooked vegetables, if using these, to the parboiled rice and mix well. Then pile the rice on top of the potatoes and heap it up like a hill. Cover it with a clean cloth and put the lid on.

4. With the heat on low to medium, cook for 10-20 minutes. The exact time will vary according to whether you use white or brown rice – white takes less time to cook. The rice will steam-cook with the potatoes frying to a golden brown underneath.

5. Before the rice and potatoes are completely cooked, dot the rice with margarine to give a glossy effect ■

LEBANON

Tabbouleh (Bulgur salad)

Serves 4

One Arab version has it that the tree of knowledge in the Garden of Eden was not an apple tree at all, but a huge stalk of wheat; so wide that the serpent placed on guard could not encircle it. In desperation the reptile persuaded Eve to prune the plant and, in passing, offer some of the grain to Adam. And in this way the couple incurred God's wrath. The tale has a twist though, for the wheat that caused their downfall inside the garden became their mainstay outside it, and the wheat berry is still highly regarded in the Arab world.

INGREDIENTS

1 cup / 225 g bulgur or cracked wheat, prepared (see p. 146)

1 pound / 450 g tomatoes, cubed

1 medium onion, finely sliced

handful of fresh parsley, chopped

handful of fresh mint, chopped

6 tablespoons olive oil

juice of 2-3 lemons to taste

1 cup / 150 g black or green olives

salt and pepper

1. Take a salad bowl and put in the bulgur or cracked wheat, chopped tomatoes and onion together with the parsley and mint. Mix well.

2. In another bowl, beat the oil with the lemon juice and season with salt and pepper. Then pour it over the salad and mix thoroughly.

3. Put the olives on top, and then chill the salad in the refrigerator for about 2 hours before serving. Garnish with a little more parsley and chopped tomato if desired ■

143

LIBYA

Olive salad

Serves 2-4

Only five per cent of Libya's land is cultivable, around the oases and along the northern coast so almost half the country's food is imported. This salad is one of the many Middle Eastern appetizers or *mezzes*, dishes providing an array of textures, colors and flavors. They can be eaten as side dishes or as appetizers.

INGREDIENTS

1 cup / 150 g green olives

1 cup / 150 g black olives

juice of 1 lemon

2 tablespoons parsley, chopped

1 teaspoon paprika

¹/₄ teaspoon chili powder

1 clove garlic, crushed

¹/₂ teaspoon ground cumin

2 tablespoons oil

1. In a bowl, mix the oil with the cumin, chili powder, paprika, parsley, garlic and lemon juice. Then pour this dressing over the olives in a bowl and stir round so that they are well coated.

2. Put the salad in the fridge to chill before serving ■

(Opposite) Family tea-time in Marrakesh, Morrocco.
Photo: Ron Giling/Panos Pictures

Salatit (Lettuce and raisin salad)

Serves 6

Libya's food crops include the staple, barley (**see Staple Food p. 160**), olives, dates, citrus fruit, tomatoes, almonds, potatoes, wheat and peanuts. Oil production rather than farming is the basis of the economy; Libya is Africa's biggest oil producer after Nigeria.

INGREDIENTS

1 iceberg lettuce or equivalent

2 tablespoons fresh parsley, chopped

¹/₂ cup / 50 g raisins or sultanas

oil

vinegar

1 teaspoon paprika

1 teaspoon ground cumin

4 tomatoes, sliced

a few olives

salt and pepper

1. First shred the lettuce and place it in a large salad bowl with the parsley and raisins or sultanas.

2. Now make a dressing with the oil and vinegar, add the paprika and cumin and the salt and pepper. Whisk and then pour it over the lettuce and mix well.

3. To serve, arrange the tomato slices and olives on top ■

145

MIDDLE EAST

Bulgur and cracked wheat

Serves 2-4

Originating in the Middle East, bulgur soon spread to other parts of the world – it was eaten in Northern Norway over 2,000 years ago and even earlier in China. It is high in vitamins and each quarter pound contains as many nutrients as you will find in a whole loaf of wholemeal bread.

Bulgur and cracked wheat are similar but not the same, although they both come from wheat grains. Bulgur is wheat that has been steamed and then dried before grinding. Cracked wheat on the other hand is uncooked wheat which has been dried and then cracked apart. Both make a pleasant alternative to rice.

INGREDIENTS

1 cup / 450 g bulgur or cracked wheat	3 cups / 700 ml water
	salt

1. Bulgur does not require cooking first. Simply pour boiling water over it in a bowl, add a little salt and leave to soak for about 40 minutes, then drain it.

2. If using cracked wheat, allow it to boil in salted water for 20 minutes and then let it remain in the pan to absorb any moisture, or cook according to the instructions on the packet. If necessary, drain before serving.

3. Use the bulgur to make tabbouleh (see p. 143) or stuffed tomatoes (see p. 141) ■

Tomato and onion salad

Serves 4

Onions and garlic were used as foods as long ago as 3200 BC in Egypt, and leeks were eaten by the Israelites before the time of their exodus from Egypt in 1500 BC.

Long valued for medicinal purposes in India, they are a bactericide and fungicide. As well as keeping vampires at bay, garlic also is useful in fending off the common cold.

INGREDIENTS

4 tomatoes, sliced	1-2 cloves garlic, crushed
1 medium onion, sliced into rings	2 tablespoons fresh parsley, chopped
3 tablespoons olive oil	salt and pepper
1 tablespoon lemon juice	

1. First lay the tomato and onion rings in overlapping layers on a shallow dish.

2. Then mix the oil, lemon juice, garlic, salt and pepper together and pour this over the salad. Garnish with the parsley and serve right away ■

Salatah Arabiyeh (Arab salad)

Serves 4-6

Inscriptions inside the Pyramids reveal that the radish, used here, was already an important food in Egypt some 4,000 years ago. *'Did but the radish digest its own self'* is an Egyptian lament – for although radishes aid digestion of other food they themselves apparently remain indigestible in the stomach.

INGREDIENTS

1 green bell pepper, sliced thinly	2 tablespoons parsley, chopped finely
1 small onion, sliced finely	4-5 cilantro / coriander seeds, crushed or $\frac{1}{2}$ teaspoon ground cilantro / coriander
3 tomatoes, cut into thin wedges	
4 radishes, cut into thin rounds	3 tablespoons olive oil
1 clove garlic, chopped finely	juice of 1 lemon
	salt and pepper

1. In a salad bowl, mix all the ingredients together except the olive oil and lemon juice.

2. Now combine these two and pour over the salad, turning it gently to distribute the dressing before serving ■

A coffee stall in Sudan. *Photo by: Maggie Murray/Format.*

AFRICA

Peanut bread

Serves 8-12

By happy coincidence peanuts are one of the few food crops grown for export in Africa that also play a major role in feeding people locally. They are a basic source of protein and can be cooked as sauces and stews, turned into sweets or made into bread as in this recipe.

I N G R E D I E N T S

4 tablespoons peanuts, finely chopped

3 cups / 375 g flour

4 teaspoons baking powder

2 tablespoons sugar

salt

1 egg

1¹/₂ cups / 350 ml milk

Heat oven to 350°F/180°C/Gas 4

1. Using a mixing bowl, first sieve the flour, baking powder, sugar and salt into it.

2. Crack the egg into another bowl, beat it and then stir in the milk. Now pour this into the dry ingredients and mix together.

3. When this is done, add the peanuts and blend them into the mixture. Spoon the bread into a greased tin and leave it to stand for 20 minutes.

4. After that, put the bread into the oven and bake for about 1 hour. Then turn it out of the tin and let it cool on a wire tray. Serve with savory dishes, or else with jelly/jam or syrup ■

Soybean scones

Serves 8-12

Soybean flour has a high protein and low carbohydrate content and is used sometimes as an ingredient in ice-cream, among other things. For breads and cakes it is usually mixed with wheat flour.

I N G R E D I E N T S

1 cup / 125 g soy flour

3³/₄ cups / 450 g wheat flour

salt

1 egg

2 tablespoons sugar

a little milk or water

2 tablespoons oil

1. Begin by mixing the soy and wheat flours together with the salt in a bowl.

2. Then, in a separate bowl, beat the egg and sugar together and stir this into the flour, adding enough milk or water to make a stiff dough.

3. Heat the oil in a heavy pan and carefully put in spoonfuls of the mixture. Let these cook on both sides for about 10 minutes until done. Repeat until all the mixture is used up, and serve hot or cold with main dishes or with jelly/jam ■

KENYA

Corn/maize meal cake/bread

Serves 4-6

Corn breads are common in America and Africa but not so much in Europe. They are often slightly sweet and are usually served with a savory stew or soup. The corn meal has a coarser texture than wheat flour and a distinctive flavor.

I N G R E D I E N T S

²/₃ cup / 100 g self-raising maize / corn meal (or plain, but then add 4 teaspoons baking powder)

1 cup / 125 g wheat flour

salt

2 tablespoons sugar

1 egg, beaten

2 tablespoons / 25 g margarine, melted

¹/₂ cup / 120 ml milk

Heat oven to 350°F/180°C/Gas 4

1. First, sieve the flours, baking powder (if used), salt and sugar into a bowl.

2. Then add the beaten egg, melted margarine and enough milk to make a fairly stiff mixture.

3. Mix well together and then spoon it into a greased loaf or cake tin. Spread the mixture evenly and then cook the bread for about 20-30 minutes. After this, leave it to cool a while before serving. You can eat the bread with margarine and jelly/jam or honey or plain as an accompaniment to meals ∎

Paw-paw/papaya and mango fool

Serves 4

Britain's colonial period has left its mark on Kenya, not least in the kitchen. One local cookbook has recipes for English Yorkshire pudding and custard, as well as for more local dishes such as fried white ants and *irio* (maize/corn and bean mash, see p. 31). The two cuisines sometimes merge nowadays, as with cassava cheese pie (p. 29), or as in this recipe.

I N G R E D I E N T S

1 cup / 200 g paw-paw/papaya, mashed

1 cup / 200 g mango, mashed

2 tablespoons lemon juice

sugar

¹/₂ cup / 120 ml double or whipping cream

1. Begin by putting the mashed or puréed fruits in a bowl. Then stir in the lemon juice and add sugar as required, mixing everything well so that the sugar dissolves.

2. Now whip the cream in a large basin until it is thick and firm. Gently fold in the fruit mixture. Then turn the fool into a serving dish and place in the fridge to chill ∎

IN ALL RECIPES
- PEPPER AND SALT ARE TO TASTE
- CHILI AND SUGAR ARE GIVEN AS GUIDE QUANTITIES ONLY. VARY TO TASTE
- MEASURES FOR BEANS AND GRAINS REFER TO DRY INGREDIENTS.

KENYA

Fruit salad

Serves 6

The papaya or paw-paw tree, originally from the Americas, is now grown widely in tropical regions. Sometimes known as the 'medicine tree', in India there are papaya remedies for beri-beri (a vitamin-deficiency disease), indigestion and for wounds. Tough meat can be wrapped in papaya leaves for a day to benefit from their tenderizing effect.

INGREDIENTS

2¹/₂ cups / 450 g paw-paw/ papaya *	3 bananas
1 small pineapple	4 passion fruits/ granadillas+
2 large mangoes	juice of 3 oranges
3 pears or apples	+ optional ingredient

* If using canned fruit, drain off the liquid. The quantities you end up with may be different from the amounts given in the recipe but as long as you have a good mix of fruit, the actual quantities do not matter too much.

1. First peel and slice or cube all the fruit except the passion fruits.

2. After this, put the fruit into a large bowl and mix well. Now cut the passion fruits in half and scoop the pulp into the bowl, add the orange juice and mix everything round. Chill in the fridge before serving ∎

Passion fruit/granadilla dessert

Serves 6-8

Originating in South America, passion fruits/granadillas are now grown commercially in Australia, the US and parts of Africa. The passion flower and leaves are used in traditional medicine as they have a sedative effect. This is a dish for special occasions, since the fruits can be expensive.

INGREDIENTS

12 passion fruits/ granadillas	juice of 2 oranges
1 cup / 240 ml water	1 tablespoon gelatine, soaked in a little cold water
sugar to taste	2 eggs, separated

1. Cut the passion fruits in half and scoop out the pulp and seeds into a pan. Add the water and bring to the boil. Then turn down the heat and simmer for 1 minute.

2. When this is done, sieve the mixture into a bowl. Add the sugar, orange juice and soaked gelatine.

3. Now pour the mixture into a pan and heat it gently, stirring until the gelatine is completely dissolved.

4. Allow the mixture to cool. When it is lukewarm, beat the egg yolks lightly and stir them in. Put aside until the mixture begins to set.

5. At this point, whisk the egg whites until they are stiff and fold them in. Put the dessert into a dish and refrigerate until it is completely set. Serve with cream or plain yogurt and wafer biscuits or shortbread ∎

MALI

Meni-meniyong (Sesame seed/sim-sim and honey sticks)

'Good luck. You need it,' wrote Bob Geldof in a visitors' book in Timbuktu, in reference to the uphill task facing Mali after the years of drought and as one of the 15 poorest countries in the world.

'To raise some much-needed cash, kids in Donentza sell these sesame nuggets, and they taste very good.' *Rosemarie Daly, London, UK*

I N G R E D I E N T S

1 cup / 100 g sesame seeds

4 tablespoons / 50 g margarine

1 cup / 350 ml honey or 1 cup / 175 g sugar

1. In a shallow pan, toast the sesame seeds without any oil until they begin to jump about and turn golden. Shake the pan so they do not stick or burn. When they are ready, put them to cool on one side.

2. Now, using a heavy pan, heat the margarine or oil and then add the sugar or honey. Stir continuously until it begins to caramelize.

3. Pour the sesame seeds into the warm mixture and stir thoroughly.

4. Transfer the mixture to a flat tin. As it cools, shape it into sticks either by cutting or by rolling the mixture and then coating it with more sesame seeds if required ∎

SUDAN

Ful-Sudani (Peanut macaroons)
Makes 10-12

Peanuts are one of Sudan's main export crops along with cotton, dates, sesame, sugar-cane and gum-arabic. This last item comes from certain types of acacia trees and is used in ink, food thickeners and pills: Sudan is the world's major supplier.

I N G R E D I E N T S

1 cup / 125 g unsalted peanuts

1 egg white

pinch of salt

3/4 cup / 150 g sugar

1/2 teaspoon vanilla, almond or lemon flavoring

waxed / greaseproof paper

Heat oven to 350°F/180°C/Gas 4

1. Brown the peanuts under the grill, shaking them and turning frequently so that they do not burn. Then chop or grind them coarsely.

2. Whisk the egg white with a pinch of salt until stiff, and then fold in the sugar and vanilla flavoring and whisk again. Add the peanuts.

3. Put some waxed/greaseproof paper on a baking tray and grease it lightly.

4. Using a teaspoon, put small heaps of the nut mixture onto the baking tray and cook for about 20-25 minutes until the macaroons are golden ∎

151

BURMA/ MYANMAR

Semolina cake dessert

6-8 servings

Burma's 'teak curtain' came crashing down in 1964, severing ties with the outside world as the government tried to prevent warring regions from fragmenting the country into a patchwork of tiny states. In 1975 the curtain was lifted a little for aid, but tourists to the country may still only stay for seven days.

Semolina, used here, comes from durum or 'hard' wheat.

INGREDIENTS

3/4 cup / 150 g semolina

1/2 tablespoon sesame seeds

1/4 cup / 30 g almond slivers

2 1/2 cups / 590 ml milk

1 egg

1/2 cup / 85 g sugar

seeds from 1 cardamom pod, crushed

1/2 cup / 150 g creamed coconut, melted in 1/2 cup/ 120 ml warm water

Heat oven to 350°F/180°C/Gas 4

1. First, toast the sesame seeds and almond slivers separately, either under the broiler/grill or in a pan with a drop of oil until they begin to turn golden.

2. Now put the semolina into another pan and cook, dry, over a moderate heat till it turns light golden brown, stirring and shaking frequently to prevent burning. Then remove it from the heat to cool.

3. Pour the milk and coconut cream into a saucepan and heat them gently, stirring to blend them. Now remove from heat.

4. When this is done, beat the egg and sugar together in a bowl with a wooden spoon until the mixture becomes light and smooth. Stir in the crushed cardamom seeds and the almond slivers.

5. After this, pour the milk and coconut cream mixture

into the pan containing the cool semolina. Cook gently over a low heat, stirring constantly to prevent burning and lumps forming, until it is very thick. Remove from the heat and then stir in the egg and sugar mixture.

6. Now place the cake in a greased 6 inch/15 cms square cake tin and smooth the top. Sprinkle on the sesame seeds, cover with foil and cook in a larger tin of hot water in the oven for about 1 hour. Leave to cool completely and then cut into pieces. Store the cake in the fridge ■

CHINA

Peanut and sesame crunch

Makes 24-30 pieces

'Walking on two legs' characterizes a policy adopted by China since the early 1960s. It means striking a balance between very modern and traditional technology, upgrading old methods of production or transport at very little cost – like fitting rubber tyres onto cart wheels to make them easier to pull.

INGREDIENTS

2 cups / 250 g unsalted roasted peanuts

1/2 cup / 50 g sesame seeds

2 cups / 350 g sugar

1/3 cup / 80 ml white wine vinegar

4 teaspoons water

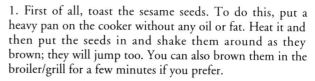

1. First of all, toast the sesame seeds. To do this, put a heavy pan on the cooker without any oil or fat. Heat it and then put the seeds in and shake them around as they brown; they will jump too. You can also brown them in the broiler/grill for a few minutes if you prefer.

2. Then mix the sugar, vinegar and water in a pan over a low heat, stirring until the sugar dissolves.

3. Now bring the mixture to the boil and let it cook without stirring until it is golden and reaches 295°-300°F

to 146°-149°C – 'hard-crack' stage. If you have no candy thermometer, test for this by taking a teaspoon and dipping it into the mixture. Then allow the syrup to drop into a saucer of cold water. It should harden and snap with a clean break if it is ready. If it does not, continue to boil and test it again.

4. Grease a baking tray 11 x 7 inches/28 x 18 cms. Sprinkle half of the sesame seeds and all the peanuts evenly over the bottom of the tray.

5. Pour the sugar mixture over the nuts and seeds and then sprinkle on the remaining sesame seeds. Allow to cool slightly and cut into small pieces. Leave the mixture in the baking tray to cool and harden completely ■

INDIA

Banana fudge

Makes 12

Sweetmeats like this one from South India are often given as presents at Hindu festivals.

I N G R E D I E N T S

1 large banana

seeds from 3 cardamom pods, crushed

2 tablespoons / 25 g margarine

1/4 cup / 50 g semolina

1/4 cup / 50 g ground almonds

1/3 cup / 60 g sugar

1-2 teaspoons water

1. To begin, put the banana into a bowl and mash it with a fork. Add the crushed cardamom seeds and mix well.

2. Now melt the margarine in a pan and gently cook the semolina until it turns golden. When this is ready, add the banana mixture, ground almonds, sugar and a little water, taking care that it does not become too wet.

3. Bring to the boil and cook, stirring constantly, until the mixture comes away from the sides of the pan.

4. Spoon it into a shallow greased tin and let it cool a little. Then put it into the fridge to set. Cut into small pieces or roll into balls to serve ■.

Coconut candy

Makes 15 pieces

Over 90 per cent of India's children are enrolled in primary education, compared with 74 per cent in 1965 – but less than half go on to secondary school.

Both adults and children, whether in school or out, will enjoy these sweets. Coconut palms grow along the Indian coast and lend their bounty to many aspects of the cookery there, particularly in the South.

I N G R E D I E N T S

3/4 cup / 180 ml evaporated milk

1/2 cup / 85 g sugar

1 1/4 cups / 100 g desiccated coconut

1. First of all, pour the evaporated milk into a pan and add the sugar. Heat gently, stirring from time to time. When it boils, turn down the heat and simmer until the milk has reduced by half.

2. Now put in the coconut and continue stirring until the mixture sticks together in a ball. Then remove it from the pan and transfer it to a greased shallow dish or toffee tray. Spread it evenly, using the back of a spoon.

3. Leave the mixture to cool and then cut it into pieces ■

153

INDIA

Kulfi (Ice-cream with pistachio nuts)

Serves 4-6

This requires patience as the milk has to reduce quite substantially, and of course the second you look away it boils over. But the result is worth the trouble. However, if you can find one of those gadgets, often a thick glass disk, that are designed to let milk simmer without boiling up then this will be a lot easier.

I N G R E D I E N T S

2 quarts / 2 liters milk

10 whole cardamom pods

4-5 tablespoons sugar

1 cup / 125 g almonds, chopped

1/2 cup / 60 g shelled, unsalted pistachio nuts *

* If you cannot find unsalted pistachios, use salted ones but wash and dry them after shelling.

1. To start, bring the milk to the boil in a heavy pan. As it begins to rise, turn down the heat and let it simmer without boiling over.

2. Add the cardamom pods now and continue to simmer the milk until it has reduced to one-third its original quantity. Stir frequently.

3. When this is done, take out the cardamoms. Then add the sugar and almonds and simmer again for 2-3 minutes.

4. Now remove the milk from the heat and pour it into a bowl. Leave it to cool.

5. After this, add half the pistachios. Cover the bowl with foil and put it in the freezer, taking it out and stirring every 15 minutes to prevent crystals forming.

6. When it is almost frozen, transfer the kulfi to a serving dish that has been cooled in the freezer, sprinkle the remaining pistachios on top and put it back in the freezer to harden before serving ■

Lassi (yogurt drink)

Serves 4

The cow is sacred to Hindus and dairy products are an important part of people's diet in India, especially in the North. The country is now self-sufficient in milk powder and butter.

Lassi, made from yogurt, is a common accompaniment to curry meals, but as it is so easy to make you can drink it any time as a change from other soft drinks.

I N G R E D I E N T S

2 small cartons plain yogurt

2 1/2 cups / 590 ml cold water

juice of 1/2 lemon

2 teaspoons sugar +

+ a little salt can be used to flavor instead of sugar, or you can serve it plain.

1. Simply whisk or liquidize all ingredients until frothy and pour into glasses ■

Tea with cardamom

Serves 2-4

'This recipe is exactly as given to me by a Sikh friend. She serves it mid-afternoon with samosas.' *Susan Spindler, London, UK.*

I N G R E D I E N T S

seeds from 6 cardamom pods, crushed

4 cups / 1 liter water

1 teaspoon tea leaves

3 tablespoons sugar

2 1/2 cups / 590 ml milk

1. To make the tea, boil the water with the cardamom seeds for 5 minutes, using a saucepan.

2. After this, add the tea leaves and continue to cook for a few minutes.

3. Now put in the sugar and cook, stirring until it dissolves. Finally, pour in the milk, bring to the boil again and simmer for 10-15 minutes before serving ■

INDONESIA

Fruit salad

Serves 4-6

Most of the fruit in this recipe is now available in stores in the West, some in cans but some can be bought fresh. The one ingredient you probably will not come across is the *zalak* – a fruit which grows on a spiny palm growing in coastal areas of Malaysia and Indonesia. You could substitute *lychees, longans* or *mangosteens,* or simply use a pear or apple. If using canned fruit you may like to drain off any syrup or else cut down on the sugar you add.

I N G R E D I E N T S

1 large can or medium fresh papaya / paw-paw

2 bananas

1 wedge watermelon

1 mango

1 zalak, 4 lychees or 1 apple

4 slices pineapple

juice of 1 lime or lemon

1 tablespoon brown sugar

dash of rum +

cream / coconut milk +

+ optional ingredient

NOTE: If using fresh papaya/paw-paw you can serve the salad in the halves of the fruit itself. Otherwise, a glass dish or other bowl will do.

1. Cut the papaya/paw-paw into two halves, remove the seeds and carefully scoop out the flesh using a teaspoon so that the fruit curls into balls.

2. Slice the other fruit into cubes and then arrange all the fruit either in the papaya/paw-paw skins or in a bowl. Sprinkle with lemon or lime juice, sugar and rum if desired. Serve with cream or thick coconut milk ■

Skewered bananas with sauce

Serves 4

The little sweet red-skinned bananas found in Malaysia and Indonesia are very good cooked. They do not travel as well as the thick-skinned large yellow varieties grown in the Caribbean and South America, which is probably why we do not often see them in the West.

Watch out for the chili in this recipe – it's a dessert with a twist for Western palates.

I N G R E D I E N T S

8 small or 4 big bananas, peeled

4 tablespoons lemon or lime juice

1 - 2 tablespoons liquid honey

1 fresh red chili, chopped finely, or 1 teaspoon chili powder *

* The chili is what makes the dish distinctive, but if the idea does not appeal for a dessert, either omit that ingredient or serve the dish to accompany a savory meal such as curry.

1. First, mix all the ingredients together in a bowl, except the bananas.

2. Now thread the bananas lengthwise onto skewers and cook them over a charcoal barbecue or under the broiler/grill, turning constantly so they cook on all sides without burning.

3. Now let the bananas cool a little and then take them from the skewers and dip them into the sauce as you eat them ■

> **IN ALL RECIPES**
> ● **PEPPER AND SALT ARE TO TASTE**
> ● **CHILI AND SUGAR ARE GIVEN AS GUIDE QUANTITIES ONLY. VARY TO TASTE**
> ● **MEASURES FOR BEANS AND GRAINS REFER TO DRY INGREDIENTS.**

SRI LANKA

Vattalappam (Spicy coconut dessert)

Serves 2-4

Coconuts are one of Sri Lanka's main exports. They are also used locally for cooking and for making oil, matting and other products. Fish add to the local diet, and prawns, shrimps, lobsters and *bêche de mer* (sea cucumbers) are also exported.

This is a rich dessert, one to be tried at least once for the fragrance given by the cardamoms.

I N G R E D I E N T S

2 large eggs

2 cups / 470 ml milk

3 tablespoons full-cream milk powder

1/2 cup / 50 g creamed coconut melted in 1/2 cup/ 120 ml hot water

seeds from 3 cardamoms, crushed

1/2 teaspoon ground cinnamon

1/2 teaspoon grated nutmeg

1-2 tablespoons black molasses / treacle

1-2 tablespoons brown sugar

Heat oven to 350°F/180°C/Gas 4

1. Start by beating the eggs lightly in a bowl.

2. Then, using a fresh bowl, mix the milk with the milk powder, add the creamed coconut and then heat in a pan until it is just beginning to boil. Put in the spices and molasses and mix thoroughly.

3. Pour the hot milk mixture into the bowl containing the beaten eggs, stir well, and transfer this to an oven-proof dish.

4. Set the dish in a larger basin containing hot water and then place in the oven for about 1 hour or until the pudding is set.

5. Sprinkle on brown sugar and raise oven heat to crisp the top. Serve warm or cold ■

VIETNAM

Xoi nuoc dir a (Coconut cream and rice dessert)

Serves 4

This recipe uses glutinous rice (which however does not contain gluten), and you can find it in Indian or oriental groceries. Other short-grain and brown varieties could be used instead. Coconut cream is available in blocks from health shops or you can make your own using desiccated coconut (see p. 126).

I N G R E D I E N T S

1 cup / 200 g glutinous/ short-grain rice

1 cup / 100 g creamed coconut mixed in 3 cups/ 700 ml warm water (thin coconut cream)

1/2 cup / 50 g creamed coconut mixed in 1/2 cup/ 120 ml warm water (thick coconut cream)

salt

2 tablespoons sugar

1/2 cup / 120 ml water

1/2 teaspoon ground cinnamon

dash of vanilla essence

1. First, put the rice in pan with the thin coconut cream and a little salt if desired. Cover the pot and cook over a moderate heat until it begins to boil. Then turn down the heat and simmer for about 10-20 minutes depending on the type of rice you are using. If using glutinous rice, it will form a thick paste.

2. Now spoon the rice into a greased 10 inch/25 cm baking tray. Cover it with foil, pierced in two places to let the steam escape. Set the tray over a pan of boiling water and steam it until the rice is firm. Put to one side to cool and then chill in the fridge.

3. Meanwhile, prepare a sauce by dissolving the sugar in the water. Bring to the boil and simmer without stirring until the mixture becomes slightly sticky. Add the cinnamon and vanilla and stir to mix them in. Now remove the sauce from the heat, let it cool and then chill it also.

4. To serve, cut the rice and put it into individual bowls, then spoon on a little sauce and the thick coconut cream ∎

AMERICA

Pone (Cornmeal pan cakes)

Serves 2

Pone, meaning bread made from maize/corn, comes from the North American Algonquin indian language. Corn pones are part of American cooking, and variations turn up in the Caribbean, often with the addition of coconut. You can use white or yellow cornmeal or polenta, and serve the pones with honey, syrup or margarine.

I N G R E D I E N T S

1 cup / 150 g cornmeal

1 teaspoon baking powder

1-2 tablespoons melted margarine

1/2 cup / 120 ml milk

1 tablespoon oil

1. To begin with, mix the cornmeal and baking powder together in a bowl. Then make a well in the center and pour in the melted margarine followed by the milk, adding as much as is necessary to make a smooth but not liquid batter.

2. Now heat a little oil in a heavy pan and drop in the batter using a spoon, shaping it into 4 round flat cakes.

3. Cook on each side for 2 minutes or so until they are browned and then serve straight away with margarine, honey or syrup or plain with a savory dish ∎

BOLIVIA

Pisara

Serves 4

'Quinoa grain is one of Bolivia's staple foods (see p.160) along with maize/corn and *chuño*, the potatoes that are frozen on the *Altiplano* and dried in the sun so that they keep for many months until you need them. As well as using quinoa for porridges and soups, it is turned into desserts too, as in this recipe for *pisara*.' *Alonzo Urquizu, Potosi, Bolivia*

I N G R E D I E N T S

1/2 cup / 110 g quinoa, toasted lightly

2 1/2 cups / 590 ml water

sugar or honey

1. Heat the water in a pan and when it is boiling put in the toasted quinoa. Cover the pan and simmer for about 15 minutes or until all the moisture is taken up.

2. Stir in the sugar or honey to taste and serve at once ∎

157

BRAZIL

Sweet potato pie

Serves 4

Brazil abounds with superlatives: as the largest country in South America; the world's major producer and exporter of coffee and sugar cane; the world's second biggest producer (after the US) of soybeans; and the country that supplies 85 per cent of the world's orange juice. But production of staples like rice, potatoes, beans, cassava/manioc and maize/corn has fallen. Brazil has to import much of its food and fuel and earns another superlative – the biggest debtor country in the region, owing around $92 billion. So about a quarter of the money earned from exports has to be used to repay the debt.

I N G R E D I E N T S

3 cups / 450 g sweet potatoes, cooked and mashed

1 medium can pineapple chunks, drained

1-2 tablespoons melted margarine

1 tablespoon sugar +

3 cloves, crushed or $^1/_2$ teaspoon ground cloves

$^1/_2$ tablespoon lemon juice

$^1/_2$ cup / 50 g breadcrumbs or toasted oats +

+ optional ingredient

Heat oven to 400°F/200°C/Gas 6

1. Mix all the ingredients together in a bowl, saving a few pieces of pineapple for the topping.

2. Now turn the mixture into an ungreased dish or cake tin, sprinkle on the breadcrumbs and decorate with the pieces of pineapple.

3. Bake for about 30 minutes. If using toasted oats, sprinkle these on before serving ∎

CARIBBEAN

Banana bread

One loaf

From the early 16th century for 300 years Africans were taken as slaves to the Caribbean islands to work the sugar plantations. After slavery was abolished Chinese and Indians were brought in as indentured laborers, a form of servitude not unlike slavery.

Farming is the main source of livelihood for ordinary people on the islands, with fruits including mangoes, coconuts, avocados, pawpaw/papaya, guavas, pineapples and bananas.

I N G R E D I E N T S

3 large ripe bananas

$^3/_4$ cup / 175 g margarine

1 cup / 175 g sugar

$1^3/_4$ cups / 225 g flour

pinch of salt

$^1/_2$ teaspoon ground cinnamon +

2 teaspoons baking powder

1 large egg

1 cup / 125 g walnuts, coarsely chopped

1 cup / 100 g raisins or sultanas +

+ optional ingredient

Heat oven to 350°F/180°C/Gas 4

1. Peel the bananas and then mash them, using a large bowl. Then beat in the margarine. When this is combined, shake in the sugar and add the sieved flour, salt, cinnamon and baking powder. Mix this well with a wooden spoon.

2. Now crack the egg and blend it in before adding the chopped walnuts and raisins or sultanas.

3. Grease a 2 pound/1 kg bread or cake tin and spoon in the mixture.

4. Bake the bread for about $1^1/_2$ hours, and test for readiness by pushing a knife or skewer into the middle. It should come out cleanly if the bread is done.

5. Turn out onto a wire rack and leave it to cool completely before serving the cake ∎

Cassava biscuits

Makes 24

The indigenous Arawak and Carib Indians lived by fishing and growing cassava/manioc, yams and sweet potatoes. Spanish conquistadores brought maize/corn, tomatoes and peppers to the islands from South America. With the slaves from Africa came okra or *gumbo*, black-eyed peas, and yam varieties. People from India brought rice, mangoes and foods such as curry.

Cassava or manioc is a common ingredient in the Caribbean, in parts of Africa and South America. The hard dark-brown root has to be peeled and cooked before using, and normally for a recipe like this one the flesh is grated and then wrapped in a cloth and squeezed hard to remove the juice.

INGREDIENTS

2 pounds / 900 g cassava/manioc, peeled

³/₄ cup / 175 g margarine

1 cup / 175 g brown sugar

2 eggs

3 cups / 225 g desiccated coconut

1 teaspoon baking powder

4 teaspoons ground cinnamon

3 cups / 375 g flour

Heat oven to 400°F/200°C/Gas 6

1. First grate the peeled cassava finely. Now place it in the center of a clean cloth or tea towel, draw up the corners and then twist and squeeze it to extract as much juice as possible.

2. After this, take a large bowl and cream together the margarine and sugar. Then add the eggs, grated cassava and coconut and mix them well.

3. Sieve in the baking powder, cinnamon and the flour, adding enough of this to make a stiff dough.

4. Now take the dough from the bowl and knead it for at least 5 minutes.

5. Roll it out on a floured surface to ¹/₂ inch/1 cm thickness and cut into biscuit shapes with a cutter or into other shapes with a knife.

6. Put the biscuits on baking sheets, about 2 inches/5 cms apart and bake them for 15-20 minutes until they are golden brown ∎

Ginger beer

Makes approx. 1 quart/1 liter

Ginger is used 'to gain the affection of a woman' in the Melanesian islands, and presumably it works on men as well since it has a long history as an aphrodisiac and sexual cure-all in many countries. Here's a recipe that may 'ginger up' proceedings …

INGREDIENTS

1 large fresh ginger root, peeled and grated

4 sticks cinnamon

4 cloves

1¹/₂ cups / 260 g sugar

2 lemons or limes

4 cups / 940 ml water

1. Put the ginger into a pan and add the cinnamon, cloves, sugar, juice and zest/thinly pared skin of the lemons or limes. Pour in the water.

2. Bring this to the boil, stirring all the time, and allow it to continue boiling for 10 minutes.

3. When this is done, strain the liquid into a pitcher/jug and allow it to cool. Test the flavor, adding more water lemon or lime juice, or sugar as required.

4. Chill, and then serve with ice cubes and slices of lime or lemon on top ∎

159

OTHER STAPLE FOODS

Many regions of the world have staple foods which are really only eaten locally, such as teff grain in Ethiopia, barley in Tibet or sago in parts of Malaysia and Indonesia.

Other carbohydrate-rich crops are used as secondary and additional staples, for example sweet potatoes or the group of corms known as aroids.

Of these additional staples, *barley* is cultivated on a wide scale, but mainly now as animal feed in the West. It is a classic subsistence crop, needing little human input and tolerating high altitudes and cold wet weather. In Tibet it is made into **tsampa** (porridge) and also fermented into wine. Barley is the starch to accompany meat dishes in some Middle Eastern countries, while in Colombia it is tipped into soups to thicken them and impart flavor.

Teff, which was developed from millet-type grasses many thousands of years ago, is now only grown as a grain for

people in Ethiopia where it is the major cereal. It is grown also in South Africa and Kenya as a hay crop. Usually teff is ground into a brownish flour and made into pancakes called *ingera*.

Two cereal grains which are important locally, but little known outside their region, are quinoa and amaranth. Called 'the grain that grows where grass will not', *quinoa* is a herb cultivated in the Andes mountains of South America. Its tasty grains are packed with protein. It is made into bread, porridge and biscuits and also fermented into the drink, **chicha**. Cultivation of quinoa is beginning to reach outside Latin America, with some growing in the Rocky Mountains area of North America.

Amaranth's name comes from the Greek meaning immortal, and even 1,000-year-old seeds have been known to sprout. In Mexico in Aztec times, amaranth was a vital part of their cultural and religious practices. Spanish conquistador Cortez recognized how significant it was and ordered amaranth field to be burnt as a way of undermining Aztec morale, and of course depriving them of food. As well as having high food value, amaranth thrives in virtually any conditions.

In Papua New Guinea, eastern Malaysia and Thailand the *sago* palm is cultivated for food. The stems of the palm contain a starchy pith which is washed before preparation as food. Sago grains (and tapioca which comes from cassava) were sent to Britain from its former colony, Malaya, as a cereal used in milk puddings.

Taros (Eddo, Dasheen or 'old' Cocoyam) and *Tannia* (Yautia and 'new' Cocoyam) are aroids, corm, which are eaten by many people in tropical regions. The taros are native to India and Southeast Asia while the tannias come from America. They are cooked in the same way as sweet potatoes.

Sweet potatoes are grown widely in tropical Third World countries, usually alongside rice, taro and yams. They originated in South America but are now popular in China, Indonesia, Vietnam, Japan, India, Philippines, Rwanda, South Korea, Uganda and Brazil. Cooked in the same way as 'Irish' potatoes, they can also be used to make desserts and sweets.

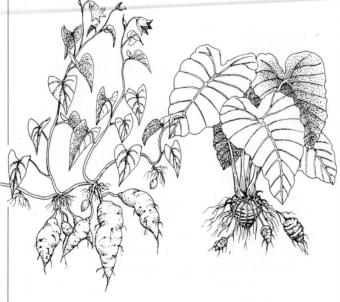

Illustration: Steve Weston

CARIBBEAN

Passion fruit/granadilla juice

Makes 1¹/₂ cups

Passion fruits are native to South America and may have acquired their name from the Jesuit missionaries' habit of illustrating the Christian Passion (Jesus' death on the cross) to local indians by analogy to the passion flower – petals and stamens representing the apostles; the style the nails; stamens, wounds; filaments, the crown of thorns. That apart, this juice makes a tasty base for flavoring drinks and fruit salads.

I N G R E D I E N T S

12 passion fruits/
granadillas

1 cup / 240 ml water

juice of 2 lemons or limes

sugar

1. Cut the passion fruits/granadillas in half and scrape the pulp and seeds into a pan. Add the water and bring to simmering point.

2. Cool and add the lemon juice and sugar. Chill the drink before using ∎

Sweet potato dessert

Serves 6-8

Although Creole cooking is often associated with the Deep South of the US, it is also popular in the Caribbean. The cuisine is based on the combining of the dishes of French and Spanish slave-owners with those of the slaves from Africa.

This dessert however could well have been influenced by the British (who were also slave-owners of course), with their love of sweet puddings.

I N G R E D I E N T S

3 cups / 450 g sweet
potatoes, cooked and
mashed

2 tablespoons margarine

¹/₂ cup / 85 g sugar

2 eggs, beaten

3 tablespoons milk

+ optional ingredient

grated rind and juice of 1
lemon

1 teaspoon allspice or
ground cinnamon

1 teaspoon baking powder

a little desiccated coconut +

cream +

Heat oven to 350°F/180°C/Gas 4

1. To begin, put all the ingredients except the desiccated coconut and cream into a bowl and mix well.

2. Then spoon the mixture into a greased baking tin or oven-proof dish, smoothing down the top. Cook for about 40 minutes and then remove it from the oven. Cool and then sprinkle on some desiccated coconut and serve with cream if liked ∎

GUATEMALA

Baked bananas

Serves 4

Guatemala, like many Third World countries, is dependent on selling its cash crops (coffee, cotton, bananas, cardamom, sugar) to earn foreign exchange. And when the price for those goods falls, the country cannot buy what it needs – often including the food it does not grow itself because land and resources have been taken up by crops for export.

I N G R E D I E N T S

4 large bananas

1 tablespoon margarine

2 tablespoons honey

juice of 1 lemon

small carton soured cream
or plain yogurt

1 cup / 125 g nuts
(cashews or walnuts or a
mixture of both) +

1/2 cup / 100 g raisins or
sultanas +

+ optional ingredient

Heat oven to 350°F/180°C/Gas 4

1. Peel the bananas and cut them in half, lengthwise. Place them in a greased baking dish and dot with the margarine.

2. Then mix the honey and lemon juice together and spread this over the bananas. Put the dish in the oven and bake for 10-20 minutes. Serve hot with soured cream or yogurt and nuts and dried fruit ■

IRAQ

Halawah Temar (Date Halva)

Makes 12-15 pieces

Helweh is an Arabic word for sweet and from it comes halawah or halva, the name of a popular dessert. Some are made with semolina while others, like the recipe below, just use fruit and nuts. Iraq is one of the world's biggest exporters of dates; its other main crops grown for food are barley and wheat.

I N G R E D I E N T S

2 cups / 200 g dates, stoned
and finely chopped *

1/2 cup / 60 g walnuts,
chopped

1/2 cup / 60 g almonds,
chopped

a little icing sugar

* Fresh dates are best if you can get them, and if they are not too expensive. Otherwise, use boxed dates but wash them a little first to rinse off some of the sweetness.

1. Begin by mixing the dates and nuts in a bowl to compact them.

2. Now sprinkle some icing sugar onto a board and roll the date mixture into a cylinder shape with your hands. Then simply cut it into small pieces and serve ■

MIDDLE EAST

Apple and almond dessert

Serves 4

Apricots, used here, originated in China along with peaches and they are now grown across the whole temperate zone from China through India and Iran to the Mediterranean countries.

INGREDIENTS

4 large cooking apples, peeled, cored and chopped

a little water

1 tablespoon sugar

1/4 cup / 50 g ground almonds

1/4 cup / 25 g raisins or sultanas, soaked in water for one hour

1/2 cup / 50 g dried apricots, soaked in water for one hour and chopped into small pieces

1/2 cup / 60 g whole almonds

Heat oven to 325°F/160°C/Gas 3 – if serving hot: see 4 below

1. First of all, put the apples into a saucepan with a little water. Bring to the boil and then reduce the heat and simmer until the apples are very soft. Some varieties of apple will purée themselves while cooking and this is fine for this dish.

2. Next mash the apples with a spoon adding sugar as required. Then add the ground almonds and mix well.

3. Scatter the raisins or sultanas, apricots and whole almonds over the surface.

4. Put into the oven for 10 minutes, or serve warm as it is. The dish can also be chilled and served cold ∎

Halva with almonds

Serves 2-4

At one time *halva* was made with rice. Nowadays, semolina tends to be the basic ingredient; it comes from the roughly-milled nutritive tissue of the durum or 'hard' wheat type. This variety, used today for making pasta, was one of the earliest cultivated wheats. It may well have been the *kussemet* mentioned in the Bible when the Israelites are told to take 'golden wheat, barley and beans and make bread thereof'.

INGREDIENTS

1/2 cup / 85 g sugar

1 1/4 cups / 300 ml water

8 tablespoons / 100 g margarine

1/2 cup / 125 g semolina

1/2 cup / 50 g raisins or dates, chopped

1/2 cup / 60 g almonds, chopped

1/2 teaspoon ground cinnamon

seeds from 1 cardamom pod, crushed

1. Cook the sugar and water together over a medium heat until they make a syrup.

2. In another pan, melt the margarine and brown the semolina in it. Then put in the raisins or dates, almonds, cinnamon and cardamom and stir well.

3. Now pour the syrup into the pan containing the semolina mix, stir it in and let it cook for 3-4 minutes. Spoon the dessert into a shallow dish and serve cold cut into squares ∎

163

MIDDLE EAST

Khoshaf (Dried fruit salad)

Serves 4

The world population of date palms is put at around 93 million trees, found in oases and other parts of the Middle East. Iraq, Iran and Egypt are the leading producers of dates which are a staple food for many Arab people. Making this fruit salad a few hours before it is needed improves the flavor.

INGREDIENTS

1 cup / 100 g dried apricots

1 cup / 100 g dried prunes

1 cup / 100 g dried figs or dates

1/2 cup / 50 g raisins or sultanas

1/2 cup / 60 g almonds or pine nuts / pignoles

1/2 cup / 120 ml cold tea

1 cup / 240 ml orange juice

1. Soak the fruit for 1 hour in the tea and orange juice (the liquid should just cover the fruit; add more or less as required).

2. To serve, place the softened fruit and liquid into a bowl and sprinkle the nuts over. Then you can either serve it as it is, cold, or put it into a gentle oven for 20-30 minutes and serve warm ■

(Opposite) Pick of the crop – fruit stall in Sri Lanka.
Photo: Hugh Sitton/Tony Stone Worldwide

Muhallabia (Rice and almond dessert)

Serves 2-4

Orange-blossom water or rose-water together with the almonds give *muhallabia* a delicate flavor. The scented water is available from Middle Eastern or Indian stores and other specialist groceries. If you cannot find them, then use a little vanilla essence instead.

INGREDIENTS

1/4 cup / 50 g ground rice

2 1/2 cups / 590 ml milk

2 tablespoons rose-water or orange-blossom water

1/4 cup / 50 g sugar

1/4 cup / 50 g ground almonds

1/2 tablespoon almonds, sliced lengthwise

1/2 tablespoon unsalted, shelled pistachios, chopped

1. Put the ground rice into a large bowl and gradually pour in about 1/2 cup/120 ml of the milk, stirring all the time to make a smooth paste.

2. Now bring the rest of the milk to boiling point in a saucepan. Then blend it into the rice mixture, stirring thoroughly so that it remains smooth.

3. After that, pour the mixture back into the pan. Heat and stir until it begins to boil and thicken. Now spoon in the orange-blossom water or rose-water and cook for a further minute, before adding the ground almonds. Stir and mix well and then pour into a serving dish. Decorate with the sliced almonds and pistachios and chill before eating ■

TURKEY

Kibrizli cake (Semolina cake)

Serves 6-8

Semolina, made from hard or durum wheat, is almost exclusively used for making pasta. But in Britain until recently semolina was most commonly served up as a milk pudding considered wholesome for children and topped with a spoonful of jam. For those who do not wish to be reminded of milk puddings, this cake is a pleasant way to use semolina.

INGREDIENTS

¹/₂ cup / 125 g semolina

5 eggs

1 cup / 175 g sugar

grated rind and juice of 1 lemon

¹/₂ cup / 125 g ground almonds

¹/₄ teaspoon baking powder

²/₃ cup / 150 ml water

a little salt

1 tablespoon sesame seeds

2 tablespoons honey

Heat oven to 350°F/180°C/Gas 4

1. First, lightly grease a deep 8 inch/20 cm cake tin and line it with waxed/greaseproof paper.

2. Now crack the eggs and separate the whites into a large bowl, putting the yolks in another.

3. Add the sugar and lemon rind (save the juice for the glaze, see step 7) to the egg yolks and beat them together until the mixture is a pale color.

4. Now put in the semolina, ground almonds, baking powder and water and mix till smooth.

5. Add the salt to the egg whites and whisk them till they are becoming firm. Then, using a metal spoon, fold them into the yolk mixture and pour this into the cake tin.

6. Sprinkle the sesame seeds on top and bake the cake in the centre of the oven for about 40-45 minutes until the cake is firm to the touch.

7. Just before the cake is cooked, warm the honey in a small saucepan and then boil it hard for 4 minutes. Remove from the heat and stir in the lemon juice.

8. When the cake is ready, spoon the warm syrup over it while it is still hot and in the tin. Allow the cake to cool and then loosen it carefully before turning out ∎

Honeyed coriander tea

1 cup

Coriander seeds, used here in their ground form, taste very different from fresh cilantro/coriander leaves. The ground coriander has a lemony flavor with a slight caraway or aniseed tang. This is an easy-to-make, caffeine-free tea …

INGREDIENTS

¹/₂ teaspoon ground coriander

1-2 teaspoons honey

1. Mix the coriander with the honey in a mug and then pour on boiling water.

2. Stir well and then strain the mixture or allow it to settle before drinking ∎

Spiced tea

Serves 4

Spiced teas are popular in this region and make a pleasant alternative to regular tea. Anise, which is used here, is native to the Middle East. Its licorice flavor is used in alcoholic drinks in many countries – in French aperitifs, Turkish *raki* and in Latin American *aguardiente*.

INGREDIENTS

2 inch / 5 cm fresh ginger root, peeled and sliced

2 teaspoons cumin seeds

4 cloves

2 cinnamon sticks

1 tablespoon anise or caraway seeds

4 whole almonds or 8 pignoles / pine nuts

1. Using enough water to make four cups of tea, gently boil all the ingredients except the nuts for about 5 minutes.

2. Divide the nuts into each cup. Strain and pour on the hot tea ∎

Spices from India. *Photo by: Annal/Camera Press.*

Glossary

GLOSSARY

Amaranth see Staple Food p.160

Allspice
Named because it combines the flavor of several spices (cinnamon, cloves and nutmeg), allspice comes from the dried unripe berries of a small evergreen tree belonging to the myrtle family and native to tropical America. Most allspice is grown in Jamaica.

Arrowroot
Arrowroot powder, used as a thickening agent, is preferred to cornstarch/cornflour as it imparts less flavor. Its starch is easy to digest, making it good invalid food. The name may have come from the Arucu indian name for it, *aru* root. It is grown in tropical regions, and the main producer is St Vincent island in the Caribbean.

Bananas see Staple Food p.76

Barley see Staple Food p.160

Bean-curd/tofu
Made from soybeans that have been cooked and puréed, then solidified into curds by the addition of vinegar and epsom salts, fresh bean-curd/tofu is white and custardlike and packed with protein. There are also smoked and fermented varieties.

Bulgur and cracked wheat
These are similar, both coming from wheat grains and both being very nutritious, but they are not the same. Both are staples in the Middle East. Bulgur is wheat that has been steamed and then dried before grinding whereas cracked wheat is uncooked wheat which has been dried and then cracked.

Cassava see Staple Food p.118

Cashewnuts
These grew originally in tropical America and were transplanted in Asia and Africa by the Portuguese and Spanish. The nuts grow on trees and make a curious sight as they hang from the bottom of the cashew 'apple'. After picking the nuts are roasted and then shelled by hand, a tedious process made worse as the shells contain an irritant. Kerala state in India, Mozambique and Tanzania are the main producers.

Cardamom
Cardamoms are the dried fruits of a herb related to the ginger family found in India and Sri Lanka. The spice is usually sold in pods which contain clusters of seeds. Cardamom's sweet pungency makes it popular for flavoring curries and desserts.

Cayenne pepper
This comes from two varieties of powdered dried chilis, and its name derives from a Brazilian Tupi indian word *quiynha*.

Chilis and peppers
The Americas' most important contribution to the world's spices, chili peppers, together with cayenne, tabasco, paprika and sweet or bell peppers come from the pod-like berry of various species of capsicum. Their spicy hotness arises from *capsaican* occurring in varying degrees in the different types. They were called 'pepper' because Columbus was looking for that spice when he reached what he thought was the East Indies (the Caribbean). When taken by the Europeans to Africa, India and Asia in the 16th century, chilis overtook regular pepper as the main condiment there.

Cilantro/coriander
The leaves and seeds of this plant are widely used in the Middle East (where it originated), Mexico, parts of Africa and Asia. The leaves resemble parsley and impart a strong flavor, while the seeds are mild and aromatic. The word coriander comes from the Greek for 'bug' referring either to the small bug-like seed, or to the fetid odor given off by the leaves.

Cinnamon
Cinnamon, used in curry powder and to flavor desserts, comes from the peeled bark of an evergreen tree native to Sri Lanka. For the best flavor, buy it in its curled stick form. Cassia is often sold as cinnamon; it comes from Vietnam and has a stronger flavor.

Cloves
Cloves are the dried flowerbuds of an Indonesian evergreen. Their export was a Dutch monopoly until plants were smuggled out in the 18th century, when Zanzibar and Pemba islands off East Africa became the leading producers.

Coconut and coconut milk
Originating in Southeast Asia, coconut palms provide leaves for roofing; coir (outer husk of the coconut) for matting; copra (the dried white flesh) used for cooking oil, soap, margarine and animal feed; the trees also give timber and shade; the coconuts give food, drink and alcoholic 'toddy'. The Philippines is the largest producer of copra. Coconut milk is an important part of tropical cooking.

Coriander see cilantro

Corn see Staple Food p.100

Cumin
Cumin or *jeera* is native to the eastern Mediterranean, but it has been cultivated also for a long time in India and China. It comes from the dried fruit of a plant related to the parsley family. Either the whole seeds or the ground spice is used.

Curry leaves
The Tamil word for seasoned sauce is 'kari' from which we get 'curry'. Curry leaves, from India and Sri Lanka, look like small bay leaves and when

crushed release a curry fragrance. In the West usually only the dried leaves are found. Indonesian bay leaves, *daun salaam* can be substituted, or use curry powder instead.

Curry powder
A combination of spices which should be cooked in a little oil to bring out the full flavor, curry powder usually includes turmeric, coriander seeds, black peppercorns, cloves, cumin seeds, cardamom, nutmeg, mace, cinnamon, ginger, chilis or cayenne powder, fenugreek, garlic, and mustard oil. Try mixing your own.

Dill
Dill comes from the Middle East and its anti-flatulence properties have ensured its popularity. Its pungent seeds are used as a pickling spice and for flavoring some Indian dishes. The milder feathery leaves are also used for aroma and decoration.

Fennel
Originating in southern Europe, fennel resembles dill in appearance. Its licorice-flavored seeds are an important spice, while the more delicately flavored leaves are used as a herb. The vegetable variety (Florence or Roman fennel) has aniseed-flavored leaf stalks which are good in salads.

Fenugreek
Native of the Mediterranean, fenugreek is related to clover. The plant is used as a vegetable while the seeds can spice curries.

Fish sauce and fish paste
This sauce is a thin salty liquid made from dried, fermented fish which adds a hint of seafood. Fish pastes are also used especially shrimp paste or *blachan* in Malaysia; their strong smell disappears on cooking.

Garam masala
A mix of spices ground to produce an aromatic flavoring for Indian foods, garam masala may include black pepper, coriander, cumin, cardamom, nutmeg, cloves and cinnamon. It is aromatic rather than hot.

Ghee
Many Indian dishes call for ghee or clarified butter, which is made by gently heating butter to produce a clear liquid. This does not burn when frying, and as it has no milk solids it does not turn rancid. It is a saturated fat and you may prefer to substitute an unsaturated margarine or cooking oil.

Ginger
The knobbly ginger rhizome comes from Southeast Asia and is a popular ingredient there. The fresh 'root' is crunchy and strong in flavor. Dried ginger root and ground ginger do not have the same pungency.

Granadillas see Passion fruit.

Kefalotiri cheese
A hard Greek cheese used for grating, kefalotiri is shaped like a head. Its name comes from the Greek word *kefali* (Latin *cephalo*) meaning head. Parmesan cheese can be substituted.

Lemon grass
A lemon-flavored thick-stemmed grass that is widely used in Southeast Asia, lemon grass is often combined with the flavors of coconut, chili and ginger. Fresh lemon grass can sometimes be found, but it is more commonly available as dried in the West, from oriental stores.

Macadamia (Queensland) nut
This is originally from the tropical part of northeast Australia but it is now grown in Africa, South America and Hawaii which is the largest exporter. It is named after Dr MacAdam who introduced it to Europeans.

Maize see Staple Food p.100

Millet see Staple Food p.50

Miso
A fermented soybean paste used as a seasoning and soup base. 'White' miso is made with the addition of rice while 'red' miso incorporates barley and has a stronger flavor.

Molassses
Molasses is a by-product of sugar-cane refining and comes in differing strengths according to whether it is the first boiling (light), the second (darker) or the third (blackstrap). It is used to sweeten dishes such as Boston baked beans and to pour over pancakes.

Monosodium glutamate(MSG)
The Chinese name for this, *wei ching* means 'essence of taste'. The white crystals, extracted from grains such as corn/maize, and vegetables, have no special flavor of their own; they are meant to enhance the taste of the dish they are added to. MSG is an unnecessary additive and has been linked to unpleasant side-effects such as dizziness; it is a sodium-related (salt) item.

Nutmeg and mace
These are both part of the same fruit of a tree native to the Molucca Islands in Indonesia. Mace is the delicately-flavored red lacy covering encasing the stronger aromatic nutmeg seed. The main producers are Indonesia and Grenada.

Okra
One of Africa's indigenous vegetables and related to the cotton plant, okra travelled to the West Indies with the slave ships. Other names for the dark green pointed pod include *gumbo, bhindi* and *lady's fingers*. When cooked, they become glutinous and help thicken soups and stews.

Oyster sauce
A Cantonese seasoning, oyster sauce is a flavor enhancer and adds body to dishes. It is made from ground oysters, soy sauce and brine but does not impart a fishy flavor.

Orange blossom water and rose water
These essences, made from distilling fresh orange blossoms or rose petals, are used widely in the Middle East and India to flavor drinks and desserts also.

169

Paprika see chili peppers

Papaya or paw-paw
The papaya tree originated in tropical America and is now found in most tropical regions. The fruits resemble melons, with a cluster of black seeds in the middle. The leaves, latex from the fruit's skin and the fruit itself are used to tenderise meat, but mostly papaya is eaten as a fruit with a squeeze of lime.

Passion fruits or granadillas
Passion fruits grow on climbing plants found in South America. The flowers are used as a sedative while the fruits are eaten raw or used in ice-cream and fruit juice. One explanation of the name is that the Jesuit missionaries used the plant to illustrate the story of Jesus' death on the cross to the indians.

Peanuts (groundnuts)
These 'nuts' are really legumes and grow as subterranean pods. Peanuts originated in South America and were taken to West Africa. They are now grown more widely in Africa than the indigenous Bambara groundnut. China and India are the biggest peanut producers with Nigeria exporting the most.

Pepper
Pepper, whose vines grow wild on the Malabar coast of south India, has been the most important spice in the world; the stimulus of risky sea-voyages, pirating and bloodshed by Arabs, Romans Portuguese, Dutch and British. Originally pepper was used in India to add pungency to curry powders — a

function now mainly served by chilis which arrived from South America in the 16th century. Today it is mainly grown in Asia, with India the largest exporter. White and black pepper are made from the same peppercorns but treated differently before grinding. For black pepper, unripe peppercorns are dried in the sun. White pepper results from soaking ripe peppercorns and removing the outer casing.

Pine nuts or pignoles
There are two main types of pine nut, the Mediterranean and the Chinese, the former being the more delicately flavored. These are the seeds from the cones of the umbrella-shaped Portuguese or stone pine tree. The nuts are eaten raw or roasted, and they are also used in confectionary especially in the Middle East.

Pistachios
These nuts grow on a small tree found in Central Asia. The green kernels are prized for their decorative color and fragrant flavor. They are eaten salted like peanuts, or

incorporated into nougat and ice-cream. Turkey, Iran and the US are major producers.

Potatoes see Staple Food p.14

Pulses — beans, peas and lentils
Of the pulses used in this book, black beans, broad beans, haricot, lima or butter beans, pink, pinto, and red kidney beans all originated in South America. Lentils are from the Mediterranean; black-eyed beans and cowpeas from Africa; pigeon peas from Africa or India; soybeans from China; chickpeas (garbanzos) and mung beans (green gram) from India and ful medames from Egypt.

Quinoa see Staple Food p.160

Rice see Staple Food p. 88

Saffron
The most expensive spice in the world comes from the dried style of a crocus — it takes 80,000 flowers to yield one pound/454 g of the spice. The best saffron comes from Spain, Turkey and India, adding delicate fragrance and vivid color to rice dishes. A Mexican variety, *azafran*, comes from safflower — grown for its seeds which are made into oil.

Sorghum see Staple Food p. 32

Sesame seeds and tahina
Sesame seeds are rich in calcium and protein. In the Middle East the uncooked seeds are turned into a thick paste, tahina, which flavors the chickpea dip, hummus.

Soy sauce and Tamari
Made from fermented soybeans and wheat or barley, yeast and salt, the fragrant brown liquid comes as 'light' and 'dark' types. The dark one is enriched with caramel or molasses. As well as its use in Asian cookery, it is an excellent marinade ingredient for beef. Tamari is a mellow version.

Sumak
Sumak is a purple-red powder and comes from the dried berries of a bush related to the cashew family. Lemon juice can be used instead.

Sweet potato see Staple Food p.160

Tabasco see chili peppers

Tahina see sesame seeds

Tannias and Taros see Staple Food p.160

Teff see Staple Food p.160

Turmeric
Native to Southeast Asia, turmeric is a rhizome of the ginger family with a musty flavor and yellow coloring effect and for this purpose it is a cheaper option than saffron.

Vanilla
Vanilla comes from the pods of an orchid plant found in the Caribbean and Central America. Madagascar is the main producer.

Wheat see Staple Food p.142

Yams see Staple Food p.160

See also Notes to the Recipes p.7, and introductions to individual recipes.

Boy grinding spices in Benin. *Photo by: Claude Sauvageot.*

A HISTORY OF FOOD

A HISTORY OF FOOD

About 12,000 years ago there was a revolution, without war, without bloodshed, which altered the way people obtained their food. After years of roaming, foraging and hunting, groups began to settle in one place secure in the knowledge that they would have enough to eat. It was almost certainly women, the gatherers of berries and seeds while men hunted, who realized that plant-growing was not completely haphazard, that there was a connection between putting seeds into the ground and harvesting the grains given the right weather, luck or a deity's will . . .

This realization likely came first in the Middle East — and somewhat later in India, China and Central America. Techniques for improvement in agriculture soon abounded. One of the first was irrigation — channelling water from a stream or river to nourish crops. Then, as food production became more reliable, settlements expanded into cities.

Each region had its staple crop; in some cases this has remained unchanged to the present day. The earliest crops of all, in the Middle East, were hairy precursors of modern wheat

and barley; while in what is now Mexico around 7,000 years ago people had begun to cultivate the foods that still sustain them — corn, beans and squash. Further south, in the Andes, potatoes were already popular. In China the basic grain was millet in the North and rice in the South, while in Africa millet grew in the Sahara, then lightly wooded, with red rice in the great bend of the Niger River.

The domestication of animals began at about the same time as settled agriculture. Dogs had been the only animals tamed by humans in the Old Stone Age but now there followed sheep, goats and eventually cattle. In ancient China pigs were found in every hut; they were so common that the word for meat is synonymous with pig.

The Sumerians, who formed the first great civilization some 5,000 years ago, had a very varied diet. It included wheat, barley, millet, chickpeas, lentils, beans, garlic, leeks, cucumbers, cress, mustard and lettuce; goat, mutton and pork, with some beef for the rich. There were even fried-fish vendors in Ur of the Chaldees where Abraham was born. And to wash down the food, what better than barley ale? Most of the brewers were women, and nearly half of the Sumerians' grain yield went into ale. It was the main drink: for water was often contaminated and as yet there was no tea, coffee or wine.

Bread-making probably began in Egypt where bakeries existed over 4,000 years ago. At one time there were 40 different kinds of bread, some using honey, milk or eggs. The process of leavening — making the bread rise — was probably discovered when somebody tipped in beer instead of water to mix the flour and yeast began its work. Again, the Egyptian diet was varied (for the rich at least) including quail, fish, wild celery, mullet, eel and pork. Pork was not outlawed in the Near East until after 1800 BC when the latest wave of nomadic invaders decided that they preferred herdable sheep and cattle to the unruly non-grass-eating pig — the ban on pork thus found its way into Judaism and later into Islam.

The Greeks did not have much land for pasturing cattle. Families would grow a little barley or wheat, olives and figs and rear pigs and goats. Barley was the mainstay for rich and poor, the 'strong grain' fed to soldiers. It was the food of

Roman gladiators too, who were called *hordearii* or 'barley-men' because they ate so much of it in their training.

Often stretched to the limits to feed its large urban population, Rome imported wheat from Egypt and North Africa. Distributing free bread — *annona* — was the Roman response to its urban poverty. At the height of the Roman Empire, one in three Roman citizens was dependent on this food. But the rich ate well, developing their taste for the spices that Arab traders were already beginning to bring to the Mediterranean.

Pepper was the foremost spice for food, highly prized and expensive. Cinnamon from Malaya and the Spice Islands (the Moluccas and Indonesia) was carried to Madagascar and then up the east coast of Africa to the Red Sea. Traders carried ginger and cassia (similar to cinnamon) from China to markets at the mouth of the Ganges for on-shipment to India and the West. To try and break the Arab grip on this trade, Rome sent its ships and soldiers to India, trading gold for pepper in Malabar.

Meanwhile, with this range of food and spices in many parts of the world that are poor today, what was happening in northern Europe?

The average rural diet there would have been founded on bread and porridge, enlivened by nettles, cress and thistles together with roots like carrot, leek, turnip and onion. The lowly Briton or Gaul may have cast envious eyes at the sophisticated foods eaten by their Roman overlords, but their own basic diet was both nutritious and balanced.

Almost all traditional cultures found foods that blended together in a wholesome way. The rice and pulses of Asia; the corn and beans of Africa and the Americas; the wheat and dairy products of the Middle East: all complement and enhance each others' protein to produce a nutritional balance that is hard to beat. In addition, these 'twinned' foods tend to be healthy for the environment: beans, for instance, are planted between rows of corn and fix nitrogen back into the soil to nourish that cereal.

In nearly all regions and cultures most people gained their protein from pulses and grains. Meat was a rarity for high-days and holidays.

Plunder and plantations

From the beginnings of settled agriculture there had been trade in food — usually in spices that enhanced the taste of a diet rather than in the basic foodstuffs themselves. But it was

Illustration: Bill Sanderson

not until Europeans from the fifteenth century onward started to make use of their new shipbuilding technology and explore to the West, South and East that there was any major change to the patterns of world agriculture.

When Europeans first reached China they were astonished to find how advanced it was, both industrially and agriculturally. Farmers worked with plows and tools made of steel; fertilizers were used, seeds were selectively bred, irrigation and water control was sophisticated. As the world's most industrialized country at the time, China had developed printing which enabled literate officials to disseminate new techniques in agriculture throughout the empire.

In Central and South America the first Europeans were similarly stunned by the advanced states they found there. Tenochtitlan, now Mexico City, had a population of around 150,000 which was twice the size of Spain's then largest city, Seville. The Aztecs in Central America and the Inca in the Andes had well-developed political, legal, social and economic systems. The Spanish marveled at their engineering feats that had produced sophisticated terracing and irrigation.

As in China, it was these productive agricultural systems which made possible the establishment of cities, handicrafts and class societies. In Aztec Mexico, for instance, production of food only required about two months' intermittent work in the season, releasing labor for other projects. Corn or maize was the main staple but there was also *amaranth* (a grain), beans, squash, tomatoes, onions, peppers and fruit. Animal protein came from fish, turkey, duck and dog. The Inca people meanwhile grew corn and chili peppers, potatoes and *quinoa* grain, along with a wide range of fruit and vegetables. Plant breeding, seed selection and hybridization (creating new plants) were well developed and guano (bird manure) was used as fertilizer.

Not surprisingly, the Spanish believed they had found paradise: at this time (the early sixteenth century) people in Europe regularly suffered from lack of food.

These civilizations were not paradises in social terms. Land was communally owned but, as everywhere else, there were very rich and very poor. Hierarchical class systems forced ordinary people to labor for and pay tribute to their rulers. But for all the undoubted repression the elite needed the poor to grow food, to build cities and to fight in the army. So it was in the interest of the rulers that people were fed adequately.

The Europeans had different priorities. Their cultural base was thousands of miles away. Their religion was Christianity. Their imperative was to transfer wealth to their own countries. Here's how Christopher Colombus put it: *'Of gold is treasure made, and with it he* (sic) *who has it does as he* (sic) *wills in the world.'*

Thus local food crops were displaced by crops that suited European needs and palates. The conquest of the Inca spelled the end of their agricultural systems; and formerly fruitful land became desert. More tragically still, the Spanish passed on diseases that were hitherto unknown in the Americas - epidemics wiped out whole communities, killing so many adults that fields went untilled and famines resulted. Between 1500 and 1650 over two-thirds of Latin America's native people had been killed by disease, slaughter or forced labor in the silver mines.

In Brazil, mining was not yet an option to the Portuguese who began to settle there in the mid-sixteenth century. On the other hand, the prospects for growing sugar cane were promising, except for a lack of local slaves to do the work. And so Portugal cast its eyes to Africa. Armed with Pope Nicholas V's authority to 'attack, subject and reduce to perpetual slavery the Saracens, pagans and other enemies of Christ southward from Capes Badajor and Non, including all the coast of Guinea (West Africa).'

The Portuguese began to ship out slaves to Brazil to work on the sugar plantations. Over the next 300 years, as the Dutch, British and French followed Portugal's example, between 10 and 12 million Africans were transported to South America and the Caribbean.

The global spread of plants

The 'triangular trade' of slaves to the Americas, sugar to Europe and manufactured goods to Africa was lucrative. And the enforced movement of people from continent to continent went hand in hand with a spread of plants beyond their traditional growing regions. The cocoyams and plantains found in the Caribbean today came with the slaves from Africa. In the opposite direction, from South America, corn and peanut plants were carried by the Portuguese to West Africa and grown there to provision the slave ships. Rubber trees, sisal, tobacco and cocoa were other New World crops replanted in African soil by the Portuguese and later conveyed by them, the Dutch and British to what are now Malaysia and Indonesia.

Sugar became increasingly important in Europe as supplies of honey, the traditional sweetener, dwindled — the main bee-keepers had been monasteries which were now being closed in Protestant kingdoms following the Reformation. Sugar's popularity grew when its preservative

Photo: Peter Stalker

qualities were recognized for jam-making, and it later married happily with tea and coffee, the booming beverages of Europe. By the 1670s sugar was so sought after for trade that the Dutch were prepared to give up New York to the British in exchange for the sugar lands of Surinam.

But concentrating on sugar-growing meant that soon both Brazil and the Caribbean islands became dependent on imported food: Britain sent bacon, salt pork and tripe; from Newfoundland came salted cod. The same thing happened on the Indonesian island of Java. There Dutch entrepreneurs grabbed land and forced peasants to grow sugar and coffee — where taxes failed to persuade the peasants to contribute to the export crops, corporal punishment normally succeeded. The result was devastation. When the first Europeans arrived, in the sixteenth century, reports showed little sign of poverty in the islands. There was a good system of health care and no evidence of hunger. They had a stable agricultural base, mainly growing rice, indigo, timber and spices.

By 1860 Indonesia's picture of health had altered irrevocably. With less land available for food, there were rice shortages and famines, followed by epidemics as people's health declined. As in other colonies around the world, the wealth from agriculture was transferred to the European power for its own economic development. The Dutch at least were open in acknowledging this — that the colonies existed to enrich the mother country — not for them the 'white man's burden' apology.

In Africa by contrast, in the late nineteenth century, the idea of the 'white man's burden' was called up to justify just about everything. Unlike South America and Asia, this continent was not endowed with rich and fertile earth. There was plenty of land however. To adapt to these realities, people hunted and gathered, or herded animals for their livelihood. Where there was cultivation, it was the shifting sort, which does not make great demands on fragile soil.

Knowing the limitations of their land, African women and men rarely outgrew its ability to support them. Sorghum, bulrush millet and finger millet were grown, plants which can tolerate dry soils and light rainfall. Wild rice, guinea forest yam and oil palms grew in West Africa along with vegetables and the cowpea, an important protein source. On the east coast foods had been introduced by Arab traders from South-East Asia: bananas, coconuts, yams and taro, a root staple.

The commerce in slaves upset the balance. Apart from robbing the continent of its strongest young people, the trade put the emphasis on war rather than on agriculture. Instead of gathering or growing food whole West African peoples were led to war against their neighbors by kings and chiefs eager to exchange captives for European guns and blankets.

And when, in the nineteenth century, the Europeans divided up the continent between them, the old balance was utterly lost. Land which had until then grown food for local people was now turned over to crops that would satisfy the industrializing nations of Europe: cotton, coffee, cocoa, peanuts, oil-palms, bananas, rubber, tea and sisal. This

reached an absurd situation: by the 1970s, West African countries such as Senegal were diverting precious water to be sprinkled on green beans, tomatoes and strawberries to be jet-freighted to the markets of France or Britain.

Devoting large areas of land to one crop is dangerous even in fertile regions; in Africa it is particularly unwise. The traditional pattern of growing several food crops together, which looked messy and therefore inefficient to some regimented Europeans, is kindest to the soil. What one plant takes out in the way of nutrients, another replenishes. If one crop fails, another will surely survive.

Some colonial administrators of course recognized the value of local farming methods. Writing in 1890, British agricultural scientist A. J. Voelker noted in India 'land scrupulously clean from weeds, ingenuity in device of water-raising appliances, knowledge of soils and their capabilities, as well as of the exact time to sow and reap. It is wonderful, too, how much is known of rotation (of crops), the system of "mixed crops" and of fallowing . . . I at least have never seen a more perfect picture of cultivation.'

Feeding the modern world

The colonial model which succeeded this 'perfect picture of cultivation' continues to shape world agriculture, even in an era when nearly all of the countries of Africa, Asia and Latin America have gained their formal independence. The pattern is of a world which produces enough food to give every woman, child and man 3,600 calories a day — which is plenty — and yet still sees people suffering from malnutrition and dying from lack of food.

In the Third World, every region except Africa has since 1950 kept food production ahead of population growth. Asia and Latin America both now produce food surpluses.

So if there is enough food to go round, why are people hungry? It is not because there are too many people: the facts show there is plenty of food for each of us. But the distribution of that food is decided by people's ability to pay for it. And too many do not have the wherewithal to buy what they need.

When NI editor Chris Brazier visited Burkina Faso in 1985, the country was in the grip of famine: *But just three miles away from the hungry village where I stayed was a town where there was grain, vegetables, meat, French bread and cans of food. It is poverty that starves people,' he concluded, 'not acts of God or a callous whim of nature.'*

That poverty has its roots in the emphasis on raising cash crops instead of food in many countries. These export crops are meant to earn foreign exchange to improve everyone's standard of living but they rarely do because of the vagaries of the world market, and the unequal internal distribution of wealth and power.

The poverty springs too from the growing number of landless people in rural parts of the developing countries, estimated at 600 million in the early 1980s. These people have no means of growing their own food, and little means of

buying it.

The poverty arises also because of male prejudice. For women, whose labor produces half the world's food, have been ignored as farmers. Expertise and resources have been directed at men; land and loans for women are hard to obtain. The UN Food and Agriculture Organization sums it up in this way: 'In the Third World agricultural productivity cannot be substantially increased, nor can rural poverty be alleviated, unless women's access to key productive resources and services is substantially improved. The consequences of patriarchy for agricultural productivity are very expensive. Developing countries cannot bear their heavy cost.'

At the **New Internationalist** we believe that because the problems of world hunger are man-made they can be remedied. But it will take time, and inclination, and true democracy.

This is not impossible. The history of food after all is one of millennia, not decades. And with that perspective, today's extremes of feast and famine — the food mountains in Europe beside the starvation in parts of Africa — look all the more unnatural because today we have enough food to feed the world. The need for a 'balanced' diet, a fair sharing of resources both individually and internationally, is starkly apparent. Our task is to speed this process. Through this *Food Book,* both within our kitchens and on the wider political stage we hope to promote a wholesome diet — enough for everyone — for all the world's family.

INDEX BY REGION AND COURSE

177

INGREDIENT INDEX

Special thanks for help with recipes to Peter Stockton. We should also like to acknowledge the following publications: *The Politics of Hunger* J W Warnock (Methuen 1987); *Food in History* R Tannahill (Penguin 1988); *The Von Welanetz Guide to Ethnic Ingredients* D & P von Welanetz (Warner Books 1987); *The Oxford Book of Food Plants* G B Masefield et al (OUP 1969); *The Evolution of Crop Plants* Ed N W Simmonds (Longman 1976); *Queer Gear* C Heal & M Allsop (Century 1986); *The Grains Cookbook* B Greene (Workman 1988); *The Cookbook of the United Nations* Ed B Kraus (Cookery Book Club 1969); *The Encyclopedia of World Cookery* E Campbell (Spring Books); *The Art of African Cooking* S Lesberg (Dell 1971); *Middle Eastern Food* C Roden (Penguin 1985); *Food around the World* J Ridgwell & J Ridgway (OUP 1987); *The Africa News Cookbook* Ed T Hultman (Penguin 1985); *A Taste of India* M Jaffrey (Pan 1985); *The Book of Latin American Cooking* E L Ortiz (Robert Hale 1984); *Good Food from Mexico* R W Mulvey & L M Alvarez (M Barrows 1950); *Vegetarian Dishes from around the World* R Elliott (Pantheon 1982); *The Khalid Aziz Book of Simple Caribbean Cooking* K Aziz (Pepper Press 1982); *A Traveller's Tastes* J Dimbleby (Woodhead-Faulkner 1986); *Cooking and Eating the Chinese Way* K Lo (Granada 1985); *Captain Blackbeard's Beef Creole* (Peckham Publishing Project 1979); *A Taste of Indonesia* Ed K Mitchell (Oracle 1982); *A Taste of the Philippines* Ed K Mitchell (Oracle 1982); *Chinese Cooking Class Cookbook* Ed Consumer Guide (Publications International 1980); *South East Asian Food* R Brissenden (Penguin 1982); *Recipes from around the World* (Oxfam 1983); *Complete Arab Cookery* A Haroutunian (Granada 1985); *More with Less Cookbook* D J Longacre (Herald Press 1987); *New Indian Cookery* M Taneja (Fontana 1984); *East-West Kitchen* S Anwar et al (Food & Futures 1988); *Mary Ominde's African Cookery Book* M Ominde (Heinemann 1984).